Exciting Epistle to the Ephesians

BY THE SAME AUTHOR

Bible Cameos
Bible Gems
Bible Highways
Bible Names of Christ
Bible Pinnacles
Bible Treasures
Bible Windows
Matthew's Majestic Gospel
Mark's Superb Gospel
Luke's Thrilling Gospel
John's Wonderful Gospel
The Amazing Acts
What in the World Will Happen Next?

Exciting Epistle to the Ephesians

Ivor Powell

KREGEL PUBLICATIONS
Grand Rapids, Michigan 49501

Library of Congress Cataloging-in-Publication Data

Powell, Ivor, 1910-
Exciting Epistle to the Ephesians by Ivor Powell.
p. cm.
Includes index.

1. Bible. N.T. Ephesians—Commentaries. I. Title.
BS2695.3.P68 1988 227'.507—dc19 88-12841
CIP

ISBN 0-8254-3537-4

1 2 3 4 5 Printing/Year 94 93 92 91 90 89

Printed in the United States of America

CONTENTS

INDEX OF HOMILIES

PREFACE

The Epistle to the Ephesians was probably the greatest of Paul's writings. The apostle to the Gentiles possessed many talents, and these became increasingly evident when the Holy Spirit used him to write a major portion of the New Testament. If that indomitable missionary had not been available to God, the structure of the Bible might have been considerably changed. When Paul returned from his sojourn in Arabia, he preached a message which he called "my gospel." His claim was justified, since no other preacher of his generation mentioned the mystery which had remained unrevealed from eternity.

When I became a Christian, I was fascinated by the fact that the Letter to the Ephesians began where the Epistle to the Romans ended. Justification by faith in Christ became the theme of Peter's preaching, but only Paul seemed to understand that Gentiles had been predestined to become "fellowcitizens with the saints and of the household of God." The apostle admitted that his message was revolutionary but claimed that it had been planned by God from eternal ages. Paul had been the recipient of a divine revelation, and the Epistle to the Ephesians supplied an explanation of that amazing experience.

Many years ago when I was a young evangelist, I was invited to deliver a series of Bible messages to a party of itinerant evangelists known in Britain as "The Pilgrim Preachers." Apparently, God blessed those studies in Ephesians, for the leader, John Newton, asked if I would type my notes so that he could use a copy on a forthcoming visit to Egypt. I did as he requested, but did not know that fifty-five years later, my wife would salvage the original "hand-made book of notes" from among discarded things in my office. I was fascinated and astonished when I read what God had given to me when I was only a young Christian. The pages of that manuscript were old and discolored; some of my youthful expressions seemed quaint, but the clear, shining truth of Paul's message was unmistakable. As I continued to read those notes, the idea of writing *The Exciting Epistle to the Ephesians* became irresistible. That volume will now begin its journey around the world, and may God breathe His richest blessing upon it.

Readers will discover the basic text used has been the Authorized Version of the Scripture. Other translations have been noted when used, but I have lived with the King James Version all my life, and it is never wise to discard an old friend. As always, my wife, Betty, has scrutinized and edited every word of this manuscript. Her patience has been endless and her suggestions invaluable; she never complained. We pray that this volume will provide inspiration for the ministers who will use it in their churches around the world.

IVOR POWELL

Santa Barbara, California

INTRODUCTION

The letter known as the Epistle to the Ephesians is one of the most discussed, criticized, and mysterious of all New Testament documents. Throughout the history of the Church, it has been considered to be the work of the apostle Paul, but in recent years, eminent scholars have challenged this assertion. Continuing debates have produced many problems, and the resulting questions have been thought-provoking. Some scholars have cited statements within the letter to support their claim that the Epistle could not have been written by Paul. Others, who have accepted Pauline authorship, have claimed that it is a letter which the author desired to circulate among many churches. The Epistle, therefore, has become one of the most mysterious and intriguing sections of the New Testament. It should not be assumed that the questions have come from liberal theologians. Some of the questioning scholars were devout Christians who sought for the truth. To gain a correct perspective and appreciation of the contrasting style of this remarkable book, it is necessary to give attention to the following suggestions.

DEFINITELY DIRECTED

PROPOSITION 1. This letter was delivered by a special courier to the saints and faithful in Christ Jesus.

It is irrefutable and therefore worthy of attention that the words "which are at Ephesus" (v. 1), were not included in the earliest manuscripts. This fact alone does not prove that the letter was never meant for this local church, but it certainly suggests that the author desired to reach a wider audience than was possible in any isolated assembly. The apostle hoped his message would be sent from church to church; his words were written for Christians everywhere, in all ages. The idea of circulating letters is clearly expressed in Colossians 4:16: "And when this epistle is read among you, cause that it be read also in the church of the Laodiceans; and that ye likewise read the epistle from Laodicea."

Paul, during his second missionary journey, was compelled to bypass the great city of Ephesus. He had been forbidden by the Holy Spirit to preach the gospel in Asia (see Acts 16:6). His enforced march through the most inhospitable country left indelible memories; he had seen crowded markets and lonely villages in which the gospel had never been heard. The apostle could not forget what had been seen and was determined to return as soon as possible. Nearing the end of that missionary journey, Paul made a brief visit to Ephesus, but, later, on his third journey, he returned to Ephesus and remained there for two years. During that period, he undoubtedly led evangelistic crusades in nearby areas and, as a result of his untiring efforts, other churches were established. Assemblies were formed in Colosse, Laodicea, Perga, Pergamos, Thyatira, Pamphilia, Troas, and other populated areas. John wrote to seven of these churches when he was a prisoner on the Isle of Patmos (see Rev. 2 and 3).

Printing presses were unknown in those days; all letters and documents were written by hand and delivered by special couriers. Apart from the highest circles in government, there was no authorized postal service. Communications were written on parchment, which was usually rolled and sealed with wax. Ordinary letters or scrolls were tied with thread and entrusted to an appointed courier who delivered the message to the designated recipient. It is interesting to note that Paul's "mailman," who went to Ephesus and Colosse, was named Tychicus (see Eph. 6:21 and Col. 4:7). It is safe to assume that since the words "which are at Ephesus" were not included in the earliest manuscripts, Paul probably left a blank space so that the bearer of the communication could add the name of the church he was visiting. How and when the name "Ephesians" became identified with this Epistle will be discussed later in this Introduction.

DECIDEDLY DIFFERENT

PROPOSITION 2. This letter is different from all others written by Paul.

The only other message which resembles the Epistle to the Ephesians, is the one sent to the church at Colosse. The fact that both letters were carried by the same courier suggests that they were written during the same period in Paul's life—from his prison in Rome. Nevertheless, these books contain important, distinguishable differences. The letter to the Colossians was directed toward the local assembly; Ephesians was meant to reach Christians throughout Asia. At that time, there was no authorized collection of New Testament writings. Such letters as existed were copied by scribes and circulated among the churches.

This Letter Is Different in Style

A comparative study of other Epistles written by the apostle reveals that they were easily understood and conducive to progressive study. The writer dealt with problems existing within the assemblies; he offered advice and occasionally condemned the compromising attitude of his readers. The letter to the Ephesians did not follow this pattern. It has been said that the opening sentences of this Epistle suggest the flight of a bird, soaring into the sky and constantly changing direction, as if uncertain how to proceed. With each turn, new vistas of the heavens become visible, and every effort takes it further toward the sun! It is almost impossible to subject the verses to analysis because, with each sentence, Paul describes new wonders of the grace of God.

The difference between Ephesians and the other Pauline Letters may be illustrated by a student in a college. When he writes to his family, mention is made of circumstances, friends, and kinsmen. Yet, when he writes a thesis, none of these details are mentioned; he describes the subject under discussion. Although the two documents are written by the same hand, holding the same pen, they differ one from the other. Paul mentioned his friends in all the Epistles except the letter to the Ephesians. This was a treatise in excellence, a thesis explaining the magnificent grace of God.

This Letter Was Different in Substance

Some theologians have insisted that Paul could not have written this letter. Elsewhere, the apostle mentioned the basic facts of the gospel and explained how the Son of God came to earth to redeem sinners. Ephesians explains how God, in Christ, gave to the Church much more. The saints have not only been redeemed from the penalty and power of sin; they have been enthroned with their Lord in heavenly places. He explains that even the weakest saint can be clothed with invincibility. Certain scholars have insisted that, with the exception of the letter to the Colossians, this theme was seldom, if ever, mentioned in earlier Epistles. Therefore, they say this message must have been written by another man. This is not a convincing argument.

Although Paul was anointed by God to preach and write about the gospel, he was, nevertheless, still a man! He did not acquire his knowledge overnight! He followed the learning process and knew more at the end of his ministry than he knew at its beginning. The messages sent to the church in Asia were the product of a mature mind. They arose from a soul which had, for many years, listened to the teaching of the Holy Spirit. If, as some theologians indicate, Paul used a different vocabulary, it might have been because he had never before expounded such truths. Evidently, the apostle was endeavoring to explain that there were two ways in which to live a Christian life. A man could be carnal and content to remain immature. Or, on the other hand, the same man might become completely devoted to his Lord. The believer would not be content to remain "a babe in Christ;" he would grow to become "a perfect man, unto the measure of the stature of the fullness of Christ" (Eph. 4:13). When Paul wrote this letter, he was nearing the end of his earthly pilgrimage. He had learned much and, to the best of his ability, was communicating his knowledge to those whom he loved.

This Letter Was Different in Scope

The message, reputedly sent to the Ephesians, appears to be completely impersonal; that is, there were no special greetings sent to any members of the assembly. This is worthy of attention, for it was contrary to his usual style of writing. When Paul wrote to the church in Rome, he had never visited the city, and yet he sent greetings to many people. Evidently, his friends preceded him to the great metropolis and Paul used the opportunity to express his love for all who shared in his labor (see Rom. 16). The same fact may be seen in the letter sent to the church in Philippi (see Phil. 4:3). This feature was absent from the letter to the Ephesians. The apostle had stayed in Ephesus for two years and three months, and probably knew most of the members of the church. He had shared dangerous and soul-stirring experiences with some of the Ephesian Christians. Therefore, it seems incredible that he should not express his love and best wishes to his friends. This fact supports the suggestion that the Epistle was not written for a local church, but for the greater audience throughout Asia.

DELIGHTFULLY DISTINCTIVE

PROPOSITION 3. This letter was sent to Gentiles—"aliens from the commonwealth of Israel" (Eph. 2:12).

Ephesus was the chief city of Asia and among Asia's religious institutions, was an important Jewish synagogue. The apostle owed his life to the faithfulness of his friends and to the town clerk whose eloquence calmed a riotous mob (see Acts 19:31-41). It is astounding that these stalwart supporters remained unmentioned in the letter which bore the name of the city. Even the Hebrew converts seem far from the mind of the apostolic writer.

When Paul wrote this letter from the prison in Rome, the chains were around his wrists and ankles; a soldier stood guard at the door. Paul had reached the metropolis of the world and was at the center of all action. At that time, the bigotry of the Pharisees appeared to be of little importance. The Gentiles had been received into the family of God and their increasing enthusiasm enthralled the apostle. He probably smiled when he wrote, "But now in Christ Jesus, ye who sometimes were far off, are made nigh by the blood of Christ. For he is our peace, who hath made both one, and hath broken down the middle wall of partition between us. Having abolished in his flesh the enmity, even the law of commandments contained in ordinances, for to make in himself of twain one new man, so making peace" (Eph. 2:13-15).

Evidently, Paul was thinking of the many Gentile converts living in Asia, and it was to them he wrote this letter. If this were not true, some of his statements would be confusing. He had been the founder and pastor of the assembly in Ephesus, and the members of that church had often heard the apostle expounding and preaching the message of God. Nevertheless, he wrote: "Wherefore I also, *after I heard* of your faith in the Lord Jesus . . ." (Eph. 1:15). Someone had told Paul of the increasing faith of the Asian Christians. His information was based on hearsay, not personal experience. Later, in 3:2 he wrote, "*If ye have heard* of the dispensation of the grace of God which was given me to proclaim . . . ." Had this message been directed exclusively to the saints in Ephesus, his statement would have been ludicrous. The Ephesians were aware of the facts relating to Paul's call and ordination; he himself had told them.

DEVOUTLY DESIRED

PROPOSITION 4. This letter, after it had been read by the churches of Asia, ultimately returned to the care of the chief church, where it was preserved by the friends of the writer.

It would be interesting if we knew more of the history of this Epistle. We know that it was written by hand and copies were carefully made from the original manuscript. From that time until a man named Marcion began collecting the Epistles of Paul, almost half a century passed. Although the manuscripts were handled very carefully, it would have been impossible to prevent their becoming worn. Constant use would inevitably lead to deterioration, and therefore the question arises, how was the manuscript preserved? Paul supplies additional information in Colossians 4:16, "And when this epistle is read among you, cause that it be read also in the church of the Laodiceans, and that ye likewise read the epistle from Laodicea." Evidently, Paul wrote a letter to the people in the other city, but that letter is unknown today. Marcion, to whom reference has already been made, believed the two letters were one and the same, and other scholars have shared his convictions.

Dr. William Barclay, in his entrancing volume on the Letter to the Ephesians, makes a thought-provoking suggestion. He writes of an ancient custom known as *damnatio memoriae*—the damnation of a man's memory. Irrespective of any service rendered to Caesar, if a man committed a grave offense, his name was erased from monuments and removed from the writings of the empire. The church in Laodicea unfortunately became very complacent, and the Lord said to them, "So then because thou art lukewarm, and neither cold nor hot, I will spue thee out of my mouth" (Rev. 3:16). Dr. Barclay suggests the possibility that the Laodiceans suffered the fate of *damnatio memoriae*. The church in Ephesus, knowing the Laodiceans possessed a letter from Paul, asked for it. That message later became known as "The Epistle to the Ephesians." This is an interesting theory, but we may never know all the details of the survival of that manuscript. Theologians may discuss and argue about several features, but the church in Ephesus evidently preserved Paul's letter and became the guardians of one of the world's most valuable documents.

DELIBERATELY DEDICATED

PROPOSITION 5. Ultimately there arose men who collected the sacred writings, and finally, accepting some and rejecting others, the leaders of the churches formulated the canon of the New Testament. This was signally blessed by God and remains to this day.

Ancient records referring to Marcion, Clement of Rome, Polycarp, and others, reveal that these men were conversant with the Gospels as well as the Epistles of Paul, and considered the manuscripts to be the inspired Word of God. During the first three centuries of church history, many manuscripts were circulated among the assemblies, and it was inevitable that ultimately there would arise a demand for an authorized collection of writings.

Some circulating letters were obviously of lesser value and did not bear the imprint of divine inspiration. Dr. Guthrie, writing in the *Zondervan Pictorial Encyclopedia of the Bible*, vol. 1, p. 740, supplies interesting material: There is a list affixed to the canons of the church at Laodicea (A.D. 363) . . . it contains all the books (of the New Testament) except the Apocalypse. . . . Thirty years later the Council of Hippo in Africa agreed to a list identical with that of Athanasius. At Carthage four years after that (A.D. 397), another canonical list was agreed upon which comprised all the New Testament books. Augustine was present at this council. It should be noted that in this list there was reluctance to class Hebrews as written by Paul. This council marks the fixing of the New Testament canon until the time of the reformation, when certain problems concerning it were reopened.

Many years have passed since the formation of the first canon of the New Testament, but throughout the centuries, the Epistle to the Ephesians maintained its place of importance within the churches. If Paul did not write this letter, the question must be asked, who did? As far as is known there was not another Christian at that time capable of producing such a document. This was the language of a man to whom God had given a special revelation of truth. Even John could not have produced anything to compare with this letter. Evidently the writer expressed things not known by most followers of Christ. Paul was certain that in Christ "dwelleth all the fullness of the Godhead bodily" (Col. 2:9).

DECISIVELY DIVIDED

PROPOSITION 6. The letter divides into two equal sections.

The Epistle to the Ephesians was written in a way which does not encourage homiletical division. The sentences are long and sometimes appear to be unrelated. The first half of the Epistle is completely different from the second. Chapters 1, 2 and 3 explain the riches to be possessed in Christ. Paul wants his readers to learn certain facts. His key word is KNOW. He writes, "Wherefore I also . . . cease not to give thanks for you, making mention of you in my prayer. That the God of our Lord Jesus Christ, the Father of glory may give unto you the spirit of wisdom and revelation, in the knowledge of him: the eyes of your understanding being enlightened. . . . *That ye may know* . . ." (Eph. 1:16–18).

The theme for the final section is completely different. The apostle explains that those who *know* such things are expected to live exemplary lives. Their knowledge should influence their conduct. The key word for the second half of the Epistle is WALK. The apostle wrote of walking worthily (4:1); walking differently (4:17); walking in love (5:2); walking as children of the light (5:8); walking circumspectly (5:15). The first section may be summarized as doctrine *announced*; the second part reveals doctrine *applied.*

A BRIEF SYNOPSIS OF EPHESIANS

THEME: *The Preeminent Glory of Christ and His Purposes Concerning the Church*

OUTLINE:

I. Far Above All in His Position (Eph. 1:20-21)
II. Far Above All in His Power (Eph. 3:20)
III. Far Above All in His Purpose (Eph. 4:10)
IV. Far Above All in His Protection (Eph. 6:11-18)
V. Far Above All in His Preacher (Eph. 6:20)

It will be seen from a study of the six chapters, that the continuing theme of Paul's message is the scintillating splendor of the Lord Jesus. The apostle repeatedly mentions this theme, and the verses, when considered together, are not only interesting, but they also provide a thrilling progression of thought. Paul was a prisoner in a Roman dungeon when he wrote this letter, but instead of being preoccupied with unpleasant, threatening circumstances, he was thrilled by fellowship with the risen Lord. Although he knew the end of his earthly journey was approaching, he saw ahead a glorious reunion with the Lord, whom he had met outside the gate of Damascus rather than meeting with the executioner. His soul was never imprisoned by damp, dark walls. Even while he sat in his cell, his spirit soared like a bird toward realms of infinite blessedness where his Lord was enthroned far above everything that existed. The apostle was so filled with joy that, had he not written his letter, everything within him would have protested. When he began his Epistle, his face was radiant; his eyes were those of a seer.

FAR ABOVE ALL IN HIS POSITION (Eph. 1:20-21)

Paul wanted his readers to be aware of God's mighty power "which he wrought in Christ, when he raised him from the dead, and set him at his own right hand in the heavenlies; FAR ABOVE ALL principality, and power, and might, and dominion, and every name that is named, not only in this world, but also in that which is to come." Paul provided one of the most graphic word pictures to be found within the New Testament. At that time, he was unaware of the immensity of the universe; his knowledge was confined only to certain parts of planet

Earth. He had been given a limited, but exciting experience when he was "caught up into paradise, and heard unspeakable words, which it is not lawful for a man to utter" (see 2 Cor. 12:1-4). Yet, even the apostle was reluctant to describe the details of that memorable experience. Whatever he saw and heard, his knowledge of the immensity of the universe remained limited in its scope. When he wrote in his prison cell, limitations were unknown. He remained convinced that his Savior had been enthroned in splendor FAR ABOVE ALL and was then seated at the right hand of the Majesty on high. Perhaps he was aware of his inability to describe everything he knew about heaven, but at least he was determined to try. It was because of that resolution that the Epistle to the Ephesians was completed and sent to the faithful saints in Asia.

FAR ABOVE ALL IN HIS POWER (Eph. 3:20)

When Paul was about to terminate the first half of his letter, he wrote some amazing words, "That Christ may dwell in your hearts by faith: that ye, being rooted and grounded in love, may be able to comprehend with all saints what is the breadth, and length, and depth, and height; and to know the love of Christ, which passeth knowledge, that ye may be filled with all the fullness of God." Then, the apostle reached his climax and wrote, "Now unto him that is able to do exceeding abundantly above all that we ask or think, according to the POWER that worketh in us . . ." (Eph. 3:17-20). Since the Lord was already seated at the right hand of God, nothing was impossible for Him to accomplish; the world was at His feet! God had promised to make His enemies a footstool. Paul emphasized that since there were inexhaustible supplies at the Lord's disposal, He would be able to "do exceeding abundantly above all that we ask or think." The Lord was able to accomplish anything He desired. He was no longer limited by space or circumstance; He was almighty. Paul was convinced that in view of this great fact, Christians should learn how to pray!

FAR ABOVE ALL IN HIS PURPOSE (Eph. 4:10)

"He that descended is the same also that ascended up far above all heavens, that he might fill all things." The apostle went further along the pathway of divine revelation. With all power and authority vested in Himself, the Lord began to complete what had been planned in eternal ages. Paul was thrilled when he began to reveal details of those plans. "THAT HE MIGHT FILL ALL THINGS." Even after two thousand years of Christian experience, it is hardly possible to comprehend all that was implied in the apostle's statement. Nevertheless, certain things are easily discerned. Sinners have been overwhelmed by guilt and shame, and every attempt at saving them has sadly failed. Paul rejoices in the fact that everything has changed. The risen Lord, in His inimitable way, overcame innumerable problems, banished racial pride, and united people of all nations in the fellowship of His Church. This was the secret of Paul's happiness. Through the victory of His atoning death, Jesus subjected all things to Himself.

FAR ABOVE ALL IN HIS PROTECTION (Eph. 6:11-18)

Paul outlined and explained his faith. He warned of inevitable conflicts and told his readers how they could succeed in difficult times. It would be necessary to put on THE WHOLE ARMOR OF GOD. The apostle illustrated his facts by referring to the equipment of Roman soldiers. He was careful to explain that everything necessary had been supplied by Christ and would protect believers from the wiles of the devil. Nevertheless, unless Christians availed themselves of that which had been supplied, they would be outwitted by the powers of evil. The apostle explained how Christ would be their Protector. Clothed with the righteousness of their Lord, they would "be able to stand, and having done all, to stand." Paul wrote of truth, righteousness, the gospel of peace, faith, salvation, and the sword of the Spirit. Christ had made possible each piece of equipment and had supplied the best possible defense for His followers (see Eph. 6:11-18). Finally, he described the power of prayer and requested that he be included in their intercessions.

FAR ABOVE ALL IN HIS PREACHER (Eph. 6:20)

The apostle had become an "ambassador in bonds" (Eph. 6:20) and was no longer an ordinary follower of the Lord. He had been PROMOTED TO HIGHER AND GREATER SERVICE. He was the appointed representative of heaven, laboring in an alien land. God was pleased with His servant and had honored Paul with an opportunity to serve in higher circles of society. This privilege had been earned—it was not a gift! Writing to the Philippians, Paul said, "But what things were gain to me, those I counted loss for Christ. Yea, doubtless, and I count all things but loss for the excellency of the knowledge of Christ Jesus my Lord; *for whom I have suffered the loss of all things*, and do count them but dung, that I may win Christ" (Phil. 3:7-8). It must be said to the eternal credit of the apostle that from the moment of his conversion, he never turned back!

His obituary was written by his own hand. "For I am now ready to be offered, and the time of my departure is at hand. I have fought a good fight, I have finished my course, I have kept the faith. Henceforth there is laid up for me a crown of righteousness, which the Lord, the righteous judge, shall give me at that day . . ." (2 Tim. 4:6-8). Every Christian should ask, "Is Christ FAR ABOVE ALL IN ME?" Christ was, and still is, far above all in position, power, purpose, and protection. He was certainly preeminent in the life of His dedicated servant. Unfortunately, He may not be occupying that place in the lives of many of His people. This is the greatest hindrance with which God has to deal. The Lord desires to lift His people to the throne, but this cannot be done until Christians learn how to die upon His cross.

Oh, to be saved from myself, dear Lord:
Oh, to be lost in Thee!

The First Chapter of Ephesians

THEME: *The Perfect Will of God*
OUTLINE:

I. The Renowned Messenger of God (Verses 1-2)
II. The Revealed Will of God (Verses 3-12)
III. The Redeemed Children of God (Verses 13-19)
IV. The Resplendent Son of God (Verses 20-23)

THE RENOWNED MESSENGER OF GOD

Expository Notes on Paul's Greetings to His Friends

Paul, an apostle of Jesus Christ by the will of God, to the saints (which are at Ephesus) and to the faithful in Christ Jesus. Grace be to you, and peace, from God our Father, and from the Lord Jesus Christ (vv. 1-2).

THEME: *Paul's Introductory Salutation*
OUTLINE:

A. Something Planned
B. Something Perceived
C. Something Preached

Many years ago when I was a pastor of a church in Wales, I had among my deacons a young man named William Hopkins. He spoke very deliberately, very thoughtfully, and what he said was always worthy of attention. I remember a morning when he said to me, "Oh, Pastor—what a time I had last night!" When I asked what had happened, he gazed into my eyes, but I felt that he was not seeing me—he was far away! Then, suddenly, he continued: "It was nearly midnight; my wife and children had gone to bed, and everything was peaceful and quiet. I opened my Bible and read the words of Paul in Ephesians, chapter one, 'Paul, an apostle of Jesus Christ by the will of God.' I began to think about that statement. Paul was an apostle by the will of God. Evidently, the Lord had planned such a career for His servant, and Paul became what he was meant to be! Then I began to wonder if the Lord had a special plan for me; was I cooperating in the divine program? Was I being responsive to the promptings of heaven?

Time was forgotten. Pastor, when I looked at the clock, I had been there forty-five minutes and had only read a part of one verse. What a time I had! It was wonderful!" I never forgot that testimony, and now after some fifty years, his words introduce what must be said concerning the remarkable introduction written by Paul to the Christians of his generation.

SOMETHING PLANNED

It was significant that of all the New Testament writers, Paul alone claimed to have become an apostle "by the will of God." He began his Epistle to the Romans, the First and Second Epistles to the Corinthians, Ephesians, Colossians, and First and Second Timothy with almost identical words. Writing to the Galatians, he said, "Paul, an apostle (not of men, neither by man, but by Jesus Christ, and God the Father, who raised him from the dead)" (Gal. 1:1). When he wrote to Timothy, he strengthened his claim by stating, "Paul, an apostle of Jesus Christ, by the commandment of God our Savior and Lord Jesus Christ, which is our hope" (1 Tim. 1:1).

Evidently, the apostle had no illusions concerning his call to service. He believed God had predestined him to become what he was. Nevertheless, he thought it necessary that all his readers should be equally convinced of that important fact. He was aware of criticism emanating from certain sections of the church. He had not been one of the original twelve disciples, and this led some people to ask, "Who is Paul?" (see 1 Cor. 3:1-6). The church in Corinth was guilty of encouraging factions which Paul denounced. When his teaching brought conviction and condemnation to carnal believers, they questioned his authority, stating that he had not been commissioned by the Savior. To offset such arguments, the apostle prefaced most of his letters with his claim to have been divinely ordained. He affirmed that what he preached had been endorsed and inspired by the Lord, and this conviction produced his strongest indictment of heresy. He wrote, "But though we, or an angel from heaven, preach any other gospel unto you than that which we have preached unto you, let him be accursed. As we said before, so say I now again, if any other man preach any other gospel unto you, than that ye have received, let him be accursed" (Gal. 1:8-9).

SOMETHING PERCEIVED

"To the saints which are at Ephesus, and to the faithful in Christ Jesus" (v. 1). It would be interesting if Paul could explain whether or not "saints" and "faithful" were synonymous. During the passing of the centuries, the term "saints" has become the title of sanctified and devout people. The Church of Rome frequently canonized special people whose service was outstanding. Once this was done, thereafter all Catholics referred to them as "saints." This was not the practice within the early church. All people who professed allegiance to Christ were known as "saints." Every member of the Church enjoyed that distinction, and when a letter arrived addressed to the saints in Rome, every believer realized he or she was one of the designated recipients. Paul wrote, "To all that be in Rome, beloved of God, called to be saints: grace to you and peace from God our Father, and the Lord Jesus Christ" (Rom. 1:7). It must be admitted that not all saints were faithful! Even the greatest of the assemblies had within its ranks those whose faith and service might have shone with increased luster!

Some years later, when John wrote the letter to the Ephesians, he quoted the Lord as saying, "I have somewhat against thee, because thou hast left thy first love" (Rev. 2:4). The question must therefore be asked, was Paul drawing a line of demarcation between two types of believers found in the Ephesian church? If he was not, then he supplied the most wonderful testimony to the quality of the assembly in that city. If he was, then his statement produces another question. What were the characteristics which transformed a believer into a faithful saint? Was the apostle referring to faithfulness in preserving the gospel message? Was he thinking of the people who triumphantly overcame temptation and never fraternized with sin and sinners? Maybe he was thinking of those who, without hesitation, would have been willing to die for their Lord. It might be wise to ask if we could be identified with the "faithful in Christ Jesus." This was something Paul perceived; perhaps our eyesight would not be as keen!

SOMETHING PREACHED

Paul's statement could be easily paraphrased, "May God's grace and peace through our Lord Jesus Christ be to you as it has been to me." The apostle's thoughts were arranged in couplets. He wrote of himself and the will of God, the saints and the faithful, and God the Father and the Lord Jesus Christ. Since Paul believed himself to be the chief of sinners (1 Tim. 1:15), it was to be expected that he would consider himself to have been the greatest recipient of God's amazing grace. He had been a persecutor and a murderer, but the kindness of God had delivered him from the delusion and thralldom of evil. His guilty conscience had been touched by the forgiving hand of the Almighty; he was at peace with his Maker.

These characteristics are never seen to better advantage than in the Epistle to the Ephesians. Within the letter Paul mentioned "grace" *twelve* times and "peace," *seven*. The apostle never lost an opportunity to tell readers about Him who could give both of these qualities to the soul of a penitent sinner. The word "grace" has been used as an acrostic—Great Riches At Christ's Expense. That simple but thrilling fact became the theme of the apostle's preaching. He believed it to be the greatest message ever communicated by God to human beings.

It is significant that most of Paul's Epistles are prefaced in the same way. There were times when it became necessary for him to scold and even condemn his readers, but his approach to people never changed. He who had received so much grace from God desired to manifest that same quality in his associations with everybody. He supplied a marvelous example for all who followed in his footsteps.

THE REVEALED WILL OF GOD

SECTION ONE

Expository Notes on Paul's Expressions of Praise

Blessed be the God and Father of our Lord Jesus Christ, who hath blessed us with all spiritual blessings in heavenly places in Christ: according as he hath chosen us in him before the foundation of the world (vv. 3-4a).

THEME: *The Revealed Will of God*
OUTLINE:

A. Contentment in His Soul
B. Confidence in His Savior
C. Challenge in His Statement

This passage of Scripture has always been acknowledged to be one of the most difficult sections to analyze. Paul appears to be in a desperate hurry while having too much to say in too short a space! It might be said that the sentences are long; the paragraphs, unbalanced and poorly written.

These verses remind me of the time I spent in South Africa. During my evangelistic crusades in that wonderful country, I enjoyed the fellowship of a great man, Mr. Lawrie Fordham. He was a diamond merchant and an expert in his profession. There was a day when we spoke together about the fabulous diamond deposits in his country, and in the course of the conversation, he told me about the mouth of the Orange River, a territory constantly patrolled and guarded. He explained that after great storms the river became a raging torrent rushing through canyons, causing soil erosion and widespread damage. I wondered what this had to do with the patrolling of the distant shoreline, but he went on to explain something exceedingly fascinating. When the Orange River reaches the coast, its surging waters spread out along the adjacent beaches, and often rare and costly diamonds are deposited on the sand. Natives who live in the area frequently find gems of great value. Every year, so it is claimed, unscrupulous adventurers secretly try to reach the area where treasures may be awaiting discovery. It has been claimed that they are always caught and sent to prison, where they have time to remember their stupidity.

Paul's message suggests a torrent of revelation rushing through the canyons of human intellect. Unceasing showers of blessing in God's High Country sent the living water toward the lowlands, where some of God's choicest treasures were scattered within reach of admiring people. Paul resembles a man who has reached the beach! As the excitement and thrill of discovery fills his soul, he looks around at things of incalculable worth. He describes them one after the other and his list makes exciting reading. He describes blessings in heavenly places, predestination before the beginning of time, redemption, the forgiveness of sin, and the riches of God's grace. When he tries to describe what he finds, he becomes short of breath! Words tumble from his lips; he has little thought of punctuation marks; within the Greek New Testament, verses 3-14 are one sentence.

CONTENTMENT IN HIS SOUL

It should be remembered that when the apostle wrote this message, he was a prisoner awaiting execution in Rome. Other men in that situation might have been apprehensive and filled with complaints. Writing to the church in Corinth, Paul reminded his readers that he had been "in labors more abundant, in stripes above measure, in prisons more frequent, in death oft. Of the Jews five times received I forty stripes save one. Thrice was I beaten with rods, once was I stoned, thrice I suffered shipwreck, a night and a day have I been in the deep;

in journeyings often, in peril of waters, in perils of robbers, in perils by mine own countrymen, in perils by the heathen, in perils in the city, in perils in the wilderness, in perils in the sea, in perils among false brethren; in weariness and painfulness, in watchings often, in hunger and thirst, in fastings often, in cold and nakedness. Beside those things that are without, that which cometh upon me daily, the care of all the churches" (2 Cor. 11:23-28).

It is thought-provoking to compare this long list of problems with his amazing statement in Ephesians 1:3. The apostle was about to make his greatest sacrifice, and yet he thought only of God's abundant blessings. Instead of reiterating the things he had suffered, he said, "Blessed be the God and Father of our Lord Jesus Christ *who hath blessed us*." Apparently, he was considering a tremendous revelation of the grace of God, before which all other things faded into insignificance. He had neither tears nor regrets, complaints nor condemnation; *he had been blessed*! His problems produced peace; his difficulties occasioned delight. The benediction from God had transformed his prison into a palace!

CONFIDENCE IN HIS SAVIOR

He had been blessed with all spiritual blessings "in heavenly places in Christ." Paul believed this was the result of "the good pleasure of his will" (v. 5). These things had not been coincidental nor accidental; they had been planned carefully by his Lord. It is interesting to discover that the definition "according to," appeared to be characteristic of Paul's letter. This might be freely translated, "in compliance with the dictates or requirements of the divine will." The following list illustrates the importance of this statement:

- According as he hath chosen us . . . to be holy (1:4)
- Adoption of children . . . according to . . . his will (1:5)
- Redemption . . . according to the riches of his grace (1:7)
- The mystery of his will, according to his good pleasure (1:9)
- An inheritance . . . according to his purpose (1:11)
- His power . . . to us-ward according to his mighty power (1:19)
- Ye walked according to the course of this world (2:2)
- Ye walked . . . according to the prince of the power of the air (2:2)
- A minister . . . according to the gift . . . of God (3:7)
- Wisdom . . . according to the eternal purpose (3:10,11)
- Strength . . . according to the riches of his glory (3:16)
- Accomplishment . . . according to his power (3:20)

- Grace according to . . . the gift of Christ (4:7)
- Joined together . . . according to his effectual working (4:16)
- Corrupt . . . according to deceitful lusts (4:22)
- Servants . . . according to the flesh (6:5)

The sovereign will of God was the standard by which every circumstance was measured and judged. Even the trials and tribulations of the apostle were subservient to the will of God. Nothing happened by chance, and this belief enabled Paul to glory in tribulations and rejoice when problems overwhelmed him (see Rom. 5:3).

CHALLENGE IN HIS STATEMENT

Paul was careful to mention that the saints had been blessed "in the heavenly places." Any blessing which had been experienced in churches, homes, or elsewhere, were the overflow of the benediction originating far above principalities and powers. The source of blessing was God, the place of blessing was the heavenly spheres, and the destination of blessing was the earth where God's servants were striving to extend the kingdom of Christ. The apostle used the term five times in his letter, and when these verses are examined together, an important progression of thought becomes visible:

- The Place of Blessing (1:3)
- The Person Who Blesses (1:20)
- The Participants of Blessing (2:6)
- The Proclamation of Blessing (3:10)
- The Preservation of Blessing (5:12)

The blessing of God was given "*in heavenly places*" where Christ was seated in splendor. Paul believed that the church was also there *with Christ* enthroned at God's right hand. These truths were not mentioned during the earlier letters written by Paul. The Epistles sent to Ephesus and Colossae were written in Rome, toward the termination of Paul's career. Was this a new revelation to the apostle, and does that account for his not having mentioned it in earlier writings? On the other hand, did Paul keep this truth until the end because the Christians in Asia would not have been able to comprehend what he was endeavoring to teach?

Throughout the history of the church, this doctrine has been known as *positional* truth compared with *experimental* truth. The saints knew they were in Asia; they realized they were being represented in heaven by a great High Priest. But would they have understood *they were already in heaven before they had arrived there*? Would they have understood that God reckoned them to be with Christ, enthroned in splendor far above all principalities and powers, and that by faith in Christ, they had authority over the forces of evil and were invincible? These lessons would have mystified immature Christians.

Paul indicated that there was a great difference between merely living the Christian life and living it victoriously. He knew that problems were like clouds obscuring the sun; people looked through accumulating gloom. Paul endeavored to tell his readers that, since through God's grace they had already been lifted to the right hand of God, they could look down at those same clouds, knowing they were beneath their feet. God had planned, that through the power of the enthroned Church, the forces of hell were to be made aware of His unerring wisdom. This fact challenged Christians to rise above their circumstances and to know experimentally what otherwise would only be ideas.

According as he hath chosen us in him before the foundation of the world, that we should be holy and without blame before him in love (v. 4).

GOD'S CHOICE . . . How Sublime

"He hath chosen us in him" (v. 4a). This statement is probably one of the most enchanting, mysterious, and thrilling declarations in the New Testament. Throughout the entire Epistle Christ occupies the central place in God's plans. It should never be forgotten that all this happened before time began. Human life was unknown, planets and worlds had not appeared. Yet, in those early ages, God saw the end from the beginning, and important decisions were made within the Divine Family. People did not choose God, He chose them. The term "in Him" is one of Paul's most delightful expressions. Unfortunately, it takes a lifetime for some humans to choose God, yet He chose them when humanity was only a thought in His mind.

It will be seen that predestination was the product of foreknowledge; either one without the other was meaningless. If foreknowledge is divorced from predestination, the result dishonors the Almighty. God saw men when they were without hope in the world. He loved them and desired to make them His children. He was able to understand what would happen in the course of time. The Lord knew that many would believe on His Name and, knowing this, planned that those believers "should be conformed to the image of his Son . . ."

(Rom. 8:29). Paul knew that he had been chosen before Adam was created! Jeremiah would have understood Paul's faith, for he was taught the same doctrine. "Then the word of the Lord came unto me, saying, before I formed thee in the belly, I knew thee; and before thou camest forth out of the womb, I sanctified thee, and I ordained thee a prophet unto the nations" (Jer. 1:4-5).

GOD'S CHOICE . . . How Surprising

" . . . before the foundation of the world" (v. 4b). Let it be admitted that this sublime fact brings humans to the limit of their understanding. How can finite minds grasp infinity? How can we comprehend the limitlessness of omniscience? We are told in Genesis 1:26, "And God said, let us make man in our image, after our likeness. . . ." The vision of the apostle went much further back into eternal ages—to the time when the Divine Family made their momentous decision. God looked through the corridors of time to see humans—sinners—us. Doubtless, He saw humans at their best and at their worst. Holiness frowned at the stupidity of men, but love desired to help them.

John was sure that, at that time, plans were made whereby help could be offered. He spoke about "the Lamb slain from the foundation of the world" (Rev. 13:8). God evidently knew that many people would respond to the promptings of His love and chose them to be the material with which to complete His greatest creation. He did not compel men to believe; neither did He force them to cooperate. He planned to call sinners to repentance so that then, His predestination plans could begin to function.

GOD'S CHOICE . . . How Special

"That we should be holy, and without blame before him in love" (v. 4c). When the apostle wrote the second half of this letter, he used identical words. He was careful to indicate that God's planning envisaged perfection; His chosen ones would be holy and without blame. When he wrote of the future of the Church, Paul said, "Christ also loved the church, and gave himself for it; that he might sanctify and cleanse it with the washing of water by the word; that he might present it to himself a glorious church, not having spot, or wrinkle, or any such thing; but that it should be holy and without blemish" (Eph. 5:25-27). The Living Bible translates the verse, "Long ago, even before he made the world, God chose us to be his very own, through what Christ would do for us; he decided then to make us holy in his eyes—without a single fault."

Evidently, God intended to do something special! The creation of innumerable worlds would not even compare with the glory of His creation in Christ. The expressed love of a trusting believer would surpass the glories of inanimate objects. The simple but sincere expression, "Lord, I love Thee," would never emanate from mountains, trees, oceans, nor the rest of this creation. God desired more than recognition in His achievements; He wanted to be loved and worshiped by appreciative sons and daughters. He, therefore, chose us in Christ, because without the reconciling death of the Lord Jesus, the redemption of sinners would be impossible.

SECTION TWO

Expository Notes on the Foreknowledge of God

Having predestinated us unto the adoption of children by Jesus Christ to himself, according to the good pleasure of his will; to the praise of the glory of his grace, wherein he hath made us accepted in the beloved (vv. 5-6).

THEME: *The Fact and Purpose of Predestination*
OUTLINE:

A. The Truth of Predestination . . . "*unto the adoption of children*"
B. The Thrill of Predestination . . . "*the good pleasure of his will*"
C. The Triumph of Predestination . . . "*accepted in the beloved*"

These verses might be described as a handful of stars! The facts relating to the greatness of God's grace appeared to have fallen from heaven, thus enabling Paul to grasp some of those shining treasures. The apostle expressed superlative truth in each verse, and, therefore, every statement deserves special attention. Students should make haste slowly!

THE TRUTH OF PREDESTINATION . . . "unto the adoption of children"

The Greek word translated "predestination," is *proorisas*. It comes from the verb *proorizo*, which means to predetermine to decide beforehand. It was closely associated with another word *ekloge* which means an act of picking out, a choosing. "It is used of that act of God's free will, by which before the foundation of the world, He decreed His blessings to certain persons . . . a decree made from choice (Rom. 9:11) that by which, He determined to bless certain persons through Christ" (Thayer). Together, these words express one of the most profound biblical doctrines, but unfortunately, the conflicting interpretations given by theologians have caused irreparable damage within the church. It should never be forgotten that predestination was a fact based upon foreknowledge. Paul said, "For whom he did *foreknow*, he also did predestinate to be conformed to the image of his Son, that he might be the firstborn among many brethren" (Rom. 8:29). Unfortunately, emphasis has been placed on the purpose of the Almighty, not upon His omniscience.

I shall never forget an elderly lady in Northern Scotland, who shed tears when she confessed, "she had not been chosen." Completely convinced that she had been predestined to be damned, she looked through tear-filled eyes and said, "I would willingly give my right arm if only I could be saved, but I have not been called." I sat in the home of a delightful family and listened as my hostess explained her view of predestination. She described a tray filled with steel filings and sand and spoke of an electrical magnet passing over the mixture. With great sincerity, she indicated that the steel would be irresistibly drawn to the source of power, but the sand would remain motionless. She explained how the steel filings represented the elect of God—those who had been predestined to become the children of the Almighty. Although "the elect" lay buried in the sand of humanity, it was inevitable that they would respond to the power of the magnetic gospel. I reminded her that if such were the case, the lost could never be blamed for their unresponsiveness, for they never had a chance of cooperating with God; their eternal damnation was more God's fault than theirs! She shrugged her shoulders and replied, "Well, that is how it is!"

This widespread fallacy has brought misery to millions of deluded people. God never predestined sinners to be lost, nor sinners to be forgiven! He looked down the corridors of time to see and know the people who would believe and because He knew the identity of those responsive souls, made plans for their future. He predestined that they—*the believers*, would be conformed to the image of His Son and that they should be trained, educated, prepared, and made ready for service in His eternal kingdom.

When a child is born, the parents anticipate the time when their son or daughter will go to college. The baby is completely incapable of appreciating that fact, but the foreknowledge of the parents is followed by careful and detailed planning. It has become the custom for such parents to arrange an insurance policy which matures at the expected time of need. Years later, because of wise preparation, the child is able to enter college and prepare for whatever vocation has been chosen. Predestination reveals that God, the eternal Father, did precisely the same thing. Even before His children were born, He foresaw their arrival and, looking beyond that exciting moment, prepared for their "higher education." His wise planning for the future was determined by His ability to see what lay ahead. When Christians graduate from the university of experience, they will be ready for service in God's eternal kingdom.

THE THRILL OF PREDESTINATION . . . "the good pleasure of his will"

"Having predestinated us unto the adoption of children" (v. 5a). Among the Jewish people, "the adoption of children" was different from the birth of a baby; it represented a time when the maturing son was invested with the privilege of manhood. This fact can still be witnessed in the ceremony known as "bar mitzvah." Paul was instructed in every facet of Hebrew life, but it should be remembered that when he wrote this letter, he was imprisoned in Rome. At that time his thoughts were influenced possibly by a different style of adoption. A senator had the power to adopt anybody! If a slave saved the life of his master or rendered any other outstanding service, it was within the power of the Roman to free the slave and adopt him as a son. All people who saw the film *Ben Hur* remember how this was the privilege bestowed upon the Hebrew who saved the life of his Roman master. When Ben Hur was adopted by the consul Quintias Arias, he wore his father's ring and exercised his power. His father said, "Young Arias becomes the legal bearer of my name and heir to all my property." The Hebrew, a member of an alien race, became a Roman, was dressed in robes of magnificence, and later became a famous charioteer.

George E. Rice, in a very illuminating paragraph, speaks of the Roman method of adoption. Paul is indebted to the Roman judicial system for one concept that beautifully portrays what God accomplished through His plan for repentant sinners. One word encompasses this concept with all its ramifications—*huiothesia. Huiothesia* is a compound word made up of *huios,* "son" and *thesis,* "a position, a placing." So the compound means "a placement as a son," or, "adoption." Under Roman law, an adopted child became a new person; he received a new name, a new identity. He was legally separated from everything that made up his past, and was given a legal right to the wealth and fortunes of his new family. In contrast, although an orphaned Jewish child may have been taken in and raised to adulthood by a Hebrew family, there was no legal adoption as in Roman society. There was no change of identity, no new name; no separation from that which made up his past. The reason for this was the preservation of the birthright. So the courts of Rome provided an illustration for the redemption that Paul could not find in his own culture. *Huiothesia* appears five times in the New Testament, always in Paul's writings (Rom. 8:15, 23; 9:8; Gal. 4:5; and Eph. 1:5). (Adapted in part from "Adoption," a delightful article in *Ministry*, an international journal for clergy, March, 1987, p. 13.)

Knowledge of such possibilities enabled Paul to visualize the truth expressed in his letter. Sinners are aliens separated from God. Redemption makes their release possible, and the predestinating grace of God brings them into the Divine Family. They are no longer slaves, they are not even servants. The adoption of children makes them sons and daughters of the living God. They enjoy His presence, wear His ring, and are clothed with a robe of righteousness. The riches of heaven are at their disposal, and this glorious inheritance is a cause for profound praise and gratitude. All of these events, which were planned in eternal ages, seem beyond comprehension.

God was thrilled to plan such an adoption. Cooperating, believing sinners could be officially welcomed into the adopted family of the Highest. This was in accord with the "good pleasure of God's will." It is important to compare certain verses. Paul wrote of: (1) The will of God (1:1), (2) The good pleasure of His will (1:5), (3) The mystery of His will (1:9), and (4) The counsel of His will (1:11). God's plans were meticulously made; nothing was overlooked or left to chance!

"The adoption of children *by Jesus Christ* to himself" (v. 5b). Paul was convinced that there was no other medium through which the divine plan could be accomplished. Neither angels nor humans were capable of performing what needed to be done. A highway had to be constructed through multitudinous problems; barriers of sin had to be removed to make possible the emancipation from slavery; and the onward march proceeded toward the ultimate goal of being "conformed to the image of God's Son." The Almighty did something through Jesus Christ, and His accomplishment harmonized with other statements made in His Word. "And all things are of God, who hath reconciled us to himself by Jesus Christ, and hath given to us the ministry of reconciliation; to wit, that God was in Christ, reconciling the world unto himself . . . " (2 Cor. 5:18-19). Christ's beneficence sought the sinner; His blood cleansed the suppliant; His blessing strengthened the saints and built them "into a holy edifice in the Lord." All things would be done according to the divine blueprints, and Christ would be the means whereby the apparently unattainable would be brought within the grasp of men and women.

It appears significant that gratitude, glory, and grace are the keynotes of Paul's message. The contemplation of God's amazing provision causes praise. To know these thrilling facts promotes thanksgiving. Even before the birth of the human race, God planned to share the unlimited resources of His abundant wealth. Beggars would be lifted from the dunghill and made to sit among princes (see 1 Sam. 2:8). The words *glory* and *grace* appear to be the identical twins of Scripture. The scintillating grace of God and the radiance of His glory filled the apostle with awe and wonder. To repeat an earlier statement, someone has aptly used the word *grace* as an acrostic: *G*reat *R*iches *A*t *C*hrist's *E*xpense, a phrase which expresses all that needs to be said.

THE TRIUMPH OF PREDESTINATION . . . "accepted in the beloved"

"Wherein he hath made us acceptable in the beloved" (v. 6). Evidently, Paul believed that without Christ, acceptance with God was impossible. "Ye who sometimes were far off, are made nigh by the blood of Christ" (Eph. 2:13).

During World War II, the Welsh nation was sometimes disgusted, but always interested, in the exploits of certain young women who tried to emigrate to the United States of America. These unwise young ladies watched Hollywood films and concluded that the road to fame was easy to find. Denied a passport, they stowed away on vessels bound for New York. Unfortunately, they were discovered and returned to Britain. What they said concerning American immigration officials cannot be printed in this book!

Later, when Adolph Hitler declared war, thousands of American soldiers arrived in Great Britain to strengthen the Allied cause, and many of these youthful men came to Wales. What transpired afterward beggars description. Amid the coal mining valleys of the principality, weddings were celebrated, and the frustrated girls suddenly discovered a new way of achieving their purpose. The "G.I." brides became famous! The British people were astounded when the American government sent specially equipped ships to British ports. Teams of doctors and nurses devoted their talents to helping these hitherto unwanted young women, and with fanfares of trumpets, the "outcasts" were brought to the land of their dreams. Red carpets were rolled out, bands played, and huge crowds gave the brides a tumultuous welcome. It would have been more economical if the girls had been welcomed when they first arrived! Nevertheless, it is all easily explained. The young ladies were not more beautiful, nor wiser! Some of them were very foolish!

The different reception was given because of a new relationship. When the girls first arrived, the U.S. government looked at them and did not like what was seen. The second time they came, the government looked at the husband, not the bride! Young men who represented their homeland had gone overseas to serve their country in the defense of freedom. It was for the sake of the husbands that the wives were welcomed to America—they were "accepted in the beloved!"

Paul evidently believed that sinners had no chance of becoming citizens of heaven until Christ left His homeland to serve and die in a foreign land. His resurrection made possible innumerable weddings when sinners accepted Him and He them. The power of Christ changed the outlook of God and humanity. Formerly, a righteous God looked at sinners; afterward, He looked at His Son and for His sake accepted His bride. That resplendent welcome into the family of God was additional evidence that the grace of God was beyond finite comprehension. It explained what Paul meant when he wrote about "the adoption of children."

> Oh, to grace, how great a debtor
> Daily, I'm constrained to be.
> Let Thy grace, Lord, like a fetter,
> Bind my wandering heart to Thee.

SECTION THREE

Expository Notes on the Riches of God's Grace

In whom we have redemption through his blood, the forgiveness of sins, according to the riches of his grace (v. 7).

THEME: *God's Grace*

OUTLINE:

A. The Means of God's Grace . . . *"through his blood"*

B. The Miracle of God's Grace . . . *"the forgiveness of sins"*

C. The Measure of God's Grace . . . *"according to the riches of his grace"*

At first glance, most of the first chapter of this letter appears to have been an excessive exuberance—an emotional outburst of the apostle's soul. When writing this section of the Epistle, Paul hardly paused to include punctuation marks. He continued to write amazing facts and produced a long sentence which, in actual fact, is no sentence at all. In the Greek New Testament, verses 3-14 are one long sentence, and critics might be tempted to describe the verses as disorganized rhetoric. Paul's continuing statements embrace eternity. First, he looked back to write, "he hath chosen us in him before the foundation of the world." Then he looked ahead to the limitless future to write, "that in the dispensation of the fullness of times, he might gather together in one all things in Christ, both which are in heaven, and which are on earth; even in him" (1:10). At first, men were on the Lord's mind; at the end, they will be at His side, redeemed by His precious blood. Bridging the gulf between the planning and the perfecting of the Church was the matchless grace of God. The various phases of that infinite grace may be summarized as seeing, seeking, saving, strengthening, and sanctifying His people.

THE MEANS OF GOD'S GRACE . . . "through his blood"

It is to be regretted that liberal theologians failed to recognize the truth of Paul's theology. They claimed that the apostle made a terrible mistake when he failed to escape from the shackles and bondage of Judaism. The age-old conception that acceptance with God depended upon a blood sacrifice was completely obnoxious; it was a tragedy when the early Christians tried to harmonize old and new ideas of truth. Critics have stated that the leaders of the first church should have severed all connections with ancient traditions to make a new start with different expressions of faith. Unfortunately, such critics have failed to appreciate even the most elementary Christian doctrine.

The Scripture taught that life was in the blood (see Lev. 17:11). When prophets and apostles spoke of the blood of Jesus, they referred to His life. When they spoke of the *shed blood* of Jesus, they referred to His sinless life outpoured on the Cross of Calvary. They did not imply that repentant sinners had to be immersed in blood, as in the waters of baptism. The early preachers believed and taught that faith in the Redeemer made it possible for an intelligent, repentant soul to obtain all that was won through the atoning death of God's Son. The phraseology of the apostles revealed that the grace of God made possible the greatest miracle ever performed by the Almighty.

It was said, "The lamb was slain from the foundation of the world" (see Rev. 13:8). Adam and Eve received coats of skins because an offering was slain; Abel was accepted because he brought to God a lamb from his flock; Cain was rejected because he did not follow that example; Isaac was delivered because a ram took his place on Abraham's altar; Israel was protected in Egypt because they obeyed God by placing the blood of a lamb on the lintels and doorposts of their houses. The daily routine in the tabernacle and temple rested upon the same ancient precept. John the Baptist expressed this faith when he said, "Behold, the Lamb of God which taketh away the sin of the world" (John 1:29). Each Old Testament type was an arrow pointing ahead to the time when Christ, the Supreme Sacrifice, would bring to fruition everything planned by the wisdom of God. He was to be the means by which the dreams and yearnings of the Father would be realized. That Deity should be concerned with finite, faltering humans was beyond comprehension. When Paul considered what had been planned and perfected, he could only say that the miracle was a production of God's amazing grace.

THE MIRACLE OF GOD'S GRACE . . . "the forgiveness of sins"

The Pharisees and Sadducees resisted the preaching of Paul because his doctrine was opposed to everything they taught. Throughout the history of their nation, the Jewish people believed that forgiveness was only obtained through merit. What men *did* resulted in what they received. Observance of the rite of circumcision was a prerequisite of pardon. Consequently, aliens were never admitted into the family of God. Unfortunately, some of the early Christians failed to renounce the ancient tenets and insisted that Gentile converts be denied full membership in the church unless they were circumcised. This serious altercation led to the convening of the first church council, in which James and his colleagues made their memorable decision (see Acts 15). When Paul preached that forgiveness could be obtained instantly, he appeared to be a heretic. Unfortunately, the teaching of the Pharisees never died!

I shall never forget the anger of a Scottish elder who became infuriated when he heard my testimony. When I said that I had been forgiven, he replied, "Young man, dinna say it; dinna say it. At the end of your journey, your good deeds will be weighed against your bad deeds, and if your good deeds outweigh the bad ones, *then*, God will tell you if you have been forgiven. Say, you HOPE to be forgiven." When I replied, "But I know NOW that my sins are forgiven," he became very annoyed and I wondered if he was about to have a heart attack! Writing to converts, John said, "I write unto you, little children, because *your sins are forgiven you* for his name's sake" (1 John 2:12). When Jesus spoke to the paralytic, He said, "Man, thy sins *are forgiven* thee" (Luke 5:20). God said to Israel, "I will forgive their iniquity, and I will remember their sin no more" (Jer. 31:34). The Bible teaches that forgiveness is a gift given by God to all who repent of their sins. Paul believed this to be a miraculous manifestation of the grace of God.

THE MEASURE OF HIS GRACE . . . "according to the riches of his grace"

It was significant that Paul wrote of the *riches* of God's grace; for casual readers, mention of the grace of God might have been sufficient. The apostle recognized each manifestation of the kindness of the Almighty as additional evidence of the indescribable, inestimable wealth of an everlasting kingdom. Such riches made the wealthiest citizens of earth appear as beggars. Paul obviously believed that everything at God's disposal had been given as a lavish expression of redemptive tenderness. When compared with the loving purposes of the eternal Father, the creation of the universe seemed trivial. The designing of flowers, mountains, valleys, and scenery was commonplace. The music of the wind blowing in the trees, the changing colors of the leaves in autumn, and all other exhibitions of creative genius were nothing when contrasted with the redemption of humanity. This was the fulfillment of His most cherished ambitions.

Grace brought eternal enjoyment to repentant sinners, but there was still more wealth to come within the reach of men and women. The exceeding riches of God's grace became visible when He came to help impoverished people. He offered peace for enmity, forgiveness for guilt, a mansion for a hovel, riches for poverty. Such an exchange seemed beyond the comprehension of finite understanding. The apostle had difficulty choosing words to describe God's amazing love; therefore, He was content to write, "The riches of God's grace." (See the homily, "In Whom We Have," p. 63.)

SECTION FOUR

Expository Notes on God's Gifts to His People

Wherein he hath abounded toward us in all wisdom and prudence; having made known unto us the mystery of his will, according to his good pleasure which he hath purposed in himself: that in the dispensation of the fullness of times, he might gather together in one all things in Christ, both which are in heaven, and which are on earth; even in him (vv. 8-10).

THEME: *A Portrait of the Omniscient God*
OUTLINE:

A. God's Generous Provision . . . *He "made known"*
B. God's Good Pleasure . . . *"the mystery of his will"*
C. God's Great Purpose . . . *"gather together in one all things"*

It has often been claimed that a man is best known through his works. A gifted artist expresses himself through paintings. An author's mind may be read in his books. An angry man becomes vicious; a gentle soul excels in kindness and tenderness. A person who never desires fellowship with people becomes a hermit; a fun-loving teenager seeks the company of kindred souls. Throughout the earliest ages God was inscrutable, He dwelled in distant heavens, and only on very rare occasions was mankind permitted to obtain a glimpse of His personality. Adam, Jacob, Moses, and a few others occasionally drew near to Him, but it was only when God decided to reveal Himself that new possibilities of understanding became apparent. Philip said to Jesus, "Lord, shew us the Father, and it sufficeth us. Jesus said unto him, have I been so long time with you, and yet hast thou not known me, Philip? He that hath seen me hath seen the Father; and how sayest thou then, shew us the Father? Believest thou not that I am in the Father, and the Father in me?" (John 14:8-10).

The Lord's statement marked the beginning of a new era of knowledge. When the apostle went into the wilderness to receive a greater revelation from the Lord, a way was prepared for humans to gain a clearer understanding of the omniscient God. Paul, whose vision embraced eternity, saw the enthralling wonder of the Creator. He looked at masterpieces of creative art and soon was lost in wonder.

GOD'S GENEROUS PROVISION . . . He "made known"

He "made known unto us the mystery of his will" (v. 9a). Later in the Epistle, Paul wrote, "If ye have heard of the dispensation of the grace of God which is given me to you-ward: how that by revelation he made known unto me the mystery; (as I wrote afore in few words, whereby, when ye read, ye may understand my knowledge in the mystery of Christ) which in other ages was not made known unto the sons of men, as it is now revealed unto his holy apostles and prophets by the Spirit" (Eph. 3:2-5). Paul desired readers to know that God had communicated knowledge; as a result, what was being preached was truth hitherto unknown. The fact that the prophets did not mention the new doctrines was not evidence of his own heresy. The prophets had been uninformed of such matters because God had not revealed His purposes.

Until God decided to disclose His plans, it was impossible for anyone—angel, priest, or prophet—to describe things of which they had no knowledge. The Almighty had now terminated His silence, and He had revealed to Paul and others "the mystery of his will." The fact that the message was new did not mean it was wrong! The secret plans of the Father had been revealed in the message of the gospel. The generosity of God became evident when He made provision whereby His deliberations could be shared with men.

GOD'S GOOD PLEASURE . . . "the mystery of his will"

"According to his good pleasure which he hath purposed in himself" (v. 9b). It is thought-provoking to read that human beings were made in the image and likeness of God (see Gen. 1:26). This suggests that God and humanity resembled each other. The Almighty could be pleased or displeased, a fact that became evident in the Scriptures. "The Lord taketh pleasure in them that fear him, in them that hope for his mercy" (Psalm 147:11). "And lo, a voice from heaven, saying, This is my beloved Son, in whom I am well pleased" (Matt. 3:17). People may either grieve or please God. ". . . and before his translation, he [Enoch] had this testimony that he pleased God" (Heb. 11:5). Paul believed that God had pleasure in His actions. As it pleased the Lord to bruise the Messiah (Isa. 53:10), so it was according to His good pleasure to reveal to the apostle's ideas, thoughts, and plans which had been cherished from eternity. The contemplation of what would be accomplished through Christ brought smiles to God's face and gladness to His heart.

GOD'S GREAT PURPOSE . . . "gather together in on all things"

"To gather together in one all things in Christ, both which are in heaven, and which are on the earth; even in him" (v. 10). Enlarging on this revelation, Paul wrote, "He made known unto me the mystery . . . that the Gentiles should be fellowheirs, and of the same body, and partakers of his promise in Christ by the gospel" (Eph. 3:5-6). Paul's vision encompassed the universe and envisaged the time when God would be all and in all (see 1 Cor. 15:28). He wrote of the "dispensation of the fullness of time" when everything and every person would be in submission to Christ. Paul described how the Lord would deliver up the kingdom to His Father, that God should be "all in all." Every aspect of evil would be banished from the thoughts of the redeemed and Isaiah's prediction fulfilled. "And he shall judge among the nations, and shall rebuke many people: and they shall beat their swords into ploughshares, and their spears into pruninghooks: nation shall not lift up sword against nation, neither shall they learn war any more" (Isa. 2:4).

We are now beginning to explore the fringes of space and are hoping, someday, to penetrate even further into the starry heavens. Scientists speculate as to what awaits discovery, and, in their long range calculations, are planning to establish human colonies on distant planets. Whether or not this will ever be accomplished is debatable. Unfortunately, our home in space is torn by discord and strife, and desire for domination has already turned Afghanistan, South America, Ireland, and the Middle East into battlefields. Jews and Arabs detest each other; saboteurs continue to kill innocent people; Lebanon, which was a beautiful country adjacent to the blue waters of the Mediterranean Sea, is ruined with little if any hope of recovery. Corruption is dominant in society, and even the highest officials have become suspect. The love for increasing wealth appears to have superseded reverence and obedience to God.

Periodically, reformers appear on the scene, and their loud protests momentarily arouse concern. Unfortunately, apathy and continuing indifference overwhelm some of the men who protest. Many people now believe humanity has become capable of self-destruction. It is refreshing to know that God promised that redeemed men and women should live eternally. He intends to create new heavens and earth in which righteousness dwells (see 2 Peter 3:13). Within His kingdom Jews and Gentiles, Arabs and Israelis, Russians and Americans, black and white people, red and yellow races will live together in unbroken harmony. "The wolf also shall dwell with the lamb, and the leopard shall lie down with the kid; and the calf and the young lion and the fatling together; and a little child shall lead them. And the cow and the bear shall feed; their young ones shall lie down together; and the lion shall eat straw like the ox. And the sucking child shall play in the hole of the asp, and the weaned child shall put his hand on the cockatrice' den. They shall not hurt nor destroy in all my holy mountain: for the earth shall be full of the knowledge of the Lord, as the waters cover the sea" (Isa. 11:6-9).

God went the extra mile—"*He abounded toward us*, in all wisdom and prudence, having made known unto us the mystery of his will." He saw and loved unenlightened people living on the lowlands of earth, and for their sake he opened the gates of His celestial reservoir, permitting sparkling waters of truth to invade their parched minds. "*He abounded toward us*." God opened His hand to scatter blessing; His mind to impart truth; His storehouse to supply food; His inexaustible resources to assist impoverished sinners. The realization that all these blessings came to men through Christ was sufficient to make Paul and his colleagues desire to sing, "Worthy is the Lamb that was slain to receive power and riches, and honor, and glory, and blessing" (Rev. 5:12). The apostle wrote, "The gospel which was preached of me is not after man, for I neither received it of man, neither was I taught it, but by the revelation of Jesus Christ. . . . But when it pleased God, who separated me from my mother's womb, and called me by his grace, to reveal his Son in me, that I might preach him among the heathen, immediately, I conferred not with flesh and blood . . . " (Gal. 1:11-16). The apostle was so convinced of the truth of his God-given revelation that he wrote, "If any other man preach any other gospel unto you, than that ye have received, let him be accursed" (Gal. 1:8-9).

SECTION FIVE

Expository Notes on the Inheritance in Christ

In whom also we have obtained an inheritance, being predestinated according to the purpose of him who worketh all things after the counsel of his own will, that we should be to the praise of his glory, who first trusted in Christ (vv. 11-12).

THEME: *An Exposition of Two Inheritances*
OUTLINE:
A. Inherited Wealth
B. Incomprehensible Wisdom
C. Indescribable Wonder

INHERITED WEALTH

It was significant that although Paul was materially poor and sometimes had to earn a living by making tents, the term "riches" often appeared in his writings. Earthly possessions did not attract him; he was continually fascinated by wealth which only God could supply. He wrote of the riches of grace (Eph. 1:7; 2:7), the riches of God's glory (Rom. 9:23; Eph. 1:8; 3:16; Phil. 4:19), the riches of God's goodness (Rom. 2:4), the riches of the glory of the mystery (Col. 1:27), and the riches of understanding (Col. 2:2). And, in one glorious outburst of praise, he wrote, "O the depth of the riches both of the wisdom and knowledge of God! How unsearchable are his judgments, and his ways past finding out" (Rom. 11:33).

Paul's impoverishment was a startling contrast to the unlimited wealth of His Lord. It was never easy to comprehend why One so wealthy should be interested in one so poor. The apostle was obviously filled with wonder and amazement when he considered how he had been "lifted from the dunghill to sit among princes" (see 1 Sam. 2:8). Paul had received a great inheritance; the kindness of God could never be forgotten. (See the homily, "A Great Inheritance . . . for Us and Christ," p. 66.)

INCOMPREHENSIBLE WISDOM

"According to the purpose of him who worketh all things after the counsel of his own will" (v. 11). Paul used two statements and indicated that they helped to make us acceptable in the beloved. God's purpose and God's praise were inseparable in the work of redemption. Even before the beginning of time, God knew what He intended to do. His master plan of predestination had been followed by various activities which were all controlled by "the counsel of his own will." Let it be admitted, even the keenest intellect cannot understand the inscrutable wisdom of the Almighty. When the future was but an idea in the mind of God, He saw and identified each soul who would respond to His affection. People may argue endlessly about the various aspects of this staggering fact, but reason dictates that it is better to rejoice in what God gave to us than to debate how He did it! The love of God began in the divine heart, came down to earth to redeem sinners, and afterward returned to the place from which it came. When sinners exclaimed, "We love him who first loved us," it became evident that God had performed a miracle . . . and it was good!

Paul believed wisdom was always one of God's greatest attributes, but many details were beyond human understanding. No one knew what existed before time began. Long before creation, God was—and there were no others. Angels, men, and created worlds were only thoughts in the Creator's mind; yet, even then, the Almighty was lonely! There was, to a degree, emptiness within the divine heart. God desired to love and to be loved; to help and to be appreciated; to speak to others and to listen to their requests. He desired fellowship and that intense yearning was never satisfied until sinners were able to say, "Abba Father."

INDESCRIBABLE WONDER

It is significant that on three separate occasions Paul used the phrase "to the praise of his glory." He used this phrase in Ephesians 1:12 and 14, as well as "to the praise of the glory of his grace" in Ephesians 1:6. These utterances might be paraphrased, "to be grateful for the magnificence of extended kindness." God's grace was the brightest star in the firmament of heaven. What God planned reflected His desires—He wanted to be loved.

Love is not admiration, and admiration is not love; yet, either one belongs to the other. When a man marries a woman, it becomes evident that his admiration is so intense he desires her to become his life-partner. When that admiration decreases, his love suffers and, ultimately, the marriage is threatened. It cannot be over-emphasized that admiration is an integral part of love. It may be assumed that angels admire the handiwork of the Creator, but it is problematical whether or not they can love as do redeemed sinners. God may have affection for angels, but His affection for humanity surpasses anything ever revealed. God loved us even when He could not admire us. When humans love God, they thrill the divine heart. Paul emphasized that all the activities of the Father were indicative of one overwhelming desire; He wanted all people, spontaneously, to "praise the glory of his grace." This may be partially realized during our lifetime on earth; but it can never be completely known until "ten thousand times ten thousand, and thousands of thousands, saying with a loud voice,

Worthy is the Lamb that was slain to receive power, and riches, and wisdom, and strength, and honor, and glory, and blessing. . . . glory be unto him that sitteth upon the throne, and unto the Lamb forever and ever" (Rev. 5:11-13).

THE REDEEMED CHILDREN OF GOD

SECTION ONE

Expository Notes on the Blessings of the Believers in Christ

In whom ye also trusted, after that ye heard the word of truth, the gospel of your salvation: in whom also after that ye believed, ye were sealed with that Holy Spirit of promise, which is the earnest of our inheritance until the redemption of the purchased possession, unto the praise of his glory (vv. 13-14).

THEME: *The Doctrines and Desires of Paul*
OUTLINE:

A. A Complete Salvation
B. A Constant Security
C. A Continuous Strengthening

There appears to have been a veiled distinction between the "we who first trusted in Christ" and the "ye who also trusted after that ye heard the word of truth, the gospel of your salvation." Paul also wrote, "Wherefore I also, after I heard of your faith in the Lord Jesus, and love unto all the saints" (v. 15). This may be evidence that Paul was writing to Gentiles scattered throughout Asia rather than to an assembly in one place. It should be remembered that this letter was written from a prison in Rome, and that a traveling Christian had supplied Paul with the latest information concerning the progress of the Asian believers. Their growth in the faith was a source of satisfaction to the apostle, who had labored diligently to establish their churches.

A COMPLETE SALVATION

"In Christ ye also trusted, after that ye heard the word of truth, the gospel of your salvation" (v. 13a). Using these choice words, Paul expressed the basic facts of salvation. His statement may be summarized as follows: telling, trusting, transforming. The Good News proclaimed in their midst had performed miracles which no other doctrine could emulate. The gospel expressed the mind of God and revealed ways whereby sinners could be accepted by Him. The glorious message of Christ explained how guilt could be removed, sins forgiven, and the depraved clothed with garments of righteousness. That inspired message had been proclaimed among the Gentiles, and their acceptance of the Savior had opened new realms of possibilities. After they believed, they trusted. They did not commence a program of self-improvement in order to acquire forgiveness. Doubtless, some of those converts had already desperately tried to reach higher levels of moral and spiritual attainment. Alas, they had failed in their endeavor. Their faith in Christ obtained in moments what had been unreachable during years of earnest effort. They heard, believed, and with childlike faith had trusted the Giver of every good and perfect gift (see James 1:17).

A CONSTANT SECURITY

"After that ye believed, ye were sealed with that Holy Spirit of promise" (v. 13b). "You became the property, the purchased possession, of your owner." Throughout the long, cold winter in the northlands of Canada, the sound of saws cutting through trees constantly disturbs the peacefulness of the forests. Huge tractors push and pull logs over the ground to stack them in piles on the frozen rivers. Every log is carefully stamped with the seal of its owner so that, months later, each tree can be identified and claimed. When the ice melts in the springtime and the rivers flow again, the logs commence their journey to the marshaling yards in distant lakes. There are no difficulties in deciding which log belongs to a company; the sealing mark makes identification easy. Perhaps Paul had such thoughts in his mind when he spoke of Christians being sealed with heaven's mark of ownership.

During the journey through this world, Christians and non-Christians mingle freely, but the fact remains that each redeemed soul is clearly stamped with God's mark; as a result, there will be no problem when the day of identification arrives. Paul wrote, "Now he which stablisheth us with you in Christ, and hath anointed us, is God, who hath also sealed us, and given the earnest of the Spirit in our hearts" (2 Cor. 1:21–22).

There are two reasons why Christians may be assured of their eternal security. First, there is the unbreakable promise of Christ: "My sheep hear my voice, and I know them, and they follow me: and I give unto them eternal life, *and they shall never perish, neither shall any man pluck them out of my hand*" (John 10:27-28). The Savior also said, "Verily, verily, I say unto you, He that heareth my word, and believeth on him that sent me, hath everlasting life, and shall not come into condemnation; but is passed from death unto life" (John 5:24). Every believer is as safe as the hand of Christ is strong!

The second reason is that the Holy Spirit resides within every believer and is aware of every attack made against the child of God. The apostle also wrote, "There hath no temptation taken you, but such as is common to man: but God is faithful, who will not suffer you to be tempted, above that ye are able; but will with the temptation also make a way to escape, that ye may be able to bear it" (1 Cor. 10:13). The mark of ownership placed upon the believer in Christ is indelible; it cannot be erased by either circumstance or Satan.

A CONTINUOUS STRENGTHENING

Paul's phrase "the earnest of our inheritance" (v. 14a) is thought-provoking. The word translated "earnest" is *arrobon.* It suggests certain things. Dr. Thayer states, "It is a word which seems to have passed from the Phoenicians to the Greeks, and thence into Latin. An earnest—that is, money which, in purchases, is given as a pledge that the full amount will subsequently be paid. Used in Ephesians, it is a pledge of future blessedness . . . a guarantee that God will complete what He commenced." To return to the illustration of the stamped, floating logs, the fact that the logs were stamped was a guarantee that later they would be claimed; the company would complete what it commenced!

Sometimes an inheritance is kept in trust until the beneficiary is mature and competent to receive it. Would it, therefore, be correct to suggest that the inheritance in Christ is, for the most part, held in trust by God until we also reach maturity? Then we shall be able to appreciate what God provided through His amazing grace. If that is the case, it explains why the Holy Spirit remains the mentor of our progress toward the ultimate goal. He remains the Supervisor of all spiritual growth as we journey toward the time when "the purchased possession" will be like Christ. Unbroken fellowship with the Holy Spirit is the guarantee that the purpose of God will be fulfilled, even as it was predestined.

Paul's appeal expressed in this Epistle substantiates that truth. He wrote, "Let no corrupt communication proceed out of your mouth, but that which is good to the use of edifying, that it may minister grace unto the hearers. And grieve not the Holy Spirit of God, whereby ye are sealed unto the day of redemption" (Eph. 4:29-30). It has often been claimed that believers in Christ are first rescued from the penalty of sin, then released from the power of sin, and finally removed from the presence of sin. The long and hazardous pilgrimage through this world will terminate when, in the glory of the eternal day, the saints will "see His face" (Rev. 22:4).

" . . . until the redemption of the purchased possession, unto the praise of his glory" (v. 14b). This will be the culmination of all divine planning. It will be the final act in the outworking of predestination, when those purchased and cleansed by the blood of Christ, will be elevated to the highest level of spiritual emancipation. Writing to the Christians in Rome, Paul stated, "For we know that the whole creation groaneth and travaileth in pain together until now. And not only they, but ourselves also, which have the firstfruits of the Spirit, even we ourselves groan within ourselves, waiting for the adoption, to wit, the redemption of our body" (Rom. 8:22-23).

Paul believed that salvation embraced the entire personality of Christians. John shared that faith, for he wrote, "Beloved, now are we the sons of God, and it doth not yet appear what we shall be: but we know that, when he shall appear, we shall be like him" (1 John 3:2). For God to make such a perfection possible, He must change the human temple in which the believer lives. Bodies are corruptible and subject to circumstance and age. Men may be devoted in worship and dedicated in service, but increasing age inevitably undermines their health and decreases their ability to serve the Lord. Their spirit may be willing but their flesh weak.

Paul believed this situation would terminate when mortal bodies put on immortality, when the corruptible would be replaced by incorruption. He wrote, "For this corruption must put on incorruption, and this mortal must put on immortality . . . then shall be brought to pass the saying that is written, Death is swallowed up in victory. O death, where is thy sting? O grave, where is thy victory?" (1 Cor. 15:53-55). God will complete what He commenced, and when the final act of emancipation is performed, "the Savior, the Lord Jesus Christ . . . shall change our vile body, that it may be fashioned like unto his glorious body according to the working, whereby he is able even to subdue all things unto himself" (Phil. 3:20-21).

Each conversion to Christ is the foreshadowing of that inevitable climax, when the entire body of Christ will be changed in a moment. Even the contemplation of that resplendent event fills the mind with awe. Perhaps even the angels will gasp with astonishment when the radiant Church, the body of Christ, will be presented "a glorious church, not having spot, or wrinkle, or any such thing . . . holy, and without blemish" (Eph. 5:27). When that spectacle of unprecedented brilliance takes place, the universe will be enthralled, and the phrase "to the praise of the glory of his grace" will be completely understood and appreciated.

SECTION TWO

Expository Notes on Paul's Continuing Prayers

Wherefore I also, after I heard of your faith in the Lord Jesus, and love unto all the saints, cease not to give thanks for you, making mention of you in my prayers (vv. 15-16).

THEME: *The Delight and Desire of Paul*
OUTLINE:

A. Unfaultering Progress
B. Unlimited Praise
C. Unceasing Prayer

When the apostle John wrote to his beloved friend, Gaius, he said, "I have no greater joy than to hear that my children walk in truth" (3 John 4). Paul endorsed this statement in his letter to the Christians in Asia.

UNFAULTERING PROGRESS

Someone had brought news to the imprisoned Paul, and as the apostle contemplated what he had heard, his face became radiant. Many years earlier, he had gone throughout Asia proclaiming the gospel, and in various places assemblies had been established. The apostle was filled with gratitude when he knew that the converts of those initial efforts had continued to serve Christ; their faith had deepened; their increasing affection for other people was known throughout their part of the world.

It is worthy of attention that he mentioned faith and love as though they belonged either one to the other. True faith, without love, was an impossibility. Love for people was only humanitarian and insufficient to gain salvation. Paul declared, "By grace are ye saved, through faith, and that not of yourselves; it is the gift of God. Not of works, lest any man should boast" (Eph. 2:8-9). This clear enunciation of the effects of the gospel upon human beings was a notable contrast to the religion of the Pharisees and Sadducees. Their faith was but a reflection of the traditions and precepts inherited from their forefathers. It was a religion without love; a philosophy which had no compassion for suffering humanity. The Pharisees saw no fault in themselves, and, therefore, spent much time criticizing others. The Christians in Asia had extended arms of compassion toward all who needed assistance, and such actions proved that "the love of God had been shed abroad in their hearts" (Rom. 5:5). Evidently, they believed John, who wrote, "But whoso hath this world's good, and seeth his brother have need, and shutteth up his bowels of compassion from him, how dwelleth the love of God in him? My little children, let us not love in word, neither in tongue; but in deed and in truth" (1 John 3:17-18).

UNLIMITED PRAISE

"I cease not to give thanks for you" (v. 16a). Paul expressed the deepest feelings within his soul when he wrote these words. Throughout all his conscious moments, day and night, he was grateful to God for blessing the message which had been proclaimed, and for the sustained watchfulness over those who had responded to the claims of Christ. The apostle's soul had become an altar upon which the sacrifice of praise was being continually offered. He believed "the praise of the glory of God's grace" should be the outpouring of every redeemed heart. It was pleasing to the eternal Father and beneficial to His children. It was better to praise than pout, to be grateful than to grumble, to be outgoing and joyful than to be introverted and silent. The writer to the Hebrews stated, "By him, therefore, let us offer the sacrifice of praise to God continually, that is, the fruit of our lips giving thanks to his name" (Heb. 13:15). These statements were inspired, at least in part, by the commandment of God given to Moses. "And this is the law of the sacrifice of peace offerings, which he shall offer unto the Lord. If he offer it for a thanksgiving, then he shall offer with the sacrifice of thanksgiving, unleavened cakes mingled with oil . . . " (Lev. 7:11-12). Unfortunately, many people received their blessings from heaven, but forgot to return thanks. Ingratitude, which resulted in forgetfulness, was a sign of degeneration within the soul (see Luke 17:17-18).

UNCEASING PRAYER

"I cease not to give thanks for you making mention of you in my prayers" (v. 16b). During my pastorate in a Welsh church, one of my elderly deacons was named Edward Hopkins; he was a saint! There came a day when he asked if I would pray especially for him, and when I promised to do so, he shook my hand and said, "Now, Pastor, don't forget. Tell the Lord it is EDWARD HOPKINS you are thinking about, and not somebody else! Mention my name just to make sure He knows!" I still remember the request of that old Christian. Perhaps his faith was a little weak, but no one could question his sincerity. He knew, as I knew, that God did not need to be reminded of any of His trusting children. If the fall of a sparrow does not pass unnoticed by our heavenly Father, the identity and need of any Christian can never be overlooked nor forgotten by an omniscient, omnipresent God. Nevertheless, there is an attractiveness about what might be termed "the pinpointing of a special request." Paul believed this truth, for he mentioned his friends, personally, before the throne of grace and thereby set an example for all Christians. Unfortunately, the ministry of prayer is often "crowded out" by other, less-important activities. When Christians become too busy to pray, their lives and ministries resemble automobiles without gasoline, engines without fuel!

The Savior was the busiest of all men. From sunrise to sunset, and sometimes much later in the evening, suffering people sought His presence, hoping that His touch would convey healing. Even when He walked through the cornfields, His disciples sought His assistance, and Jesus preached as He walked. It was difficult for the Lord to find time to pray, a fact that led to the practice of interceding at the most unusual times. "And it came to pass in those days, that he went out into a mountain to pray, and continued all night in prayer to God" (Luke 6:12). "And in the morning, rising up a great while before day, he went out, and departed into a solitary place, and there prayed" (Mark 1:35). Paul emulated his Lord's example and prayed for his friends. When the high priest of Israel entered within the veil to intercede for Israel, he wore a breastplate upon which were engraved the names of the twelve tribes. To a lesser degree, when Paul knelt before the risen Lord, engraved upon his heart, so to speak, were the names of his friends in Asia. He was able to write, "I cease not to give thanks for you, making mention of you in my prayers."

I shall always remember a small boy named Brynley Howell, who lived near my church in Wales. I watched one day as he returned from school to knock upon the door of his home. With one hand he lifted the flap of the old-fashioned letter box; then he stooped to look through the opening to see his mother responding to his knocking. He knew she was inside and would answer the pounding on the door! His faith was rewarded when she responded and embraced her boy. When Paul knocked on the door of heaven, his soul was filled with anticipation; his Father was "at home" and would answer the call.

SECTION THREE

Expository Notes on the Detailed Requests in Paul's Prayer

That the God of our Lord Jesus Christ, the Father of glory, may give unto you the spirit of wisdom and revelation in the knowledge of him: the eyes of your understanding being enlightened; that ye may know what is the hope of his calling, and what the riches of the glory of his inheritance in the saints (vv. 17-18).

THEME: *The Opening of the Eyes of Understanding*
OUTLINE:

A. A Perfect Portrait
B. A Personal Perception
C. A Predestined Plan
D. A Precious Privilege

It must be remembered that the key word of this section of the Epistle is know. Paul claimed to have received a special revelation from God and wished to share its content with the saints in Asia. He prayed constantly that the eyes of their understanding would be opened to see the riches awaiting discovery in Christ. His phraseology has unfortunately been misconstrued by his critics.

A PERFECT PORTRAIT

Paul wrote of "the God of our Lord Jesus Christ, the Father of glory" (v. 17), and expressed the hope that wisdom would be given to all who read the Epistle. He appeared to draw a line of demarcation between God, the Father, and the Lord Jesus Christ and emphasized that the Father was the author of every good and perfect gift. Biased teachers have deduced from this statement that God is superior to the Son and that Jesus is not co-equal with the Almighty. They have taught that the Son is subservient to the Father, and therefore can not be Divine. They claim that since He is the "begotten Son," there was a time when He did not exist, a belief that explains why He needed a God whom He could worship.

That conclusion is erroneous; it is contradictory to the Scripture. John declared, "In the beginning was the Word, and the Word was with God, and the Word was God" (John 1:1). The apostle described the reactions of the Pharisees and Sadducees when he wrote, "Therefore, the Jews sought the more to kill him, because he not only had broken the sabbath, but said also that God was his Father, *making himself equal with God*" (John 5:18). The Savior did not deny that accusation, for it was true. If Jesus were not what He claimed, then He was the greatest of all deceivers. Nevertheless, Paul said the eternal Father was indeed "the God of our Lord Jesus Christ," and his statement invites investigation.

Writing to the church in Philippi, the apostle said, "Let this mind be in you, which was also in Christ Jesus; who, being in the form of God, thought it not robbery [a thing to be grasped at] to be equal with God: but made himself of no reputation, and took upon him the form of a servant, and was made in the likeness of men: and being found in fashion as a man, he humbled himself, and became obedient unto death, even the death of the cross. Wherefore, God also hath highly exalted him, and given him a name which is above every name . . . " (Phil. 2:5-9). The Son of God laid aside the robes of His majesty to be born of a woman and "to be found in fashion as a man." He, therefore, came to earth to be as an individual, that is, to have a distinct identity from the eternal God. As the "last Adam," He gave allegiance to the Supreme God, spoke to Him in prayer, and every day endeavored to be "the image of the invisible God" (Col. 1:15). This was the basic feature of the revelation given to Paul. It thrilled him to such a degree that he prayed day and night that his friends would comprehend the magnitude of that message.

A PERSONAL PERCEPTION

The apostle believed that a course of self-improvement would be unable to bring this enlightenment to his readers. They needed a revelation from God. Paul expressed these identical facts when he wrote to the church in Corinth. "But we speak the wisdom of God in a mystery, even the hidden wisdom, which God ordained before the world unto our glory: which none of the princes of this world knew: for had they known it, they would not have crucified the Lord of glory . . . but God hath revealed them unto us by his Spirit: for the Spirit searcheth all things, yea, the deep things of God" (1 Cor. 2:7–10). God's mystery concerning His plans for man had been preserved throughout the ages, but an amazing change had taken place whereby believers in Christ could understand what, hitherto, had been unrevealed. Therefore, Christians were obligated to listen carefully to what was being taught. Compliance with God's desires and obedience to His commands, would enable them to make new discoveries. They had enjoyed the apostle's ministry, but there remained mountains of truth to be climbed where they would obtain a new vision of what God had planned for them in Christ. If, somehow, the cataracts of unbelief could be removed from their eyes, they would quickly discover, as did the Queen of Sheba, "the half has never been told;" the best was yet to be.

A PREDESTINED PLAN

"That ye may know what is the hope of his calling" (v. 18a). Paul's definition is interesting. A man's calling may be his occupation or vocation in life. It is the profession to which he dedicates his time and talents. He may choose to be a clergyman, an architect, an engineer, a scientist, or an educator. Paul desired his readers to be aware of Christ's calling, the supreme task to which he dedicated all he possessed. The writer to the Hebrews expressed similar thoughts when He referred to the task of "bringing many sons unto glory" (see Hebrews 2:10). The vocation or calling of Christ was to fulfill in time what had been planned in eternity. Paul desired this knowledge to be known among his friends. They were already aware of the basic truths of the gospel, but the babes in Christ needed to mature and "come unto the measure of the stature of the fullness of Christ" (Eph. 4:13). The converts had made magnificent progress since they first trusted Christ, but they had a long way to go to reach their final objective. Paul apparently believed that those who were satisfied with their progress had much to learn! He expressed his convictions when he wrote, "Brethren, I count not myself to have apprehended: but this one thing I do, forgetting those things which are behind, and reaching forth unto those things which are before, I press toward the mark for the prize of the high calling of God in Christ Jesus" (Phil. 3:13-14). Salvation would remain incomplete until the saints, clothed in the righteousness of the Lord, stood forever in the presence of the Father. This was the ultimate goal of predestination; the fulfillment of which was Christ's greatest desire.

A PRECIOUS PRIVILEGE

"That ye may know . . . the riches of the glory of his inheritance in the saints" (v.18b). The apostle spoke of *our inheritance* in verse 11. He presented the other side of the picture in verse 18 when he wrote of *Christ's inheritance* in the saints (see the homily, "A Great Inheritance," p. 66). No man receives an inheritance from himself. An inheritance is bequeathed by a benefactor; it is something given and gladly received. Paul was thrilled by the greatness of his message. His language is worthy of consideration. He spoke of "the riches of the glory;" "the exceeding greatness of his power;" "the workings of his mighty power." He spoke of superlative truth, the greatness of which would never be recognized until the eyes of their understanding were enlightened (Eph. 1:18).

SECTION FOUR

Expository Notes on the Greatness of God's Provision for His People

That ye may know . . . what is the exceeding greatness of his power to us-ward who believe, according to the working of his mighty power, which he wrought in Christ, when he raised him from the dead, and set him at his own right hand in the heavenly places, far above all principality, and power (vv. 18-19).

THEME: *The Continuation of Paul's Desire for the Saints*
OUTLINE:

A. The Grandeur of God's Power
B. The Growth of God's People
C. The Greatness of God's Provision

The apostle Paul did his utmost to explain the magnitude of the power of God, but the vastness of the subject seemed to be almost inexpressible. He had to be content with one electrifying phrase, "the exceeding greatness of his power." It is interesting to note how the apostle made use of the word "exceeding." He wrote of "the exceeding greatness of God's power" (Eph. 1:19), "the exceeding riches of God's grace" (Eph. 2:17), "the exceeding wonder of God's capability" (Eph. 3:20).

THE GRANDEUR OF GOD'S POWER

It is difficult to think of this text without considering the supernatural energy which brought worlds into existence. The apostle John wrote, "All things were made by him, and without him, was not anything made that was made" (John 1:3). Paul expressed similar thoughts when he wrote to the Colossians as follows: "In whom [Christ] we have redemption through his blood, even the forgiveness of sins: who is the image of the invisible God, the firstborn of every creature; for by him were all things created, that are in heaven, and that are in earth, visible and invisible, whether they be thrones, or dominions, or principalities, or powers: all things were created by him, and for him" (Col. 1:14-16). This thrilling fact was revealed in different ways. The omniscience and omnipresence of God were expressed when Jesus declared that God was aware of the fall of every sparrow throughout the world. The omnipotence of God was expressed by Daniel, when he told king Nebuchadnezzar his breath was in the hand of God (see Dan. 5:23). The prophet evidently believed that the Lord is almighty and that even the most powerful monarchs become helpless when God withdraws His supporting grace.

The Creator brought planets into existence and placed each one in its orbit. He designed trees, flowers, animals, and every living creature. He arranged the colors of the rainbow, composed the songs of the birds, and gave to each the inherent knowledge of survival, in what was to become a hostile world. Nevertheless, Paul believed that great as was the power exhibited in creation, it was overshadowed and superseded by the power seen in the death and resurrection of the Lord Jesus Christ. The apostle wrote, "The mighty power which he wrought in Christ, when he raised him from the dead" (Eph. 1:19-20). Mortality became man's greatest enemy. Decay ruined existence, death became predominant, and the entire world, became a victim of age. Today the astronomers speak of "the death of stars." When God raised Christ from the dead, He demonstrated that man's greatest enemy had received a fatal blow—death had died!

THE GROWTH OF GOD'S PEOPLE

"The greatness of his power *to us-ward* who believe" (v. 19). Even the apostle was amazed by the facts imparted to him by the Holy Spirit. It seemed beyond the limits of his understanding that the indescribable power of the Almighty, as demonstrated in the resurrection of Christ, was destined to be the possession of every believer in the Savior. What God did, was done *for Christians* who believe! It was one thing to be the object of God's redeeming grace, but quite another to be united with the Lord in resurrection life and power. That made possible the subjugation of those enemies by whom the saint had been enslaved.

Paul explained how believers could be raised from the dead even before their mortal bodies died! Resurrection life was not only the ultimate goal of the Christian, but it was also the continuing experience of all who shared the Spirit-filled life. Paul was not anticipating the moment when, through age, accident, or sickness, humanity became the victims of mortality. He was considering that greater aspect of Christianity when souls become unresponsive to the prompting of evil and when the self-life ceases to trouble those, experientially, risen with Christ. That hallowed and blessed state could be enjoyed, for what was seen in the triumph of Jesus was for "US-WARD who believe."

These lessons were beyond the reach of babes in Christ; the converts had only just enrolled in God's academy and had much to learn! They needed to have the eyes of their understanding opened; their growth in grace would bring new revelations of God's ability to do in and for them that which was thought impossible.

THE GREATNESS OF GOD'S PROVISION

"Which he wrought in Christ when he . . . set him at his own right hand in the heavenly places, far above all . . . " (v. 20). Paul was decisive in his statements. Continuing his opening remarks, he explained the scope of Christ's supremacy. He was enthroned "far above all principality, and power, and might, and dominion, and every name that is named, not only in this world, but also in that which is to come" (Eph. 1:21). Later, he explained how God had commissioned him to preach, "to the intent that now unto the principalities and powers in heavenly places might be known *by the church* the manifold wisdom of God" (Eph. 3:10).

Two facts appear to be irrefutable:

1. Paul believed that *there existed an organized kingdom of evil which was opposed to everything righteous.* Satan was the archenemy of God and His people. When Paul gave advice to his readers (Eph. 6:11-13), he emphasized the need to be prepared for spiritual conflict. "For we wrestle not against flesh and blood, but against principalities, against powers, against the rulers of the darkness of this world, against spiritual wickedness in high places" (Eph. 6:12). He claimed that the Lord Jesus was enthroned *far above* these enemies of God. He was not content to say "above;" he said "far above." The word of the exalted Savior superseded any command of Satan; Jesus was able to render inoperative *anything* conceived in the kingdom of darkness.
2. Paul explained that as far as God was concerned, the Church was also enthroned with the Savior and that in union with Christ, *the word of the resplendent Church was as authoritative as the command*

of Christ. The saints, when they exercised their God-given power, could thwart Satan's efforts and prevent his attempts to hinder the activities of the Holy Spirit. He insisted this was an integral part of God's provision for His people.

I would like to describe an experience which recently happened in one of my meetings. I had been writing and thinking about these truths, but did not realize they were soon to be tested. It was time for the evening service and a delightful family had come to provide special music. Their voices were filling the sanctuary with melody when a strange thing happened. A visiting lady apparently lost control of her emotions and began screaming. Let no reader misunderstand. She *screamed,* waved her arms, and appeared to be completely irresponsible.

Evidently, some of the people knew her and were accustomed to her strange behavior. A few in the congregation were already smiling. The pastor whispered that the lady was highly emotional and his people might be pardoned for their mirth. I was very apprehensive. Then I remembered how Paul said, "I was seated with Christ in heavenly places." I did not ask the Lord to intervene—I did it myself! I commanded Satan to stop interfering in the meeting and to leave the woman alone! I called for the protecting power of the blood of Christ to cover, shelter, and protect the entire service. Then, a strange quietness fell on the meeting; the woman ceased screaming. I preached for forty-five minutes, and several of the young ministers became very noisy in their responses. Their crescendo of praise rose higher and higher until their hallelujahs filled the church. Yet, all through the service, the lady who had screamed remained perfectly still and quiet. She never uttered a sound!

I am still amazed as I recall that experience. Some people would be unimpressed, declaring the incident to be a coincidence, but was it really that? The young pastor said afterward, "I saw and heard you praying, and then she stopped!" His voice became a whisper as he stared at me. Could that have been God's endorsement of the truth uttered by Paul? Intelligent, Spirit-filled Christians do not have to tolerate Satan's intervention. If God has placed invincible weapons in the hands of His Church, Christians should learn how to use them.

THE RESPLENDENT SON OF GOD

Expository Notes on the Exaltation of Christ and His Church

He set him at his own right hand in the heavenly places, far above all

principality, and power, and might, and dominion, and every name that is named, not only in this world, but also in that which is to come: and hath put all things under his feet, and gave him to be the head over all things to the church, which is his body, the fullness of him that filleth all in all (vv. 20-23).

THEME: *The Resplendent Son of God*
OUTLINE:

A. The Conquering Christ . . . "*All things under his feet*"
B. The Church of Christ . . . "*His body*"
C. The Complete Christ . . . "*the fullness of him that filleth all in all*"

The promise that Christ would become the Head of all things introduces a very comprehensive theme; it reaches into the past, embraces the present, and points to the future when everything will be subject to Him who will be all, and in all.

THE CONQUERING CHRIST . . . "All things under his feet"

When the psalmist tried to explain the greatness of man, he wrote, "What is man that thou art mindful of him? and the son of man, that thou visitest him? For thou hast made him a little lower than the angels, and hast crowned him with glory and honor. Thou madest him to have dominion over the works of thy hands; thou hast put all things under his feet: all sheep and oxen, yea, and the beasts of the field; the fowl of the air, and the fish of the sea, and whatsoever passeth through the paths of the seas" (Psalm 8:4-8). God planned that Adam should be the lord of all creation, and some of that majesty can still be seen. Nevertheless, man lost much of his authority when he permitted evil passions to control his desires.

It was to be expected, therefore, that when the last Adam arrived to supersede the first one, the same text would be associated with Him. The writer to the Hebrews stated, "But unto the Son, he saith, Thy throne, O God, is forever and ever; a sceptre of righteousness is the sceptre of thy kingdom . . . and, thou, in the beginning, hast laid the foundations of the earth; and the heavens are the works of thine hands: they shall perish, but thou remainest . . . but to which of the angels saith he at any time, sit on my right hand, until I make thine enemies thy footstool?" (Heb. 1:8-13). Evidently, the New Testament writer believed that Jesus had taken the place of the first Adam and proceeded to explain that things had changed. Creation was no longer subservient to authority, "But now we see not yet all things put under him, *but we see Jesus* . . . crowned with glory and honor" (Heb. 2:8-9). Paul supplied additional details to the Philippians. He wrote, "The Savior, the Lord Jesus Christ, shall change our vile body, that it may be fashioned like unto his glorious body, according to the working whereby he is able even to subdue all things unto himself" (Phil. 3:21). The predestination plans of God will never be completely fulfilled until everything is brought into subjection to Christ. Writing to the Corinthians, Paul declared, "He [Christ] must reign till He hath put all enemies under his feet" (1 Cor. 15:25). Eventually, the Lord Jesus Christ will be recognized as Lord of the universe and crowned "KING OF KINGS AND LORD OF LORDS" (Rev. 19:16).

THE CHURCH OF CHRIST . . . "His body"

It is thrilling to recognize that in all of God's plans, the saints were always associated with the Savior; they are never far apart! There exists between Christ and His Church an unbreakable bond. Christ is the Head of His body. Neither could exist happily without the other. In the beginning, the Church was in the Lord's mind; at the end, she will be at His side.

Paul had much to relate concerning the body of Christ; his message may be summarized as follows:

1. The head and the body are joined together—either needs the other.
2. The function of the body is to obey the head. The brain dictates actions and healthy bodies respond.
3. All members of a body should work harmoniously with others. They should never be jealous or envious of another member's accomplishment.
4. Members of a body are completely useless if severed from the body itself. Hands, arms, and legs are but parts of a corpse when life is denied to the body itself.
5. Bodies need nourishment. Christians who never feed on the Bread of Life cannot be healthy or useful.
6. Members of a body need exercise. Christians who seldom if ever work for or speak of Christ are useless in the extension of God's kingdom.
7. A body which has been hurt needs the immediate attention of a skilled doctor. Procrastination in seeking medical assistance is the harbinger of a funeral! Jesus was called "the Great Physician;" His patients should consult Him often.

THE COMPLETE CHRIST . . . "all and in all"

" . . . the church, which is his body the fullness of him that filleth all in all" (v. 23). It is impossible to add to "fullness." A vessel which is completely full cannot hold another drop of liquid. It is only possible to fill something not already full! It is significant, therefore, that the Church is described as "the fullness of Christ who filleth all in all." That can only mean that the redeemed, resplendent Church of Christ represents the maximum of God's creative power. The bringing of many sons and daughters to glory supersedes in excellence of anything God ever did (see Heb. 2:10). Jesus, the Son of God, fills eternity with His radiance. He is the Supreme Head of angelic hosts, the theme of prophetic utterances, the joy of grateful people. He will be adored by innumerable saints who will sing, "Thou art worthy . . . for thou wast slain, and hast redeemed us to God by thy blood, out of every kindred and tongue, and people, and nation" (Rev. 5:9).

A SUMMARY OF THE FIRST CHAPTER

The study of the first chapter of the Epistle to the Ephesians has now terminated. Ere we proceed, it might be beneficial to consider again what the apostle Paul said. This summary may be divided into five sections:

1. Looking Into Another World (vv. 1-6)
2. Lost in Absolute Wonder (vv. 7-14)
3. Learning About Astonishing Wisdom (vv. 15-19)
4. Liberated From Awful Weakness (vv. 20-22)
5. Loving Through Adoring Worship (v. 23)

LOOKING INTO ANOTHER WORLD (vv. 1-6)

Paul's vision scanned eternity. First, he saw timeless aeons where there was no form of created life; God alone existed. That era will remain eternally hidden in inscrutable mystery. It is not known from where God came, and it would be foolish to speculate on such profound matters. Philosophers state that all things must have a beginning, but that reasoning is unconvincing. If God had a beginning, then men would ask who was responsible for His creation? God said, "I AM THAT I AM" (Exod. 3:14). He did not say "I WAS;" neither did He say, "I WILL BE." He had no beginning and will have no end! Paul looked into that timeless era and saw the Divine Family in conference. He listened and afterward said, "He hath chosen us in him before the foundation of the world . . . " (Eph. 1:4).

LOST IN ABSOLUTE WONDER (vv. 7-14)

The phrase "to the praise of his glory" appeared three times in quick succession in Paul's opening statements. He was overwhelmed by what he heard, but to express the amazing facts seemed beyond his capability. The apostle appreciated the immensity of the plans of God, and marvelled at the grace which brought Christ to earth. The Redeemer fulfilled everything predicted of Him and revealed that God, who sent Him, was the embodiment of love. Paul described the blessings of the Almighty as "gifts according to the riches of God's grace." Men gave according to their capabilities; they could not give what they did not possess. God was exceedingly wealthy. Paul spoke of the "riches of His grace." He saw the divine Benefactor as the One who held all things in the hollow of His hand.

LEARNING ABOUT ASTONISHING WISDOM (vv.15-19)

Between the omniscience of God and the limited, intellectual ability of the apostle existed a gulf as broad as eternity. Therefore, it became necessary to find a means of communication whereby Paul could understand what otherwise would have been incomprehensible. The apostle was able to write, "He hath abounded toward us in all wisdom and prudence, having made known unto us the mystery of his will" (Eph. 1:8-9). When he wrote to the Corinthians, he expressed identical facts. "Eye hath not seen, nor ear heard, neither have entered into the heart of man, the things which God hath prepared for them that love him. But God hath revealed them unto us by his Spirit: for the Spirit searcheth all things; yea, the deep things of God. . . . Now we have received, not the spirit of the world, but the Spirit which is of God, that we may know the things which are freely given to us of God. Which things also we speak" (1 Cor. 2:9-13).

LIBERATED FROM AWFUL WEAKNESS (vv. 20-22)

Paul was aware of the inherent weakness of human nature; in common with other Christians, he was assailed by all the temptations known to man. He wrote to the church in Rome to say, "I am carnal, sold under sin. For that which I do I allow not, for what I would, that do I not; but what I hate, that do I. If then I do that which I would not, I consent unto the law that it is good . . . for I know that in me (that is, in my flesh), dwelleth no good thing" (Rom. 7:14-18). Aware of innate shortcomings, Paul was thrilled to proclaim the glorious deliverance made possible through the Savior. The Church had been raised with Christ and made to sit in heavenly places. Christians had been given power which exceeded anything known among their enemies. They could reign with Christ. Poverty could be replaced by power, weakness by worship, defeat by glorious deliverance. Paul was able to exclaim triumphantly, "I can do all things through Christ which strengtheneth me" (Phil. 4:13).

LOVING THROUGH ADORING WORSHIP (v. 23)

Perhaps this was best expressed by Paul when he wrote: " For this cause, I bow my knees unto the Father of our Lord Jesus Christ" (Eph. 3:14). The far-reaching effects of God's provision, the all-embracing power of His grace, amazed the apostle to the Gentiles. When he considered the details of the salvation offered by Christ, he appreciated the statement which said he had been lifted from the dunghill and made to sit with princes (see 1 Sam. 2:8). During the inspiring moments when speech became difficult, Paul bowed his head to worship. Perhaps, during those times of meditation, his thoughts might have been expressed in the words of an old chorus.

There on Calvary's Cross,
He gave His life for me.
At such an infinite cost,
He died to set me free.
I cannot tell why He loved me,
Perhaps its too much to know:
I only can tell how He saved me,
And cleansed me as white as snow.

HOMILIES

Homily No. 1

"IN WHOM WE HAVE"

The apostle Paul was probably the greatest evangelist of all time. His service to the Church was of incalculable worth. Although he had very little money, he was the wealthiest of all Christians—not in earthly assets, but in spiritual power. This outstanding fact is clearly seen in his letter to the Ephesians.

IN CHRIST WE HAVE REDEMPTION THROUGH HIS BLOOD . . . Pardon (v. 7)

It is noteworthy that most of the inhabitants of Ephesus were Gentiles who had worshiped the goddess Diana. Their city was notoriously sinful, but the gospel so transformed the district that before the end of the second century, many of its citizens had become Christians. It would have been expected that Jews would understand the message of redemption through the blood of sacrifice, but when pagans accepted this truth, it testified to the effectiveness of Paul's ministry. He did not hesitate to speak about the atoning death of the Lord Jesus, for he knew, that for all people, this alone was the power of God unto salvation. It was thrilling to read Paul's words, "the forgiveness of sins, according to the riches of his grace." God's grace was marvelous, but the apostle spoke of *the riches* of His grace. That indicated grace in all of its fullness. Pardon given to undeserving sinners was measured by the infinite grace of a compassionate God.

IN CHRIST WE HAVE AN INHERITANCE . . . Provision (v. 11)

An inheritance is something claimed after the donor has died. The writer to the Hebrews wrote, "For where a testament is, there must also of necessity be the death of the testator, for a testament is of force after men are dead; otherwise it is of no strength at all while the testator liveth" (Heb. 9:16-17). It was the desire of the Lord that redeemed sinners should receive an inheritance to supply their need through time and eternity. This was only made possible when the Testator's death validated His will. Later in the Epistle to the Ephesians, Paul itemized the details of the provision made by the Prince of Heaven.

IN CHRIST WE HAVE BEEN SEALED . . . Possessed (v. 13)

So that there could be no mistake in the identity of claimants to this eternal fortune, the stamp of ownership was placed on every believer. That the Christian was eligible to receive an inheritance could never be challenged in a court of law; the stamp of heaven was indelibly placed upon his soul. Paul wrote, "Ye were sealed with the Holy Spirit of promise." Many logging companies have felled trees in the Canadian forests, but these are immediately stamped with the special mark of the owner. The logs, thereafter, float down rivers to the lake where they are examined and separated. There is never a problem of identity, for each log "is sealed" with a stamp of ownership. Christians may mingle with millions of other human beings but, sealed by the Holy Spirit, their identity can never be confused.

IN CHRIST WE HAVE BECOME A HABITATION . . . Privilege (v. 22)

Paul went to great lengths to explain that within the fellowship of the Church, racial bitterness should be non-existent. Jews and Gentiles were united. Old barriers had been removed to create God's substitute for the temple at Jerusalem. Formerly, it was claimed that Jehovah lived in the sanctuary made by men; Paul affirmed that something new had been created. Christians had become a home for the indwelling Spirit of God (see 1 Cor. 3:16).

IN CHRIST WE HAVE BOLDNESS . . . Pleasure (Eph. 3:12)

This was no "flash in the pan" doctrine, something about which to argue, something which might be proved false. It was "according to the eternal purpose which God purposed in Christ Jesus." What had been planned in eternity had been accomplished in time. Paul was absolutely sure of the provisions in his inheritance, and he said that every believer should share his confidence. Neither shame nor hesitancy should be evident when the believer stated his case before men. There could be no doubt about the realities claimed; God had endorsed what had been said.

IN CHRIST WE HAVE ACCESS. . . Permission (Eph. 3:12)

Access into the ancient Holy of Holies had been denied to all except the high priest of Israel. He had been permitted, once a year, to go beyond the veil to stand before the mercy seat. All prohibitions had been swept away by the death of Christ. Jesus had opened a new and living way to the heart of the Father, and all who desired could "come boldly unto the throne of grace to obtain mercy and find grace to help in time of need" (see Heb. 4:16). Paul was a wealthy believer, but we also may claim an identical inheritance . . . if we know how! (Homily taken from the author's book, *Bible Gems*, pp. 131-132.)

Homily No. 2

A GREAT INHERITANCE . . . for Us and Christ

I shall always remember the old lady who decided to bequeath to me her fortune. "My boy", she said, "I am a wealthy woman. I have property in England and South Africa, but since I cannot expect to live much longer, I have decided to leave my possessions to you." When she smiled, she seemed to be an angel! Thereafter I walked on air until one of the local people asked how I was getting along with my hostess. Possibly, he saw the excitement in my eyes, for he said, "She is a wonderful old lady, but she has one weakness. Has she spoken to you about her last will and testament? She makes one every month and probably gets a real kick out of doing it. Has she told you she intends to leave everything to you? Ah, I thought so! She is always approaching new people with the same story. Her lawyer must be a very patient man." Yes, that kindly lady made me her sole beneficiary, but she forgot to die—in time. "For where a testament is, there must also of necessity be the death of the testator. For a testament is of force *after* men are dead: otherwise it is of no strength at all while the testator liveth" (Heb. 9:16-17). An inheritance depends upon three things: (1) someone must have something to bequeath, (2) the testator must die before the will becomes valid, and (3) the beneficiary must claim the inheritance and rejoice in its provision.

OUR INHERITANCE IN CHRIST (Eph. 1:11)

Paul speaks of our inheritance in Christ and then affirms that the Lord Jesus also has an inheritance in us (see Eph. 1:18). The Savior had something to bequeath, and His death made it possible for beneficiaries to register their claims. Against the background of slavery, the apostle speaks of redemption through the blood of Christ, but in Ephesians 2:5–7 his statement describes the greatness of God's purposes for the Church. In the past, He quickened us together with Christ; in the present, He has made us to sit with Him in heavenly places; in the future, He intends to display His eternal kindness before the assembled hosts of heaven. When royalty honors a subject, the act is reported around the world. Similarly, " . . . in the ages to come he might shew the exceeding riches of his grace in his kindness toward us through Jesus Christ." The forgiveness of sins, eternal life, the filling of the Holy Spirit, the enduement of power, and the assurance that someday we shall be like Him are part of our great inheritance.

Sometimes, earthly inheritances are conditioned by restrictive clauses; for example, a man may not be able to register his claim until he has reached a certain age. However, our inheritance may be claimed *now*. The Savior made His last will and testament before the foundation of the world. He desired to share His wealth with us, but when He died, His will became valid and operative. Then Christ rose from the dead to become His own executor in order to administer His estate. Nevertheless, there is one restrictive condition. Unless an inheritance is claimed, it remains useless. A beggar could have millions of dollars in a bank and yet die of starvation on the steps of that same building. It is useless to have a vast fortune in a bank if the beneficiary ignores it. Even millions of dollars cannot save a man's life if he refuses to eat!

CHRIST'S INHERITANCE IN US (Eph. 1:18)

It must be remembered that when Paul rejoiced in the first inheritance, he prayed for wisdom to grasp the full significance of the second. He prayed for three things.

1. That Christians might understand the purpose of God's call—*the hope of His calling*. There were things Christ fervently desired. The apostle spoke of *an inheritance*. He envisaged the joys of ownership and thought not only of a soul forgiven, but of one possessed! An accepted inheritance may be used by its owner to further his purposes and increase his pleasure. Christ plans to reach a world, but for Him to do so, He needs dedicated people through whom to work. Second only to the joy of possessing men is the thrill of using them. There is great wealth in the human soul and this may be bequeathed to the Savior.
2. Nevertheless, in spite of every noble resolve, *our will can only be validated when we also die*—"For a testament is of force after men are dead." We need to be crucified with Christ, for it is then that the Lord Jesus can claim his inheritance of the saints. It was for this reason Paul prayed for His friends' enlightenment. He desired them to see "the riches of the glory of his inheritance in the saints."

3. The apostle desired his converts to know "*the exceeding greatness of Christ's power to us-ward who believe*." The cross of Calvary stands at the center of everything spiritual. Through His death it is possible for us to inherit the riches of heaven; through our identification with Him, He can inherit the riches of His earthly family. He was glad to lay down His life for us; it is problematical whether or not we are glad to emulate His example. Elsewhere, Paul spoke of our being laborers together with God—we are partners in a great concern. Together we work toward a great climax. However, we should consider a question. We have been able to claim our inheritance; has He been able to claim His?

> Oh, teach me how to die, dear Lord;
> To die upon a cross:
> To give to Thee that which is Thine,
> And count all else but dross.
> Then teach me how to live, dear Lord,
> To take Thy hand in mine:
> To work, and pray, and seek for souls,
> Until the world is Thine.

(Homily taken from the author's book, *Bible Highways*, pp. 161-162.)

The Second Chapter of Ephesians

THEME: *The Greatness of Our Inheritance in Christ*
OUTLINE:

I. The Plight of the Sinner (Verses 1-12)
II. The Purpose of the Savior (Verses 13-18)
III. The Privileges of the Saint (Verses 19-22)

THE PLIGHT OF THE SINNER

SECTION ONE

Expository Notes on the Guilt of Unrepentant Sinners

And you hath he quickened, who were dead in trespasses and sins; wherein in time past ye walked according to the course of this world, according to the prince of the power of the air, the spirit that now worketh in the children of disobedience: among whom also we all had our conversation in times past in the lusts of our flesh, fulfilling the desires of the flesh and of the mind; and were by nature the children of wrath, even as others (vv. 1-3).

THEME: *What the Christians Had Been*
OUTLINE:

A. They Were Dead in Sin
B. They Were Dupes of Satan
C. They Were Dominated by Self

Many teachers believe the first two chapters of this Epistle belong together, and some have expressed regret that the division into chapters had ever occurred. This is one possible point of view, but a scrutiny of the second chapter suggests God's guiding hand might have been upon those responsible for the separation. Paul, in his opening section, directed the attention of his readers to the eternal ages where God made momentous decisions. Although many things were veiled in mystery, some details of God's activities were revealed. "According to the good pleasure of His will," He predestined that sinners should be accepted into His family. The first chapter shows that Paul's attention was centered upon the eternal ages when there was no created life. The second chapter supplied something very different. The apostle directed attention to the planet earth and its sinful inhabitants. If the first chapter described what God planned in eternity, the next chapter revealed how that plan was fulfilled. It was, and still is, impossible to understand the magnitude of the divine plan unless there is an understanding of the state of fallen humanity. Paul went to great lengths to emphasize the position of the sinner who had never known Christ. The key phrase of the chapter is "in times past" which is found, with slight variations, in verses 1, 3, 11, 12, and 13. The apostle was determined to remind his readers of the depths of sin from which they had been lifted.

His indictment might be summarized: they were un-Christlike, unholy, and unwanted. They were un-Christlike in that they walked according to the course of this world. They were unholy in their nature; their life-stream was tainted with the poison of evil. Finally, they were unwanted because they were Gentiles, outcasts from the commonwealth of Israel. They had no claim on God, no Messiah, and, consequently, no hope. They were traveling a road to nowhere! Some of them had worshiped idols, had walked according to their own evil desires, and, apparently without regret, had persisted in living a life which merited condemnation.

THEY WERE DEAD IN SIN

"And you hath he quickened who were dead in trespasses and sins" (v. 1). Since Paul was writing to living people, it is obvious that the term "dead in sins" referred to their standing before God. A dead person does not respond to promptings; a corpse can neither understand, speak, nor hear. The apostle believed that sinful people are unable to appreciate the promptings of the Holy Spirit and that, left to his own resources, humanity could never save themselves. It was incumbent, therefore, that God should make the first move regarding the salvation of lost souls. Paul was able to write, "And you hath he quickened." A remarkable story which illustrates this truth was told by the late, Bishop Taylor Smith of England.

Years ago, during my city-wide services in Glasgow, Scotland, I stayed with six other ministers in a centrally-located hotel. One of the clergymen was the Rev. Chalmers Lyons, a forthright preacher of the gospel. I shall always remember a story he told of his travels in Germany. Accompanied by Bishop Taylor Smith, he was going from place to place, and one Saturday evening, the Bishop looked at his friend and said,

"Lyons, I'll give you a sermon for tomorrow."

"Yes, Bishop, what is the text?"

"Lord, by this time he stinketh."

"But, Bishop, I can hardly speak from that text."

"Why not? I used it in an English cathedral only a few months ago. I had a great time with it."

Chalmers Lyons stared at the Bishop; it seemed inconceivable that such a text could provide subject matter for an address in a dignified cathedral! Then, as he recognized the Bishop was not leg-pulling, he continued, "Bishop, you preached from that text: What did you say about it?"

"Well, I had three points: A dead body cannot save itself, a dead body only deteriorates—it gets worse and worse, and Christ alone can do anything in the matter."

Chalmers Lyons paused in relating this story—his eyes twinkling. "You must admit," he added, "the old Bishop had some excellent thoughts there, and I told him so." Then he continued: "But the Bishop had not completed his story. He went on to say,"

"Lyons, after the service had ended, I went to the vestry to disrobe, and was surprised when the dean of the cathedral followed me in, and locked the door."

"Bishop" said the Dean, "Your text upset me greatly."

"Well" responded Taylor Smith, "It was true, was it not?"

"Yes, that is what I mean. You stressed the fact that men who are dead in sins cannot save themselves; they grow worse and worse. You said that even the finest body ultimately dies; that the coming of Christ in resurrection power is essential. Men need to be born again. Bishop, it is true, but I never knew it until tonight. I need that new life."

And there behind a locked door, they knelt to pray, and that scholarly man entered into newness of life. The Bishop concluded his story by saying, "I heard from him a little while ago. He is rejoicing, but some of his colleagues cannot understand what has happened to him. He is different! So, there you are, Lyons, the text is an excellent one. Use it tomorrow." And smiling broadly, the Bishop went his way. (Reprinted from the author's book, *Bible Highways*, pp. 150-151.)

THEY WERE DUPES OF SATAN

The word translated "sin" is *hamartia*, and to say the least, it is interesting. Dr. Thayer says it means "a failing to hit the mark;" "that which is done wrong; an offense; a violation of the divine law in thought or act." It, therefore, supplied a word-picture of a person who failed to "hit the mark," did not gain his objective, and did not reach the standard required by God. Someone might be sad because of his inability to do what was expected, but he who cares nothing about his failure is devoid of merit. He has failed to "hit the target" and has neither remorse nor disappointment. His nature rebels against discipline, and he could not care less about his failure! Such a condition reveals mental and spiritual poverty; the man's conscience remains undisturbed because his allegiance has been given to another whose desires are opposed to righteousness. Paul declared, "In times past, ye walked according to the course of this world, according to the prince of the power of the air, the spirit that now worketh in the children of disobedience." The apostle believed that Satan was the head of a diabolical organization and that unrepentant sinners were energized by him. Jesus said that these people were the children of Satan (see John 8:44). Evil governed their lives, sinners were slaves of the evil one, and only the power of God could guarantee deliverance from bondage.

Paul believed that the authority given to Adam had been lost when Lucifer assumed dominion over the earth. Humanity's fallen nature provided a workshop within the human heart from which the evil one dominated every aspect of human behavior. Jesus called the arch-conspirator "the prince of this world," and Paul, in Ephesians 6:12, stated that every Christian would have to resist him.

Some teachers deny the existence of evil and state that it is, in fact, undeveloped good! Medical professionals refer to alcoholism as a disease and sex offenders as men who need understanding. Homosexuality has become a part of national life, and such people, so it is claimed, should not be criticized. People now encourage actions once thought to be outrageous. Strange churches exist in some of America's largest cities, and even their pastors are self-confessed homosexuals. Apparently, they ignore what Paul described in Romans 2:26-28, "God gave them up unto vile affections, for even their women did change the natural use into that which is against nature; and likewise also the men, leaving the natural use of women, burned in their lust one toward another, men with men working that which is unseemly, and receiving in themselves that recompense of their error which was meet."

The world is now threatened with a major health problem; the disease known as AIDS is swiftly spreading around the world. This unprecedented epidemic is out of control, and scientists are desperately trying to find a remedy. Humanity seems to have forgotten that even in Paul's generation these conditions existed. The apostle would not have appreciated the modern approach to something he called sin! He predicted that flagrant disobedience of the laws of God would, inevitably, lead to judgment. Who, in today's world, would challenge his statement or question his conclusion? Homosexuals, both men and women, may be wealthy and educated, but, according to the teachings of the Bible, they are guilty sinners—dupes of Satan—who are not only sacrificing their bodies in this world, but endangering their souls in the world which is to come.

THEY WERE DOMINATED BY SELF

"Ye walked according to the course of this world . . . among whom, also, we all had our conversation in times past in the lusts of the flesh, fulfilling the desires of the flesh and of the mind" (vv. 2, 3). The word "ye" signified that Paul was writing to Gentiles; the word "we" indicated that Jews were as guilty as those they condemned. Paul's final analysis confessed that, in the sight of God, Jews and Gentiles were equally guilty—they each had violated the laws of God. The righteousness of God was opposed, not merely to the deeds of men and women, but to the corruption of their nature. Paul remembered how the converts in Asia had been people in whose lives God had no part. Dominated by the world in which they lived and overwhelmed by their selfishness, they pleased themselves and rejected responsibility for their deeds.

They had been "aliens from the commonwealth of Israel, and strangers from the covenants of promise." They had no association with God and no claim upon His beneficence. They had been heathens; unrepentant and condemned. They were "by nature the children of wrath." This simple statement had roots which went back to the earliest history of the human race. Adam was made in the likeness of God and was completely free from blemish. Before he could fall from his place of blessedness, it was necessary for Satan to attack him. When Adam yielded to temptation, his life became tainted, and a perfect man became a *sinner*. Adam transmitted that nature to his children and, consequently, there was no need for the Devil to tempt Cain. The thought of murder originated in the mind of a sinful man, thus indicating that Cain had received a life tainted by sin from his parent. Satan had gained a foothold within the human breast and from that center, was able to interfere in human behavior. David wrote, "Behold, I was shapen in iniquity; and in sin did my mother conceive me" (Ps. 51:5).

The converts in Asia were sinners, as were all men. They also had been given a nature capable of committing evil—they were, "BY NATURE, the children of wrath." God did not try to improve nor sanctify the old Adamic nature; He provided a completely new life through the death and resurrection of the Lord Jesus Christ. The Savior explained this to Nicodemus (John 3) and indicated that entrance into the kingdom of God was by regeneration. The old nature was susceptible to sinning; the new nature given by Christ would never sin (see 1 John 3:6-9). The Adamic nature of the human race could never be sanctified and, therefore, was unconditionally condemned. Nothing could be done by sinners to improve their standing before a holy God; if man were to find acceptance in heaven, it was necessary for God to intervene in human affairs. Paul explained how this was done. When the apostle used the word "we," he included himself in this category, and such a statement suggests certain truths.

1. Paul was a *good* man. Being good did not necessarily mean he was godly. "Among whom also we all had our conversation in times past in lusts of our flesh" (Eph. 2:3). He wrote, "Touching the righteousness which is in the law [I was] blameless" (Phil. 3:6).
2. Paul was an *educated* man. "I am verily a man which am a Jew . . . brought up in this city at the feet of Gamaliel, and taught according to the perfect manner of the law of the fathers" (Acts 22:3). Education of the mind never guarantees the enlightenment of the soul.
3. Paul was a *sincere* man. "And was zealous toward God as ye all are this day" (Acts 22:2). Sincerity does not guarantee salvation. The man who builds his house on sand might be very sincere, but sincerity never excuses stupidity!
4. Paul was a *religious* man. "And Saul . . . went unto the high priest, and desired of him letters to Damascus to the synagogues . . ." (Acts 9:1-2). Paul was a religious activist who worked ceaselessly for his espoused cause. Religion was not redemption. All his assets were afterward "counted but dung" (see Phil. 3:8).

Although Saul of Tarsus was one of the best men on the earth, he, nevertheless, needed a Savior. If this were true of him, it certainly was true of the people of Asia who had no claim on the promises of Jehovah. They had been strangers to everything considered to be sacred in Israel.

SECTION TWO

Expository Notes on What God Did Through Christ

But God, who is rich in mercy, for his great love wherewith he loved us, Even when we were dead in sins, hath quickened us together with Christ, (by grace ye are saved;) and hath raised us up together, and made us sit together in heavenly places in Christ Jesus (vv. 4-6).

Theme: *What the Christians Became*
OUTLINE:

A. A Gracious Compassion . . . *He loved us* (v. 4)
B. A Great Conquest . . . *He quickened us* (v. 5)
C. A Glorious Coronation . . . *He raised us* (v. 6)

"But God" (v. 4). The word "but" represents "a turn in the road." Having allowed his thoughts to travel in one direction, the apostle suddenly changed course, and his turning point is indicated by the conjunction "but." It is used twenty-five times in the Epistle to the Ephesians, and most of the texts indicated a change in the apostle's thoughts. It may be interesting to consider the following verses.

THE "BUTS" OF PAUL'S EPISTLE TO THE EPHESIANS

- Forgiveness: "*Ye were children of wrath . . . but God loved us*" (2:3-4)
- Fortunate: "*Ye were aliens . . . but are now made nigh*" (2:12–13)
- Fellowship: "*Ye are no more strangers . . . but fellowcitizens*" (2:19)
- Favor: "*But unto every one of you is grace given*" (4:7)
- Faithfulness: "*No more cunning craftiness but speaking the truth*" (4:14-15)
- Forsaking: "*Greediness . . . but we have not so learned Christ*" (4:19-20)
- Fruitfulness: "*No more corrupt communication . . . but that which is good*" (4:29)
- Fervent: "*Neither filthiness . . . but giving of thanks*" (5:3–4)
- Fortitude: "*Works of darkness . . . but reprove them*" (5:11–13)
- Flourishing: "*. . . not unwise but understanding . . .*" (5:17)
- Fullness: "*Not drunk . . . but filled with the Spirit*" (5:1–18)
- Fulfillment: "*Not having spot . . . but without blemish*" (5:27)
- Feeding: "*Hateth his own flesh . . . but nourisheth it*" (5:29)
- Fearlessness: "*A great mystery . . . but I speak*" (5:32)

- Fatherhood: "*Provoke not your children . . . but bring them up*" (6:4)
- Following: "*Not . . . as men-pleasers but as servants of Christ*" (6:6)
- Friendliness: "*But that ye also may know my affairs . . .*" (6:21)

A GRACIOUS COMPASSION . . . He loved us (v. 4)

" . . . his GREAT love wherewith he loved us" (v. 4). "For God SO loved the world that he gave his only begotten Son that whosoever believeth in him, should not perish, but have everlasting life" (John 3:16). Paul's conception of the magnitude of divine compassion was formulated by his own experience outside the gate of the city of Damascus. He had been an ardent persecutor; and a bigoted murderer, but the love of God had delivered him from the darkness and thralldom of sin. Such a rescue was beyond comprehension. Although the apostle could have referred to "His love," that definition appeared to be inadequate. The amazing power of God in creation had been superseded by His unspeakable love in redemption. His bringing into existence of all things, animate and inanimate, was insignificant when compared with the love expressed in the salvation of undeserving sinners.

The difficulty of analyzing Paul's Epistle has already been recognized. The apostle had much to say, and little time in which to say it. His opening remarks appear to be cascading floods of living water, rushing from the eternal hills of God's providence. Waves of truth filled the mind of the apostle, and his readers could only be amazed as Paul explained his doctrines. Having emphasized the urgent need of the people in Asia, he suddenly came to a turn in the road and exclaimed, "But God, who is rich in mercy, for his great love wherewith he loved us . . . hath quickened us together with Christ." The Savior had descended to a maelstrom of evil, and somehow managed to lift sinners to safety. Paul stressed the fact that God did this because He was "rich in mercy." The apostle was aware of the immensity of his revelation and used superlatives to express his faith. He wrote of "the riches of God's mercy" (Eph. 2:4), "the riches of God's grace" (Eph. 2:7), and "the riches of God's glory" (Eph. 3:16). The Lord always operates on a lavish scale; He is not only rich—He is very rich!

The Scriptures supply many examples of "the riches of God's mercy:"

- When Adam and Eve sinned, Jehovah supplied coats of skins and clothed the guilty couple (Gen. 3:21).
- When Abraham was about to plunge a dagger into his helpless son, God supplied a substitute and spared the lad (Gen. 22:13).
- When Jacob and his family knew nothing of the approaching famine, Joseph was sent into Egypt to provide salvation for a hungry nation (Gen. 42:25).
- When the children of Israel were slaves of the Pharaoh, God sent Moses to be their deliverer and then honored the scarlet stain on the doorways of their homes (Exod. 12:13).
- When Joshua captured Jericho, the harlot Rahab was spared because of her faith which placed a thread in her window (Josh. 2:18 and 6:25).
- When Hezekiah prayed desperately for help, God reassured and rescued him (Isa. 38:5).
- When the Jews were captives in Babylon, God raised up an alien deliverer who restored their liberty (2 Chron. 36:22-23).
- When a sinful world deserved judgment, God sent His Son to bare its sin and make forgiveness possible (John 3:16).
- When Paul was a ruthless persecutor of the church, the Lord met him at the Damascus gate and bestowed upon him incomprehensible mercy (Acts 9:1-2 and 17).

When the apostle contemplated these facts, his soul became exuberant. Recognizing that each conversion was an exhibition of God's amazing mercy, Paul wrote to the Asian converts about "his great love wherewith he loved us." Perhaps the greatness of God's mercy, grace, and glory is best understood when consideration is given to the statement in 2 Corinthians 8:9: "For ye know the grace of our Lord Jesus Christ, that, though he was rich, yet for your sakes, he became poor, that ye through his poverty might become rich." The apostle believed that God's grace was within reach of all people: "For there is no difference between the Jew and the Greek: for the same Lord over all, is RICH UNTO ALL THAT CALL UPON HIM" (Rom. 10:12).

A welcome is given by Jesus,
To all who will come to His feet,
And a welcome given by Jesus,
Is wondrously full and complete.

There's never a man who has wandered past
The reach of His infinite love:
And never a man who has fallen
Too low for the mansions above.

Within the scope of three dynamic verses, Paul expressed the greatest of his revelations. When he wrote of the gift of God, he spoke of three things: (1) The means by which it was expressed, (2) the miracle by which is was experienced, and (3) the majesty with which it should be exercised.

The Means by Which It Was Expressed

"In Christ we have redemption through his blood, the forgiveness of sins, according to the riches of his grace" (v. 7). Writing to the church in Corinth, Paul said, "Thanks be unto God for his unspeakable gift" (2 Cor. 9:15). The name of the Savior is mentioned eighteen times in the first two chapters of this letter. The apostle Paul stressed the fact that Christ is the divinely appointed way by and through whom the eternal God manifests His blessing and communicates His knowledge. If He had not revealed Himself in the person of the Savior, God would have remained inscrutable and far removed from the consciousness of created beings. When the people saw Jesus of Nazareth embracing children, they had a glimpse of God's desire to hold men and women. When the Lord affirmed that a sparrow could not fall injured to the ground without His Father being aware of it, He revealed a compassion never before discovered in the heart of the Almighty. When Paul said, "God was in Christ, reconciling the world unto himself" (2 Cor. 5:19), he revealed the limitlessness of divine love. The Lord Jesus became a new kind of Jacob's ladder by which access into the divine presence became possible. "But now in Christ Jesus ye who sometimes were far off, are made nigh by the blood of Christ." "For through him . . . we both have access by one Spirit unto the Father" (Eph. 2:13 and 18).

The Miracle by Which It Was Experienced

"When we were dead . . . he quickened us . . . " (v. 5). Dead things are incapable of action. The fact that sinners were said to be "dead in sin" indicated they had not made their own reconciliation to God and could not boast of their achievements. Paul emphasized this when he wrote, "For by grace are ye saved through faith; and that not of yourselves: it is the gift of God . . . not of works lest any man should boast" (Eph. 2:8-9). God planned salvation; the Savior made it possible; the Holy Spirit presented it to undeserving sinners. Personal faith in Christ made real the rebirth of the human soul. Adam was only a creation of soil, but God breathed the breath of life into the lifeless form and man became a living soul. Centuries later, Paul and his friends became representatives of the new humanity that God wished to create. They resembled spiritual beings but, alas, were clad only in garments of self-righteousness; they had little if any knowledge of eternal verities. Then, the miracle of regeneration changed everything, and new life came to the souls of believing men and women. When the significance of that fact dawned upon the consciousness of the converts, they appreciated the apostle's statement: "God who is rich in mercy, for his great love wherewith he loved us, hath quickened us together with Christ."

To see the scintillating wonder of God's handiwork in creation is one of the most inspiring experiences known to human beings. His color scheme in the autumn and His resurrection power in the spring of the year make even the birds to sing. The splendor of an early summer when bees make their honey and birds fuss over and feed their young contributes to the symphony of praise which fills the earth. All this evidence is invaluable, but God's love may best be seen when a redeemed sinner says, "Once I was blind, but now I see." THAT is the ultimate in God's pleasure and the secret of His undiminishing happiness.

The Majesty in Which It Must Be Exercised

"He hath made us sit together in heavenly places" (v. 6). We have been made "unto our God kings and priests" (Rev. 5:10), and, therefore, it behooves all Christians to live a serene life. Paul said, "If ye then be risen with Christ, seek those things which are above, where Christ sitteth on the right hand of God. Set your affection on things above, not on things on the earth. For ye are dead, and your life is hid with Christ in God" (Col. 3:1-3). The apostle emphasized that Christian citizenship is in heaven, and even though believers remain subjects to earthly rulers, their position and power in Christ should be continually seen. If the child of a reigning monarch ever lived in filth and poverty, it would be evident that something had interfered with the royal birthright. Christians who constantly succumb to temptation should re-examine their faith and conduct. No king should be dressed in rags; no millionaire should be a beggar on a city street!

A GREAT CONQUEST . . . "He quickened us"

It is impossible to exaggerate the immensity of the victory won by the Savior when He reconciled us to God. Mention has been made of the transformation of sinful people when they become members of the family of God. There was much more in the triumph of Christ when He "blotted out the handwriting of ordinances that was against us, which was contrary to us, and took it out of the way, nailing it to his cross" (see Col. 2:14-15).

Christ Defeated the Power of the Devil

The human race may never know how fierce was the conflict waged between the Son of God and the forces of evil. Throughout His lifetime, the Savior was attacked by his enemies, and if Christ had made one mistake, the plan of God would have been ruined. One failure would have made Christ a sinner, and if that had happened, He would have needed someone to save Him! The crusade to defeat the purposes of God commenced with Herod's attack on the children of Bethlehem and ended with the monumental attack in the Garden of Gethsemane. If Jesus had died before going to His cross, salvation would never have been offered to sinners. Paul believed that Satan rallied his forces for a supreme attack on Christ, but the Lord "made a show of them openly, triumphing over them in it" (Col. 2:15).

Satan never retreated unless he was forced to do so. Victories won by Christ and His followers were the result of warfare! Paul believed that before Christ could be enthroned anywhere, Satan had to be dethroned. The apostle wrote to the Roman Christians, "I find then a law, that when I would do good, evil is present with me. For I delight in the law of God after the inward man: but I see another law in my members, warring against the law of my mind, and bringing me into captivity to the law of sin which is in my members. O wretched man that I am! who shall deliver me from the body of this death? I thank God through Jesus Christ" (Rom. 7:21-25). Christ's victory over evil was not only for Himself, but for all His followers. His triumph was complete and convincing, and its repercussions should be known in the experience of all Christians.

Christ Destroyed the Pain of Death

"He quickened us together with Christ" (v. 5). When the Lord rose triumphantly from the grave, the Church also rose with Him to be lifted to unprecedented heights of blessedness. Christ opened a highway from the valley of death to the gates of God's celestial city. Jesus promised His disciples, "I go to prepare a place for you. . . . I will come again and receive you unto myself" (John 14:2, 3). That promise is the guarantee that all Christians will travel the highway to heaven. The poet wrote, "Because He lives I shall live also." The Savior said, "And whosoever liveth and believeth in me shall never die" (John 11:26). The Christian's faith rests upon this unshakeable foundation; he is able to exclaim triumphantly, "O death, where is thy sting? O grave, where is thy victory?" (1 Cor. 15:55).

Christ Dispersed the Problem of Doubt

"By grace are ye saved" (v. 8). The clarity and assurance expressed in Paul's statement are exceedingly interesting. Conformity to the laws of Moses has never caused confidence, for, although the sincerity of the Hebrews was often commendable, it has never been possible to fulfill every legal requirement. To break one commandment is to violate all of them. It has been, therefore, evident that acceptance with God has been beyond the reach of man. The new message preached by Paul indicated that faith was far more important than deeds. True faith rests upon what Christ has done, and not upon what man might do. Eternal life is not a reward for merit but a gift given by the Lord, whose love for needy people could never be questioned. That message, to say the least, is astounding. The thrill and satisfaction brought to believers are beyond contradiction. Their hearts become radiant temples where the sunlight of God's love continually shines. Doubts are removed, fears disappear, and songs of deliverance replace sighs of despair! Paul was able to say, "you hath he quickened," and that statement is true in many ways. Mentally, the saints have been quickened; they possessed a new faith. Physically, they are encouraged; they will never die! Spiritually, they are refreshed; they are destined to occupy a mansion in the sky.

They were pilgrims pressing onward,
To their home beyond the sky.
They were each day getting nearer
To that glorious place on high.
Earth had lost its great attraction,
Heaven alone could satisfy;
They were going home to glory,
Where they knew they'd never die.

A GLORIOUS CORONATION . . . "He raised us up"

Probably, one of the greatest illustrations of this truth is found in 2 Kings 25:27-30. Jehoiachin, the king of Judah, had been imprisoned for thirty-seven years, and his outlook was doubtless bleak. Then, "in the twelfth month, on the seven and twentieth day of the month, that Evil-merodach, king of Babylon, in the year that he began to reign, did lift up the head of Jehoiachin, king of Judah, out of prison; and he spake kindly to him, and set his *throne above the throne of the kings that were with him in Babylon*; and changed his prison garments, and he did eat bread continually before him all the days of his life. And his allowance was a continual allowance, given him of the king, a daily rate for every day, all the days of his life." Jehoiachin exchanged rags for riches, and the prisoner who had been condemned and helpless, was exalted to a place of importance. It is significant that his throne was "above the throne of the kings that were with him in Babylon." Rival monarchs could have been antagonistic, but their resentment could not harm the resplendent captive. The king of Babylon had made provision whereby Jehoiachin could be "seated in heavenly places, far above principalities and powers." The word of the king of Judah was final; he could, so to speak, trample under his feet those enemies by whom, otherwise, he would have been subdued. Had he chosen to remain a prisoner dominated by Babylonian lords, he would have lacked intelligence.

Similarly, since the King Eternal has liberated believers from the thralldom of evil and lifted them to a throne in heavenly places, they should never again be subservient to taskmasters. When Joshua entered Canaan, he was told to "possess his possessions." God made extensive provision for His delivered children, a provision for every day of their lives. Therefore, they should exclaim exultantly the words inscribed on the tombstone of the late Martin Luther King—FREE AT LAST! (See the homily, "Enthroned Far Above All," p. 112.)

SECTION THREE

Expository Notes on the Continuity of the Grace of God

That in the ages to come he might shew the exceeding riches of his grace in his kindness toward us through Christ Jesus (v. 7).

THEME: *The Kindness of the Eternal Father*
OUTLINE:

A. When? . . . "*in the ages to come*"
B. What? . . . "*He might shew the exceeding riches of his grace toward us*"
C. Who? . . . "*through Christ Jesus*"

THE UNENDING GRACE

This text was one of Paul's greatest utterances; it encompassed eternity, and went beyond the basic doctrines of redemption. The Christian readers of the first century appreciated the good news of salvation and were strengthened by Paul's Epistles. He reminded them that they had been "without Christ, being aliens from the commonwealth of Israel, and strangers from the covenants of promise, having no hope, and without God in the world" (Eph. 2:12). That the Savior had "broken down the middle wall of partition" which divided Jews from Gentiles was a cause for thanksgiving; they "who were far off, had been made nigh by the blood of Christ" (2:13).

Nevertheless, the wider scope of Paul's message was amazing. The forgiveness of sin was only the commencement of something eternal. Paul gazed into the limitless future, but as far as he could see, he saw the magnificent grace and kindness of God manifested toward, and shared with, glorified saints. What had been gained through faith in Christ would never be lost. That revelation was astounding; it exceeded everything previously preached. It did not matter what part of eternity the apostle visualized; God was there displaying kindness toward redeemed sinners. Paul would have loved the hymn, one verse of which says:

> When we've been there ten thousand years,
> Bright, shining as the sun:
> We've no less days to sing God's praise,
> Than when we first begun.
>
> — John Newton

THE UNSURPASSED GLORY

"The exceeding riches of his grace in his kindness toward us through Christ Jesus" (v. 7). Paul was never a stranger to superlatives! Writing to the Corinthians, he declared, "For our light affliction, which is but for a moment, worketh for us a far more exceeding and eternal weight of glory" (2 Cor. 4:17). He desired the saints in Asia to be aware of "the exceeding greatness of his power to us-ward who believe" (Eph. 1:19). He also wrote, "Now unto him that is able to do exceeding abundantly above all that we ask or think, according to the power that worketh in us" (Eph. 3:20). In spite of his command of language, Paul could not find adequate expressions to reveal the immensity of the truth which dominated his thoughts. He resembled the Queen of Sheba, who said to Solomon, "It was a true report that I heard in mine own land, of thy acts and of thy wisdom. Howbeit, I believed not the words, until I came, and mine eyes had seen it: and, behold, the half was not told me; thy wisdom and prosperity exceedeth the fame which I heard . . . blessed be the Lord thy God, which delighteth in thee" (1 Kings 10:6-9).

Paul's profound statement suggests a question. How will God express "the exceeding riches of His grace" throughout the countless ages of eternity? What can He possibly tell that we do not already know? The apostle's words bring us to the edge of an unexplored region; we can only speculate as to the treasures awaiting discovery in eternity. Millions of worlds hang in space, but we may never know what else exists in the heavens, until we travel through God's amazing creation. Could this be one of the ways in which He will display the riches of His grace?

John predicted that "we shall be like Christ" (1 John 3:2), but we may not understand all that is meant by this statement. We shall have bodies like unto His glorious body and be able to ascend and descend, thus defying the laws of gravity. Sharing Christ's indescribable power, we shall do things thought to be impossible. We shall share the Lord's creative genius and display His colorful artistry. God is "full of surprises." He will amaze His children with continuing displays of revelation, power, beauty, tenderness, and affection. During life on this planet, we look with awe at the loveliness of waterfalls, the grandeur of mountains, the grace of a deer, and the carpet of flowers with which God beautifies the earth in the springtime. Perhaps the beauty of earth will become insignificant when God unveils eternal panoramas of loveliness. The glorious radiance will overshadow anything known, and behind each vista of loveliness will be the smiling face of our heavenly Father. Was Paul thinking of this when he wrote, "That in the ages to come he might shew the exceeding riches of his grace in his kindness toward us through Christ Jesus"? Maybe he was entranced with the same thought when he prayed for his friends, "That Christ may dwell in your hearts by faith, that ye being rooted and grounded in love; may be able to comprehend with all saints, what is the breadth, and length, and depth, and height: and to know the love of Christ which passeth knowledge" (Eph. 3:17-19). How can anyone comprehend the incomprehensible? How can anyone measure infinity and explain the inexplicable? Eternity will be God's university, where graduation will be impossible; the learning process will never end!

THE UNSPEAKABLE GIFT

"Through Christ Jesus" (v. 7b). Paul supplied an example for all preachers of the gospel; he presented Christ! The apostle preached in synagogues and market places as well as from house to house, but his theme never changed. When he wrote his Epistles in health, in prosperity, in adversity, everything he did and said pointed to the Savior. He believed Jesus was the center and circumference of everything; the only One through whom sinners could draw near to God. Whatever mysteries might be explained in heaven, whatever blessings might be given us in the hereafter, Christ would always be supreme.

When the marriage of the Lamb fills eternity with joy and when the Bride occupies her eternal home, fellowship with the Lord will beggar description. If saints walk on streets of gold, it will be an indication that earth's most coveted treasures will have become commonplace. The absence of cemeteries, funeral parlors, hospitals, ghettos, hovels, and clinics of all kinds will remind everybody that the by-products of redemption are beyond imagination. "For ye know the grace of our Lord Jesus Christ, that though he was rich, yet for your sakes, he became poor, that ye through his poverty, might be rich" (2 Cor. 8:9).

SECTION FOUR

Expository Notes on Paul's Basic Belief

For by grace are ye saved through faith; and that not of yourselves; it is the gift of God; not of works lest any man should boast (vv. 8-9).

THEME: *The Apostle's Greatest Conviction . . . Salvation was by faith alone*

OUTLINE:

A. Paul's Experience . . . *Startling!*
B. Paul's Exposition . . . *Scriptural!*
C. Paul's Example . . . *Stirring!*

It is significant that Paul repeated a vital statement and that the two claims are only separated by the sentence, "It is the gift of God." This truth may best be understood when considered against the background of Hebrew customs.

THE APOSTLE'S STARTLING EXPERIENCE

Writing to the Philippians, the apostle stated, "If any other man thinketh that he hath whereof he might trust in the flesh, I more, circumcised the eighth day, of the stock of Israel, of the tribe of Benjamin, an Hebrew of the Hebrews; as touching the law, a Pharisee; concerning zeal, persecuting the church; touching the righteousness which is in the law, blameless" (Phil. 3:4-6). Very few people can make such a claim. Even before Paul met the Savior, he endeavored to live an exemplary life, and consequently believed he was acceptable in the sight of God. Yet, after he met the Savior, he realized that observance of the Mosaic law was insufficient to gain the approbation of the Almighty. The apparent magnificence of his moral and religious conduct became meaningless, and he candidly confessed that what he had previously valued appeared to be refuse (see Phil. 3:8).

That electrifying discovery removed everything about which he might have been proud. He had been circumcised, was morally blameless, had been an activist in religious movements, and had been a friend of the high priest of Israel. Without those assets, he had no achievement of which to be justifiably proud. When he discovered that salvation was not a reward for merit, everything appeared to be worthless. Then, when he had been stripped of his glittering record, Saul realized that what he needed most was being offered as a gift from God. That revelation thrilled his soul and became the theme of his sermons. He wrote, "For the wages of sin is death; but the gift of God is eternal life through Jesus Christ our Lord" (Rom. 6:23).

THE APOSTLE'S SCRIPTURAL EXPOSITION

When Paul commenced preaching his gospel, the Jewish elders were shocked; his claims appeared to be blasphemous and contradictory of everything taught within the nation. He maintained that circumcision was not a requisite for salvation, that the Jews were not exclusively the recipients of God's grace, and that all nations were acceptable to God through Christ. It was no cause for amazement when synagogues around the world became centers of bitter opposition. The priests and rulers considered the upstart preacher to be a menace to the faith of their fathers and were determined to silence him.

Rhetoric and eloquence were insufficient to exonerate Paul, and he began, therefore, to expound the Scriptures in which Israel professedly believed. He reminded his opponents that although they accepted the commandments of Moses, they claimed that Abraham was the father of the nation (see Rom. 4:1 and Luke 1:55). The apostle explained how Abraham was accepted by God—not because of his obedience to the law, but because he believed! "For if Abraham were justified by works, he hath whereof to glory; but not before God. For what saith the scripture? ABRAHAM BELIEVED GOD, and it was counted unto him for righteousness. Now to him that worketh is the reward not reckoned of grace but of debt. But to him THAT WORKETH NOT, but believeth on him that justifieth the ungodly; his faith is counted for righteousness" (Rom. 4:2-5). Paul said, "[Abraham] staggered not at the promise of God through unbelief; but was strong in faith, giving glory to God; and being fully persuaded that, what he had promised, he was able also to perform. And, therefore, it was imputed to him for righteousness. Now it was not written for his sake alone, that it was imputed to him; BUT FOR US ALSO, to whom it shall be imputed, if we believe on him that raised up Jesus our Lord from the dead; who was delivered for our offenses, and was raised again for our justification" (Rom. 4:20-25). It became evident to Paul that neither circumcision nor any other works could merit salvation. Eternal life was a gift from God.

THE APOSTLE'S STIRRING EXAMPLE

"Lest any man should boast" (v. 9). It is difficult to consider this statement and not remember the two men mentioned by the Lord. "The Pharisee stood and prayed thus with himself, God, I thank thee that I am not as other men are, extortioners, unjust, adulterers, or even as this publican. I fast twice in the week; I give tithes of all that I possess. And the publican, standing afar off, would not lift up so much his eyes unto heaven, but smote upon his breast, saying, God be merciful to me a sinner. I tell you, this man went down to his house, justified rather than the other: for every one that exalteth himself shall be abased; and he that humbleth himself shall be exalted" (Luke 18:10-14). The Pharisee evidently thought it was necessary to mention the meritorious things he had done; he was proud of his achievements. Yet, the publican, who was too ashamed to approach the altar, stood afar off and, smiting his chest, confessed his unworthiness. When Jesus compared the two men, He said that forgiveness was given to the penitent and not to the proud. When a person truly approaches the throne of God, the realization of personal guilt is unavoidable.

I shall always remember a missionary who described a memorable event in his career. A generator had been installed on the mission station, and to honor the native pastor, arrangements were made that the electrical power should first be installed in his thatched cottage. The natives, who had never seen electric lights, gathered for the great occasion. It seemed incomprehensible to them that when someone pressed a switch, light could flood a home. The pastor's wife was very excited and spring-cleaned her hut; she realized that all the villagers would come to her home, and she desired a clean house! The moment arrived, the master switch was pressed, and the official party approached the dwelling. Suddenly, the native woman rushed out of her hut shouting, "Don't come in! Don't come in! I thought my house was clean, but when that light began to shine, I saw the dirt. I am ashamed; don't come in!"

Paul would have applauded her confession. He had also cleaned his house, and he was able to write, "Touching the righteousness which is in the law, [I was] blameless" (Phil. 3:6). Then, as he approached the city of Damascus to arrest the Christians, "there shined round about him a light from heaven" (Acts 9:3). That moment changed his outlook; he never again boasted of his works. He wrote to his friends to say, "I do count them but dung, that I may win Christ, and be found in him, not having mine own righteousness, which is of the law, but that which is through the faith of Christ, the righteousness which is of God by faith" (Phil. 3:8-9).

SECTION FIVE

Expository Notes on God's Desire for His People

For we are his workmanship, created in Christ Jesus unto good works, which God hath before ordained that we should walk in them (v. 10).

THEME: *The Positive Purpose of Predestination*
OUTLINE:

A. The Workmanship of the Creator
B. The Wishes of Christ
C. The Walk of the Christian

THE WORKMANSHIP OF THE CREATOR

"We are his workmanship" (v. 10a). David would have appreciated Paul's statement, for he wrote, "I will praise thee; for I am fearfully and wonderfully made; marvelous are thy works; and that my soul knoweth right well" (Ps. 139:14). Medical science was not far advanced during the lifetime of the psalmist, but he evidently had some knowledge of the intricate structure of the human body. David surely knew of blood vessels and veins, of the brain and its relation to every part of his being; and when he considered these things, he was filled with wonder. He knew that "God created man in his own image; in the image of God created he him; male and female, created he them. And God blessed them, and God said unto them, be fruitful and multiply and replenish the earth" (Gen. 1:27-28). David contemplated the miracle of childbirth and wrote, "For thou hast possessed my reins; thou hast covered me in my mother's womb . . . my substance was not hid from thee, when I was made in secret, and curiously wrought in the lowest parts of the earth. Thine eyes did see my substance, yet being unperfect; and in thy book, all my members were written, which in continuance were fashioned, when as yet there was none of them" (Ps. 139:13-16). Even the construction of the human body was attributed by David to the omniscience of the Almighty. No other agency could explain the inscrutable mystery of man's beginning.

David and Paul were aware of the human capacity to commune with the Almighty. Humanity belonged to the highest order of created beings and was given dominion over the earth. Beavers could make small dams in a river, but only man could erect huge walls behind which to store limitless supplies of water. Moles dug into the earth in search of food, but only humans could sink deep shafts to produce coal and other things necessary for industrial use. Birds flew through the air in search of food, but only people designed and built space vehicles capable of taking astronauts beyond the gravitational pull of the earth. The writer to the Hebrews quoted an Old Testament scripture when he said, "What is man, that thou art mindful of him? or the son of man that thou visitest him? Thou madest him a little lower than the angels, thou crownedst him with glory and honor, and didst set him over the works of thine hands" (Heb. 2:6-7). In some strange and wonderful way, God and Adam resembled each other—they were look-alikes! Unfortunately, man lost that characteristic. When Jesus came to earth, He restored that lost quality and became the perfect representation of His Father, "the express image of his person" (Heb. 1:3). God took soil, designed a human body, and breathed into it the breath of life. Man became a living soul, the finished product of the greatest plan ever conceived in the mind of the Creator. Even before Christ came to redeem sinners, we were "His workmanship."

THE WISHES OF CHRIST

"Created in Christ Jesus unto good works" (v. 10b). Perhaps it is difficult to read the minds of birds, reptiles, animals, and other forms of life. However, it has become obvious, after prolonged observation, that these creatures possess inherent characteristics; and, under given circumstances, it is possible to predict their behavior. Nevertheless, even the most developed animal cannot be compared with intelligent man. Humans have ambitions and the capacity for improvement and can criticize themselves! He is the most intelligent of all created life; is able to respond to the promptings of the divine Spirit, and thus can fulfill God's original desire for the human race. Similarly, when God planned to create new people in Christ, it was His desire that they should live exemplary lives. The Lord said to His disciples, "Ye have not chosen me, but I have chosen you, and ordained you, that ye should go and bring forth fruit, and that your fruit should remain; that whatsoever ye shall ask of the Father in my name, he may give it you" (John 15:16). Paul indicated that this type of victorious service would conform with the predestinated purposes of God. The same message was sent to the Christians in Rome. "For whom he did foreknow, he also did predestinate to be conformed to the image of his Son" (Rom. 8:29). Christ was an example for all His followers. The apostle John wrote, "He that saith he abideth in him,ought himself also so to walk, even as he walked" (1 John 2:6).

THE WALK OF THE CHRISTIAN

The key word of the second half of this remarkable Epistle is "walk." Having explained the amazing revelations expressed in the first three chapters of the letter, Paul emphasized that the conduct of the readers should harmonize with their knowledge. He began the fourth chapter with the words, "I therefore, the prisoner of the Lord, beseech you that ye walk worthy of the vocation wherewith ye are called." This suggestion was first made in the verse now under consideration. God had created a highway along which His children should proceed. The milestones mentioned by Paul indicated direction and progress. The saints had been called, justified, and glorified. God's foreknowledge identified those who would respond, and His redemptive machinery was set in motion. His voice called sinners to repentance, the blood of His Son made justification possible, and the Holy Spirit will ultimately make saints like their Lord. (At this point in the study, it might be beneficial to consider the homily, "Paul . . . Who Had Very Firm Convictions," p. 116.)

SECTION SIX

Expository Notes on the Need to Remember

Wherefore remember, that ye being in time past Gentiles in the flesh, who are called Uncircumcision by that which is called the Circumcision in the flesh made by hands; that at that time ye were without Christ, being aliens from the commonwealth of Israel, and strangers from the covenants of promise, having no hope, and without God in the world (vv. 11-12).

THEME: *The Bankruptcy of Unbelievers*
OUTLINE:

A. Asian Christians Had Been Without Christ
B. Asian Christians Had Been Without Citizenship
C. Asian Christians Had Been Without Covenant Promises
D. Asian Christians Had Been Without Confidence
E. Asian Christians Had Been Without a Creator

It has often been claimed that certain things are best forgotten. God recognized this fact when He promised, "I will forgive their iniquity, and I will remember their sin no more" (Jer. 31:34). Yet, some things should never be forgotten, and this was in the mind of the apostle when he wrote, "Wherefore remember. . . ." Some facts must never be forgotten, and such a sentiment was expressed by the prophet Isaiah when he said to the people of his generation, "Hearken unto me, ye that follow after righteousness, ye that seek the Lord: look unto the rock whence ye are hewn, and to the hole of the pit whence ye are digged" (Isa. 51:1). It is never wise to forget the goodness of God and the way in which He helps those who trust Him. When Christians cease to be grateful, they become unresponsive to the whispers of the Lord.

THE ASIAN CHRISTIANS HAD BEEN WITHOUT CHRIST

Paul reminded his readers in Asia that they had been idol-worshipers and heathens without Christ. Jews, even at their worst, had hope of the coming Messiah; their faith was a vital part of their heritage. Other nations had nothing to strengthen their anticipation of future blessedness. They had idols which decorated their temples and adorned their streets. They prayed and offered sacrifices to those man-made objects, but their prayers were never answered. The Gentiles had no outlook for the future and no peace within their hearts. They were traveling a road to nowhere and were busy doing nothing. The citizens of Ephesus knew little, if anything, about the Savior and were the equivalent of unevangelized heathens. Had they been deprived of the ministry of Paul and his friends, they may never have heard the gospel.

THE ASIAN CHRISTIANS HAD BEEN WITHOUT CITIZENSHIP

". . . ye being in time past Gentiles in the flesh, who are called Uncircumcision by that which is called Circumcision in the flesh made by hands" (v. 11). The Asians, and all other Gentiles, had no connection with the religious life of Israel, and rabbis went as far as to describe them as "fuel for the fires of hell." Even though some Jews disgraced their faith and disappointed their leaders, they remained Hebrews and had access to the feasts and festivals of their nation; only on rare occasions were they deprived of those privileges. The Gentiles were not as fortunate; they could not change the laws of Moses and, consequently, remained aliens. The Jews considered them to be eternally damned even before they died! What Christ accomplished on their behalf beggared description. He performed the impossible and brought hope to the hopeless.

THE ASIAN CHRISTIANS HAD BEEN WITHOUT COVENANT PROMISES

". . . aliens from the commonwealth of Israel, and strangers from the covenants of promise" (v. 12b). The promises of God were the foundation upon which the Jewish faith rested. The fathers of the nation had entered into a unique arrangement with Jehovah. He promised never to forsake them; they promised to remain His faithful, separated people. Unfortunately, the Jews forgot to honor their part of the agreement. Nevertheless, throughout the centuries, God honored His covenant and rescued the nation even when the people deserved condemnation. Israel remained the chosen people of the Most High God. The promise given through Moses was never forgotten. "Wherefore, say unto the children of Israel, I am the Lord, and I will bring you out from under the burdens of the Egyptians, and I will rid you out of their bondage, and I will redeem you with a strong stretched out arm, and with great judgments. And I will take you to me for a people, and I will be to you a God; and ye shall know that I am the Lord your God, which bringeth you out from under the burdens of the Egyptians" (Exod. 6:6-7). The covenant promises of Jehovah were meant to unite God with His people forever. The Gentiles had nothing in their culture to compare with this heritage.

THE ASIAN CHRISTIANS HAD BEEN WITHOUT CONFIDENCE

" . . . having no hope" (v. 12c). The Gentiles had neither happiness in life nor confidence in death. They had no assurance that life continued beyond the grave and consequently contemplated dying with dread. They were going nowhere! Ephesus was famous for its soothsayers, and promiscuity was commonplace within their temple. It is possible that some citizens detested the debauchery within the city; and as a result of this, they gave attention to the teaching of the rabbis. The Hebrews were monotheistic; they taught there was only one God. Unfortunately, their conduct did not always endorse their theology. There is reason to believe that many onlookers were confused; they did not know what to believe and resembled travelers at crossroads where there was no signpost!

THE ASIAN CHRISTIANS HAD BEEN WITHOUT A CREATOR

" . . . without God in the world" (v. 12b). They had many idols, but the multiplicity of man-made deities could not answer the questions arising from the confusion of their minds. They worshiped Diana and knew where to purchase the silver images of the famous goddess. Yet, they surely knew that such manufactured symbols had not created mountains and rivers, birds, and flowers. They worshiped a popular goddess but found no satisfaction in their devotion. When Paul came preaching the gospel, the listeners became appalled by the ignorance which had obscured their vision. They were rescued from the power of sin, saved by undeserved grace, and welcomed into the family of God. They would have appreciated the message of the hymn:

> O to Grace, how great a debtor,
> Daily, I'm constrained to be.

They knew exactly what Paul meant when he wrote, "Wherefore, remember."

THE PURPOSE OF THE SAVIOR

SECTION ONE

Expository Notes on the Power of the Blood of Christ

But now in Christ Jesus, ye who sometimes were far off are made nigh by the blood of Jesus (v. 13).

THEME: *The Effectiveness of the Work of Christ*
OUTLINE:

A. A Change of Position . . . *"made nigh"* (v. 13)
B. A Change of Privilege . . . *"hath broken down the middle wall of partition"* (v. 14)
C. A Change of Priority . . . *"to make in himself of twain one new man"* (v. 15)

This was one of Paul's famous "turns in the road," reference to which has already been made. The apostle had emphasized the desperate situation of sinners, stating they were "without hope and without God in the world." Then he reached the turn-in-his-road saying, "But now in Christ Jesus." A miracle had been performed. It may or may not have been significant when Paul used two titles of the Lord to make the unified name: "CHRIST JESUS." *Christ*, or *Christos*, was the name of the expected Messiah; the name *Jesus* was used to express that He was the Savior of Gentiles. The citizens of Sychar, after they had met the Lord, said to the Samaritan woman, "Now we believe, not because of thy saying; for we have heard him ourselves, and know that this is indeed the Christ, the Savior of the world" (John 4:42). As Paul had taken two very definite and different names to make a superb title, so Christ had taken two races of people to make a united people—"one new man." No person could have known that such a thing was planned by the good pleasure of God's will. This subject may be considered under three headings: (1) God's Purposes—to bring the untouchables closer, (2) God's Plan—to do it through the blood of Jesus, and (3) God's Pleasure— to be the fulfillment of something which had been carefully decided in eternal ages: the fulfillment of a divine dream!

GOD'S PURPOSE . . . To Bring People Closer

A divided world can never be contented. Most men agree with that conclusion and desire ways by which to banish discord. Nevertheless, those same people often disagree when suggestions are made as to the way to make unification possible. It has become universally acknowledged that the Jews had no justification in excluding Gentiles from their temple and privileges of worship. Yet, nations fight each other to promote the same kind of division. All countries have treasured heritages; their cultures are different. Black nations actively express their religion; they shout, wave their arms, and make certain God hears their requests! Many worshipers whose skin is of a different color love to worship in silence; they approach their heavenly Father reverently, and noise of any kind is considered to be an intrusion. Both types of people are justified in desiring to preserve what they treasure. That explains how, basically, both black and white people prefer to worship in their own sanctuaries. South Africa, unfortunately, is divided by racial strife, but it appears to be inexplicable how those who denounce the apartheid policies of that country can adopt similar practices. They refuse to share a communion service with Christians from another church. A dedicated servant of God may be asked to refrain from partaking of the Lord's supper merely because he preaches in another church. I know this is true because it happened to me!

All my life I have been a Baptist, but it has been a privilege to preach for many denominations. Sometimes, I was invited to preach in assemblies, but was told bluntly that "unless I came out from among the unclean things," I could not remember Christ at His table. Is there any difference between the ancient, legalistic Pharisees and the leaders of a twentieth century church who apparently believe that they, and they alone, are the custodians of everything sacred? God never planned that His Church should be divided into warring sections. There is nothing more absurd than to see two Christians who agree on 99% of their doctrines argue because they differ on one unimportant theological detail. If men looked for good in other people, the world and the church would be happier places. God was aware of the divisions within His world, but in spite of the problems, determined He would unite enemies and produce a unified people where love, not legalism, would be predominant.

GOD'S PLAN. . . To Bring People Closer by the Blood of Jesus

This was one of Paul's most astonishing statements. How could the blood of any man destroy traditions which had survived for centuries and make stubborn people do what they vowed never to do? To place anything, blood or water, upon a black man does not make him white; to do the same with a German does not transform him into a man of another nationality. The unification of nations demands a change of character and a new outlook; it brings a miracle which replaces criticism with tenderness, bigotry with humility, ugliness with loveliness. Laws, however rigid and however enforced, cannot do the impossible. To fulfill the desires of God for His people, every person needs a change of heart; in fact, everyone needs to become a member of a new society in which all are equal. God alone can perform such a miracle, and the precious blood of Christ was the means by which He did it.

GOD'S PLEASURE. . . To Share History With Redeemed Sinners (Eph. 1:9 and John 15:11)

It is profoundly awe-inspiring to know that God, in common with man, can be either happy or sad! When the Lord placed His arms around children, His face was radiant, and that was a clear picture of God's great pleasure. When, so to speak, the everlasting arms of God's kindness encircle sinners, the Almighty knows an ecstasy which nothing else can provide. The Savior said, "Likewise, I say unto you, there is joy in the presence of the angels of God over one sinner that repenteth" (Luke 15:10). When parents attend the graduation exercises of their children, they are filled with justifiable pride. When a girl grows into the loveliness of womanhood or a son is able to succeed his retiring father, the parents experience a happiness hitherto unknown. The same is true of the heavenly Father. When His children learn to exhibit dependability and reach maturity, God must be delighted. Then joy is mutually shared. His joy becomes the possession of His children, and their happiness gives to Him a thrill which cannot be obtained in any other way. It was for this purpose that He sent His Son to earth, that people far off from the realities of "grace" could be brought within the family of the Almighty.

Rita Snowdon tells a fascinating story about the reaction of a Roman Catholic priest during the war in Europe. A sergeant and a few of his men brought the body of a dead comrade for burial. The tide of battle was sweeping across France, and the soldiers wished to be sure their slain comrade was given a decent burial before they left the area. The priest inquired if the deceased had been a Catholic, but the men confessed they did not know. He gently explained that he was bound by the laws of his church and that he could not inter the body of a non-Catholic in dedicated soil! Reluctantly and sadly, the small party of men carried their comrade outside the cemetery fence and there dug his grave. The next morning, they returned to have a final look at the resting place of their friend. They walked around the fence again and again, but could find no evidence of freshly turned soil. Then the priest came to explain that he also had been worried about the event of the previous evening. Early in the morning, he had gone to the cemetery and "with his own hands" had moved the fence so that the body of the man who had died for France might be included!

I lived through two world wars in Britain, but I confess that this story has stirred my soul more than any other. It illustrates how love can remove barriers which exclude people from the kingdom of God. The Lord Jesus came during the night of our sin, and with His own hands moved the fence! Man has always been expert in building barricades, but nothing should ever separate people from God . . . WHO LOVES THEM. (See the homily, "The Precious Blood of Christ . . . The Master Key," p. 118.)

SECTION TWO

Expository Notes on the Middle Wall of Partition

For he is our peace, who hath made both one, and hath broken down the middle wall of partition between us; having abolished in his flesh the enmity, even the law of commandments contained in ordinances; for to make in himself of twain one new man, so making peace (vv. 14-15).

THEME: *The Formation of a New Race of People*
OUTLINE:

A. The Destruction of a Wall
B. The Denunciation of a War
C. The Delectability of a Wish

DESTRUCTION OF A WALL

There are two interpretations to this text concerning "the middle wall of partition," either or both may be correct. Of the first, Paul, as a Jew, would be aware of the restrictions imposed upon Gentiles approaching the temple in Jerusalem. There were several courts leading to the sanctuary, and the outermost of them was named "The Court of the Gentiles." Aliens, or non-Jews, were not permitted beyond that area. Writing of the enclosures, Josephus said, "Thus was the first enclosure. In the middle of which, and not far from it, was the second, to be gone up to by a few steps; this was encompassed by a stone wall for a partition, with an inscription, which forbade any foreigner to go in, under pain of death" (Josephus. *The Antiquities of the Jews*. Book 15, Chapter 11, Paragraph 5). Paul was accused of a violation of this law. His enemies said he had brought Greeks into the restricted area of the temple. "And when the seven days were almost ended, the Jews which were of Asia, when they saw him in the temple, stirred up all the people, and laid hands on him, crying out, Men of Israel, help: this is the man, that teacheth all men everywhere against the people, and the law, and this place: and further brought Greeks also into the temple, and hath polluted this holy place. (For they had seen before with him in the city, Trophimus, an Ephesian, whom they supposed that Paul had brought into the temple.)" (Acts 21:27-29).

Some theologians prefer the second interpretation which suggests that Paul was thinking of the animosity which existed between Jews and Gentiles. They teach that since Paul was writing to Gentiles in Asia, the recipients of his message would have little, if any, interest in the construction of the Jewish temple and that therefore, the reference to "the middle wall of partition" indicated the hostility between Jews and Gentiles. Paul, they say, would be explaining that this enmity had been removed by the atoning death of the Savior. The argument is not conclusive. There were many Jews and synagogues throughout Asia, and some of those Hebrews had been won for Christ. They, at least, would be aware of the restrictions imposed on Gentile visitors to the temple and able to understand the apostle's statement.

THE DENUNCIATION OF A WAR

Paul was endeavoring to explain that Christ had instituted a new kind of spiritual reality. What had existed for centuries had been abolished. Racial strife and bitterness had been outlawed to make possible a new form of international fellowship. "For he is our peace . . . having abolished in his flesh the enmity, even the law of commandments contained in ordinances; for to make in himself of twain, one new man, so making peace" (Eph. 2:14-15). Moses gave to Israel strict commandments regarding their diet and conduct, but successive generations unfortunately increased legal requirements until the traditions of the Fathers became a burden too heavy to be carried. Serenity no longer depended upon a dedicated, worshiping heart, but on strict observance of laws which had no connection with spirituality. Acceptance within the precincts of Israel did not depend upon consecration, but upon what the Pharisees declared to be holy. There was a great difference. What God required had been made subservient to the wishes of the Pharisees.

Paul insisted that things had changed. The war which existed within the souls of nations should end because Christ had made possible a fellowship pleasing both to God and man. Invited and initiated into the family of God, people saw each other as brothers and sisters, not en-emies. They found pleasure in helping their former foes. True peace had become possible through the merit of Christ's death. The Savior had concluded a mission by which war ended.

THE DELECTABILITY OF A WISH

Evidently, what had been accomplished had been carefully planned in eternity. Paul referred in Ephesians 1:4 to the eternal ages of the past. In Ephesians 2:7 he mentioned the eternal ages of the future. The apostle referred to the good pleasure of God's will and carefully indicated that nothing had been left to chance. God had desired certain things to happen, and all His plans relating to predestination were connected with the supreme desire of His heart. He foresaw a kingdom of peace in which all men would be brothers. This only became possible when the Spirit of God succeeded in transforming the hearts and desires of opposing people and uniting them into the bonds of an all-embracing love which emanated from God Himself.

Dr. Kurt Frank tells a wonderful story of his father, who, because of his ability to speak Russian, was placed in charge of a prisoner-of-war camp in Germany. That particular winter was extremely cold, and the imprisoned men suffered great hardships. They had no shoes and were forced to protect their feet by wrapping rags around them. They stood ankle deep in slush. One day Mr. Frank heard loud voices coming from the enclosure and, suspecting there might be trouble, hurried to the barbed wire fence to investigate. He saw a young Russian surrounded by other prisoners who were evidently listening to what the young man was saying. The soldier was speaking about the Christian faith and saying, "We have great troubles and may never see our homes and families again, but I want to tell you about another country. We may not get home for Christmas, but we can all reach that heavenly land through the death and resurrection of the Savior."

It all seemed unbelievable that there, amid such misery, a young Russian should be testifying of the Lord Jesus. Mr. Frank went through the gateway and approached the group to say, "What that soldier is telling you is true. Christ is also my Savior." He apologized for the treatment which was given to the prisoners and by so doing, risked his own life. In Nazi Germany, such an apology was considered treason. A delightful benediction fell upon that silent group when they saw the commandant of the camp embrace their fellow-prisoner. Even if they were not aware of Paul's doctrines, they were seeing a living example of his truth; a middle wall of partition had been broken down, and of two, God had made "one new man"!

SECTION THREE

Expository Notes on the Earliest Works of Grace in the Human Heart

And that he might reconcile both unto God in one body by the cross, having slain the enmity thereby: and came and preached peace to you which were afar off, and to them that were nigh. For through him we both have access by one Spirit unto the Father (vv. 16-18).

THEME: *The Immediate Results of Christ's Work of Redemption*
OUTLINE:

A. Christ Reconciled Us (v. 16)
B. Christ Reached Us (v. 17)
C. Christ Reinstated Us (v. 18)

Obviously, these verses were the continuation of the preceding statements of the apostle. Paul had explained the wonders of God's work in redemption and, in bringing that section of his letter to conclusion, was preparing to introduce the third and final section of his message.

CHRIST RECONCILED US

"And that he might reconcile both unto God in one body by the cross . . . " (v. 16a). To appreciate what Paul said, it is necessary to understand a word he used. The apostle emphasized that God's purpose was to make "of twain one new man." The Greek word translated "new" is *kainon*, which comes from *kainos*. Another word translated "new" is *neos*, but its meaning is different. W. E. Vine in his *Expository Dictionary of Old and New Testament Words*, (Vol. 3, p. 110), states, "*Kainos* and *neos* are sometimes used of the same thing, but there is a difference. . . . The new man in Ephesians 2:15 (*kainos*) is 'new' in differing in character; but the new man in Colossians 3:10 (*neos*) stresses the believer's new experience, was recently begun, and still proceeding."

Dr. William Barclay, explaining the same words, said, "There is *neos* which is new, simply in point of time; a thing which is *neos* has come into existence recently, but there may well have been thousands of the same thing before. A pencil produced in the factory this week is *neos*, but there already exists millions exactly like it. There is *kainos* which means new in point of quality. A thing which is *kainos* is new in the sense that it brings into the world a new quality of something which did not exist before" (*The Daily Study Bible. Galatians and Ephesians*, p. 116). It would, therefore, be evident that Paul was thinking of a new creation—something which, although recently produced, was, nevertheless, something extraordinarily new. God took two elements which were old to produce something absolutely new. Quoting Chrysostom, one of the early church fathers, *The Pulpit Commentary* says, "It was as if one should melt down a statue of silver and a statue of lead, and the two should come out gold!"

It is significant that Paul emphasized that redemption or reconciliation came through the Cross; there was no other way by which the task could be concluded satisfactorily. The translation offered by the Living Bible is extremely thought-provoking. "By his death he ended the angry resentment between us, caused by the Jewish laws which favored the Jews, and excluded the Gentiles, for he died to annul the whole system of Jewish laws. Then he took the two groups which had been opposed to each other, and made them parts of himself; thus he fused us together to become one new person, and at last there was peace."

CHRIST REACHED US

"And came and preached peace to you which were afar off, and to them that were nigh" (v. 17). No one can appreciate the gospel until he has heard and understood its message. There may be a reference here to the promise given through Isaiah. "Peace, peace to him that is a afar off, and to him that is near, saith the Lord . . . " (Isa. 57:19). Probably Paul was thinking more of his own call to the ministry and the compelling desire which sent him to make known the gospel in Asia. The scope of that ministry may be explained in two ways. Paul might have been contrasting the Gentiles with Jews, who were presumably closer to God. He might have been contrasting the idolaters, who were far from God, with the orthodox Hebrews, who at least professed to be the custodians of His law. God planned carefully that the gospel should be heard throughout the world. He desired to express His love for all nations.

CHRIST REINSTATED US

"For through him, we both have access by one Spirit unto the Father" (v. 18). This thrilling verse provided the climax to Paul's exposition. The Divine Family was anxious to restore to man what had been lost. "Through him [Christ] we both have access by one Spirit [The Holy Spirit] unto the Father [God]." God planned salvation; Christ procured it; the Holy Spirit presented it. All three members of the Trinity had a part in restoring to mankind the privileges lost by Adam. The first man could have enjoyed unbroken fellowship with his Maker, but sin unfortunately closed the door of access to the divine Presence. Thereafter, the veil within the sanctuary prevented people from approaching the mercy seat, and the hostility between the Jews and Gentiles placed restrictions upon aliens who desired entrance into the inner precincts of the house of God. When Jesus made reconciliation for sin, He opened a highway to the throne of God and made possible for all men to approach the throne of grace. Jews did not have priority over Gentiles, and aliens were no longer considered to be inferior people. Through the redemptive work of Christ, enemies became brothers and sisters and were accepted into the Church.

Most of earth's citizens may never experience visiting Buckingham Palace in London, or the White House in Washington D.C.. There are many restrictions which exclude strangers. That situation no longer exists in the palace of the King of Kings. God's door is open—there are no guards to interfere, and God's "welcome sign" awaits any who desire an audience with their Lord. "We both [Jews and Gentiles] have access by one Spirit unto the Father."

THE PRIVILEGES OF THE SAINT

Expository Notes on a Miraculous Transformation

Now, therefore, ye are no more strangers and foreigners, but fellowcitizens with the saints, and of the household of God; and are built upon the foundation of the apostles and prophets, Jesus Christ himself being the chief cornerstone; in whom all the building fitly framed together groweth unto an holy temple in the Lord; in whom ye also are builded together for an habitation of God through the Spirit (vv. 19-22).

THEME: *The Unity of the True Church of God*
OUTLINE:

A. A Miraculous Transformation (v. 19)
B. A Marvelous Temple (v. 20)
C. A Meaningful Testimony (v. 21)
D. A Momentous Truth (v. 22)

A MIRACULOUS TRANSFORMATION

"Now therefore ye are no more strangers and foreigners . . . " (v. 19a). The entrance of a Gentile into the fellowship of the family of God resembled the entry of a leper into society. Apart from the intervention of the Spirit of God, it would have been an impossibility. To refer again to 1 Samuel 2:8, redemption lifted beggars from the dunghill to make them sit with princes! It was an amazing transformation from rags to riches, from the bitterness of despair to the bliss of delight. During recent years, legislation was enacted to recognize the equal rights of black people with those of white people. However, the world is aware that the passing of laws cannot remove bitterness from the hearts of men. The letter of the law is cold, unrelenting, and discouraging. For example, if the South African government granted equality to its black people, that decision would not remove the dislike and disdain from white citizens. Black and white folks could still detest each other. Russians and Americans may sit at a conference table and be exceedingly courteous to each other, but such politeness would not guarantee harmony. Arabs and Jews may sign a peace treaty which could easily be broken.

True peace rests on a change of character, a completely different assessment of the value of people thought to be enemies. When terrorists are filled with compassion for their victims, when love casts out fear and all men are consumed with a desire to help others, then, and only then, can permanent relationships be established.

Paul was aware that, on a small scale, this had happened with his friends. The entire Jewish race had not changed, neither had all Gentiles embraced the new faith. Those who had—of either race—become vital parts of God's Church. It was God's fervent desire that this would be true of the entire world—"the earth shall be full of the knowledge of the Lord, as the waters cover the sea" (Isa. 11:9).

During the second World War, I was privileged to lead an evangelistic crusade in the city of Inverness, Scotland. I shall never forget the day when I was taken into the nearby prisoner-of-war camp to speak to the German prisoners. My escort carefully showed his military pass at each gateway in the barbed-wire fences, and we ultimately reached a small hut where the service was to be held. I watched as the prisoners entered. They appeared to be sullen and rebellious. Doubtless, they were homesick, and some, at least, resented the fact that a clergyman was about to "lecture" to them about God! I did my best, under very difficult circumstances, to reassure my audience that the love of God recognized no racial barriers and that their dreams would come true. Did they believe me? I do not know. When the men had returned to their quarters, I sat with their prisoner-of-war chaplain. He told me that he had been a missionary in India and that during his furlough, Nazi Germany had conscripted him into the army. He was not a Nazi. After one terrible battle in France, he had been captured and eventually brought to Inverness. I sympathized with that devoted man; there was no enmity in either his or my heart. The fact that we belonged to nations at war was inconsequential—we were Christians; we were brothers in a faith which admitted no racial barriers.

I remember a day when I crawled into a mud hut in Central Africa. Seated near the only supporting pole of that strange house was an aged black man who wondered why I had entered his impoverished home. He could not speak a word of my language, and I could not speak a word of his. I folded my legs beneath my body and smiled at him. Then I said "JESUS," and his face immediately became a pool of radiance, and in that mysterious fashion known only by Christians, we became united in fellowship. He was just another man who had been made nigh by the blood of the Savior.

During my evangelistic crusades in Australia, one of the daily newspapers reported an incident from North Queensland. A British pilot had been intercepted by fourteen Japanese planes, and alas, the young airman had been shot down. Somehow, he managed to reach the shore, where he collapsed on the beach. When he regained consciousness, he saw two Aborigines standing above him with spears raised. One of the natives asked, "Jap?" The flier shook his head. Then the other native, pointing to the medallion of the cross hanging from the airman's neck, inquired, "Jesus-man?" The wounded airman smiled and said yes. Those Aborigines carried him to a mission station. They had learned to appreciate the value of "Jesus-men." Perhaps they too had been brought near by the power of the same gospel.

A MARVELOUS TEMPLE

"Now therefore ye are . . . fellowcitizens with the saints, and of the household of God; and are built upon the foundation of the apostles and prophets, Jesus Christ himself being the chief cornerstone" (vv. 19-20). When Paul announced that the human heart had taken the place of the temple at Jerusalem, critics questioned his sanity. The Jewish sanctuary represented all that was best in the religious life of the nation; it stood at the heart of Hebrew aspirations. It was believed that Jehovah dwelt between the cherubims whose wings covered the mercy seat. To suggest that the sacred place had been vacated in favor of a human soul was preposterous. The Scriptures taught that the heart of man was deceitful and desperately wicked (Jer. 17:9); how then could a holy God dwell in an unclean place? Paul persisted in presenting his message, for the transformation of man into a temple expressed all that was best in the gospel. As the blood of the sacrifice was sprinkled on and in front of the altar of God, so the blood of Christ could cleanse the heart of a sinner. Then, as a necessary development of that event, the Spirit of God transformed the cleansed soul into a sanctuary. Paul wrote to the Corinthians, "Know ye not that ye are the temple of God, and that the Spirit of God dwelleth in you?" (1 Cor. 3:16). It has already been stated that the key word of the first half of this Letter is "know." This was one of the great facts that the apostle wished his readers to understand.

Paul indicated that the new temple was a structure resting on men whom Christ had taught. The apostles and prophets provided the base upon which everything rested, but Christ was the cornerstone which united the walls. Oftentimes in Middle East countries, the cornerstones were considered more valuable than the foundation, and upon them could be found the name of the king who sponsored or erected the building. The idea that Christians were incorporated into God's structure suggested they had no need to visit any special shrine; they were the temple; God was not distant; He resided within them.

Communion could be a continuing delight. (See the homilies, "The Chief Cornerstone," p. 120 and "Christ . . . The Builder," p. 122.)

A MEANINGFUL TESTIMONY

"In whom all the building fitly framed together groweth unto a holy temple in the Lord" (v. 21). A. Skevington Wood, in the *Expositor's Bible Commentary* on Ephesians, p. 42, writes, "Paul refers to 'the whole building' *pasa oikodomee*, rather than to each separate building. The absence of the article implies that the work is still in progress. The phrase really means 'all building that is being done'. . . . The word used for temple is not *hieron* which includes the entire precincts, but *naos*, the inner shrine. . . . For three hundred years the Christians had no buildings of their own. The true temple is the whole Church." The Living Bible translates the verse, "We who believe are carefully joined together with Christ as parts of a beautiful, constantly growing temple for God." Today's English Version of the Bible translates the passage, "He is the one who holds the whole building together and makes it grow into a sacred temple in the Lord." Evidently Paul emphasized that God's sanctifying work was continuing; the Christians were constantly developing and, through the power of the indwelling Spirit of God, were advancing toward the goal of absolute purity. As in former ages the glory of God had filled the tabernacle, so it was the purpose of the Lord to fill His people with transcendent glory in order to make them like Himself. Their cooperation was expected, and, therefore, Paul issued the appeal and command, "And grieve not the Holy Spirit of God, whereby ye are sealed unto the day of redemption" (Eph. 4:30).

A MOMENTOUS TRUTH

"In whom ye also are builded together for an habitation of God through the Spirit" (v. 22). The possibility exists that Paul had both the Jewish temple and the temple of Diana in his thoughts when he wrote this letter. In any case the Hebrews would be conversant with the design of the temple, and all Asians would be aware of the heathen temple which overshadowed the city of Ephesus. The magnificence of both structures was known throughout the world; they represented the best in architecture. The church exhibited the best of God's workmanship which presented Christians with a standard by which to live. God was attempting to accomplish something which would have been impossible without the efforts of the Holy Spirit. If the Cornerstone bound the walls together, the omniscience of the Holy Spirit placed every stone in alignment with Christ. The Jerusalem Bible translates the passage, "Every structure is aligned on him, all grow into one holy temple in the Lord."

The temple of Diana dominated the view of Ephesus; the temple in Jerusalem stood alone in magnificent isolation. It overshadowed everything within view. It was the will of God that the Church, His new creation, should be the outstanding thing in time and eternity. It would surpass in excellence anything ever conceived in the mind of man. Paul reminded his readers that although they had been "without Christ, being aliens from the commonwealth of Israel and strangers from the covenants of promise, having no hope, and without God in the world," they, nevertheless, had been brought near by the blood of Jesus and incorporated into a living temple for their heavenly Father. Paul and his friends would have loved John Newton's words:

> Amazing grace! How sweet the sound,
> That saved a wretch like me.
> I once was lost, but now am found;
> Was blind, but now I see.

A SUMMARY OF THE SECOND CHAPTER

When Paul wrote the first chapter of the Epistle to the Ephesians, his thoughts were centered on what God had planned in eternal ages. The second chapter indicated that he was thinking of what God had accomplished on earth. His exposition of the gospel proved that the Lord had provided everything necessary for the salvation of sinners. This summary may be considered under four headings.

THEY WERE LOST

They were condemned *by past deeds*. The apostle reminded his readers of what had transpired prior to their conversion. The key statement "in past times" appeared frequently in his writings as follows: "In time past ye walked according to the course of this world" (v. 2), "our conversation in times past in the lusts of our flesh" (v. 3), "in times past, Gentiles in the flesh" (v. 11), and "that at that time ye were without Christ" (v. 12). Paul reminded his readers that they could only be ashamed of their past record. They had worshiped idols and had been enslaved to sinful lusts. Prior to their acceptance into the family of God, they had been controlled by the prince of the power of the air, "the spirit that now worketh in the children of disobedience." They had been slaves of Satan, and if their conduct resembled that of the citizens of Ephesus, they were immoral and infamous. They could have exclaimed with Isaiah, "All we like sheep have gone astray, we have turned every one to his own way" (Isa. 53:6).

They were condemned *by the law of God.* The Scripture taught that God was no respecter of persons; in His sight, sin was sin whether it was found in Jews or Gentiles. The people of Asia may not have been conversant with the writings of the prophets and were not among the privileged Hebrews. Nevertheless, their deeds were in violation of their conscience and, therefore, merited the disfavor of God. They were "without Christ . . . having no hope, and without God in the world." They had been like shipwrecked sailors, adrift on tempestuous seas and without hope of reaching the shore. They were lost!

They were condemned *by nature.* " . . . and were by nature the children of wrath, even as others." Paul indicated that what they had done was the product of what they had been. Their nature was tainted by evil, and even if their conduct had been exemplary, nothing could have excused the corruption within their souls. They had been born in sin and formed in iniquity (see Ps. 51:5), and nothing could change that fact.

They were condemned *by God's people.* God's covenants of promise made with Israel made provision whereby the high priest could intercede for his people. When he stood before the mercy seat, he represented the twelve tribes, and God listened to his supplications. Even in the most difficult periods of Israel's history, the intercessory work of the priest obtained forgiveness for guilty sinners. Provision was made whereby an offering could carry the sins of penitent people. Belonging to the "chosen race" was something not to be lightly esteemed. Unfortunately, the Gentiles had no heritage to compare with that privilege. They were detested by the Jews and denied participation in the feasts and festivals of Israel. They remained outcasts.

THEY WERE LOVED

"But now in Christ Jesus ye who sometimes were far off are made nigh by the blood of Christ" (v. 13). The apostle declared, "But God, who is rich in mercy, for his great love wherewith he loved us . . . " (v. 4). Having described the unattractive past of the converts, Paul used superlative statements to explain the transformation within their souls. The term "mercy" was insufficient to express this thought. God had been *rich in mercy!* Paul was accustomed to describing the love of God, but on this occasion he was compelled to write, "his *great love*" (v. 4).

God reconciled us *without our assistance*. We were "dead in sins" (v. 5). Salvation was, therefore, all of God. The converts had been completely unresponsive to the promptings of God's Spirit, and what had been accomplished was done without their assistance. Paul implied that the greatness of human guilt needed *great mercy*. The kindness of the Lord might be able to handle small situations, but the guilt of sinners was so vast that God went the "extra mile" and exercised *great mercy* to provide salvation.

God reconciled us *without charge*! We were "without money; without price." Writing to the Christians in Rome, Paul exclaimed, "Being justified *freely* by his grace through the redemption that is in Christ Jesus" (Rom. 3:24). The apostle was explicit when he said, "Not of works lest any man should boast." Debts may be paid in cash or service, but the immensity of human guilt was such that man could do nothing to cancel his indebtedness.

The classic illustration of this profound truth is found in Matthew 18:23-27. Jesus spoke of a servant who owed his master "ten thousand talents. But forasmuch as he had not [nothing] to pay, his lord commanded him to be sold, and his wife, and children, and all that he had, and payment to be made. The servant therefore fell down, and worshiped him, saying, Lord, have patience with me, and I will pay thee all. Then the lord of that servant was moved with compassion, and loosed him, and forgave him the debt." The ten thousand talents mentioned might have been the equivalent of $2,800,000. Evidently, the debt was so enormous that an ordinary man could never pay what was owed. The lord who forgave such a large debt was *great in mercy!* Similarly, because sinners were incapable of paying to God what was owed, He became responsible for arranging salvation and did it without price!

God reconciled us *at great cost*! We were purchased "by the blood of Christ." This was the greatest price God paid for anything! That He was willing to sacrifice His Son for undeserving people only proved His love was *great love*. The question has often been asked, "Where was God when He allowed men to crucify His Son?" Paul supplied the answer, "God was in Christ, reconciling the world unto himself" (2 Cor. 5:19). It may never be possible for humans to understand the degree of pain and anguish experienced by the Almighty; the heartbreak of paying the price of redemption was beyond comprehension.

THEY WERE LIBERATED

The Savior said, "If the Son, therefore, shall make you free, ye shall be free indeed" (John 8:36). Christianity brought to slaves freedom hitherto thought to be impossible. This became evident when masters and slaves sat together at the Lord's table; class distinction had died! Nevertheless, the types of freedom made possible through the Savior were varied.

These converts *had been idolaters*. They had worshiped the goddess Diana, and had been subject to heathen laws. Their sacrifices, superstition, and conduct all carried the marks of paganism. Their acceptance of the Lord Jesus Christ broke the traditional chains, and as Christians, they walked in newness of life. They no longer feared the wrath of the goddess; they became unafraid of the custodians of the temple. They enjoyed happiness hitherto unknown; their future was bright with prospect and hope.

These converts were indwelt by the Holy Spirit. They received a new power which enabled them to triumph over their carnal desires. If on any previous occasion they sought moral improvement, they encountered difficulty in their own inherent weakness. They were slaves of self. The coming of the Holy Spirit enabled them to say exultantly, "I can do all things through Christ which strengtheneth me" (Phil. 4:13). They had been liberated and, like Simon Peter, had left a dungeon to enjoy the freedom of God's world! (see Acts 12:11).

These converts had been released from the requirement of the Mosaic law. Throughout the centuries, rabbis taught submission to the law of circumcision was a prerequisite of the blessings of God. Uncircumcised Gentiles had no opportunity of receiving Jehovah's benediction. The painful process of obedience was essential in people's approach to Jehovah. Although that teaching continued for many centuries, Paul enthusiastically taught that circumcision was unnecessary. Salvation was a gift. Christ removed the barrier separating men from God; without ceremonies and institutions, both Jews and Gentiles could kneel at the throne of grace. Through faith in Christ, freedom of many kinds had been made possible. The Asian converts had been liberated. Chains around the feet impede progress, but through the redemptive work of the Savior, the shackles had been broken, and a world of unlimited possibilities awaited the converts. Paul would have loved the hymn which says:

> He breaks the power of cancelled sin;
> He sets the prisoner free.
> His blood can make the foulest clean;
> His blood availed for me.

THEY WERE LIFTED

Probably, this was the most sensational of all the teachings of Paul. Temples, edifices, buildings of any importance were only made possible when skillful workmen gave attention to the erection. Many years of toil were necessary before the temples of God and Diana came into being. Yet, these buildings could not compare with the new temple being constructed by the Almighty. It had been planned in the earliest ages when the master plan was drawn by the divine Architect. The stones to be used in the construction had to be hewn individually from mountains of sin; the work would be ceaseless and costly. The apostle was thrilled to write, "Ye are built upon the foundation of the apostles and prophets, Jesus Christ himself being the chief cornerstone; in whom all the building fitly framed together groweth unto an holy temple in the Lord" (vv. 19-21).

They had been *sought*. No stone ever became part of a building accidentally! The Scriptures mentioned the great activity which made the temple of Solomon possible. Special men were selected to be responsible for the supply of materials. "And Solomon had three score and ten thousand that bare burdens, and fourscore thousand hewers in the mountains" (1 Kings 5:15). Careful search was made for suitable stones which were carefully cut from the hillside. The same attention was evident in God's search for sinners. The stones did not appear miraculously; they were sought and found by the Holy Spirit, who was the Overseer of God's building program.

They had been *selected*. The Lord said, "For many are called, but few are chosen" (Matt. 22:14). There remains today in one of the ancient quarries of Egypt, a large stone which evidently was meant to occupy an important place in one of the nation's temples. Alas, at the last moment, a flaw was discovered, and the stone was abandoned by the ancient builders. There were many stones, but only those carefully selected reached the building under construction. Paul reminded the converts that they were "chosen in him before the foundation of the world" (Eph. 1:4). The apostle repeated his message, "For we are his workmanship, created in Christ Jesus unto good works, which God hath before ordained that we should walk in them" (Eph. 2:10).

They had been *shaped*. Every detail in the temple at Jerusalem was carefully planned. Each stone was cut to fit into its neighbor. Skilled masons worked continually to produce perfection. Any stone not fashioned and trimmed by the craftsmen would have become an eyesore in a magnificent structure. Paul believed the same truth applied to the temple of the Holy Spirit. Hewn from the mountains of guilt, each believer needed careful attention before he or she could be placed with others in the temple of the divine Spirit. Immature Christians had many "bumps and corners" which would need to be removed. This could be a long process, but Paul was at least glad the work had commenced. "For now is our salvation nearer than when we believed" (Rom. 13:11).

They had been *strengthened.* "And are built upon the foundation of the apostles and prophets, Jesus Christ himself being the chief cornerstone" (v. 20). One stone could never make a building; one brick could never make a house! By the same token, one pencil may easily be broken; yet many pencils, when placed together, are unbreakable. All stones in the living temple are aligned with the Chief Cornerstone, Christ, whose love binds them together. Without His strengthening influence, even the best Christian would be ineffective. Paul taught that although Christ held the Church together, the Holy Spirit inhabited the house, and God Himself was its owner. This was the predestined plan, and Paul reminded his readers of their profound privilege. They had been far away in sin, but had been sought, selected, shaped, and strengthened to occupy a place in the Lord's greatest structure.

HOMILIES

Homily No. 3

ENTHRONED FAR ABOVE ALL (2 Kings 25:27-30)

The prison was dark and somber, a place of gloom where hope had long since died. Throughout the hours of daylight, merciless guards enforced the rigors of hard labor, and during the night weary prisoners were alone with their memories. Jehoiachin, the one-time king of Judah, was a particularly sad case, for thirty-seven years of imprisonment had crushed his spirit. Year after year, he had languished in his prison cell, youth had given place to middle-age, and now he had grown old. There were occasions when he would have welcomed death, for nothing could be worse than the bondage experienced in a Babylonian dungeon.

A GREAT PRINCE

Unknown to the captive king, a young prince whose attitude contrasted greatly with that of the prevailing royal house had become favorably disposed toward him. Babylonian law knew no mercy until this prince manifested grace. Secretly, he had desired to liberate the famous priso-ner, but this had been impossible. He therefore planned for the future when supreme power would be in his own hands. "And it came to pass in the seven and thirtieth year of the captivity of Jehoiachin . . . that Evil–merodach king of Babylon in the year that he began to reign, did lift up the head of Jehoiachin out of prison." Here are veiled foreshadowings of New Testament truth, and if it were possible to change the name of that Babylonian, many Christians would prefer to call him "Prince Grace."

A GREAT PARDON

When the captive was informed of the liberation order, he had difficulty accepting its authenticity. It could not be true that his former enmity would be forgotten and that his earlier resistance to the state would be pardoned. Yet, it was true. In contrast to the previous regime, the new one offered kindness to the king of Judah. Jehoiachin had neither to earn nor to merit his pardon. It was a free gift from the new monarch. He had only to accept the king's grace, and he would be free. In like manner, the Prince of Peace offers pardon "without money and without price" (Isa. 55:1).

A GREAT POWER

Jehoiachin's initial joy might have been spoiled by premonitions of finding enemies in the new life of freedom. All Babylonians were not of the same type who now offered mercy. Brutal overlords could renew his misery and bondage. Perhaps he asked himself if he would be able to maintain what was being offered; he was aware of his weakness. But then someone explained the magnitude of the king's offer. "And he spake kindly to him, and set his throne above the throne of the kings that were with him in Babylon." The great prince who offered mercy had made ample provision for future requirements. If men tried to enslave Jehoiachin, his power would be sufficient to offset their challenge. And so it is in the Christian life! The Savior not only offers pardon to the sinner; He gives power to the faint. When each believer asks, "O wretched man that I am, who shall deliver me?" they should be able to reply, "I thank God through Jesus Christ."

A GREAT PROVISION

"And the king changed his prison garments; and he did eat bread continually before him all the days of his life." The two men lived and dined together and discovered the fellowship for which they had yearned. Thus did God set forth the mysteries of the salvation to be provided in Christ. "My God shall supply all your need according to his riches in glory by Christ Jesus" (Phil. 4:19). Jehoiachin would have been a very foolish man had he rejected the king's amazing offer. "How shall we escape if we neglect so great salvation?" (Heb. 2:3). (Homily reprinted from the author's book, *Bible Cameos*, pp. 61-62.)

Homily No. 4

PAUL . . . Who Walked Through Ephesians!

Many Bible students regard the Epistle to the Ephesians as the most profound of the Pauline letters. The apostle had been a pastor in this famous city of Asia and during his ministry had introduced people to the vital doctrines of Christianity. It was to be expected, therefore, that his letter would continue this tradition. The first three chapters embody the revelation of Christian doctrine; the key word is "know." Chapters 4-6 present Christian responsibility; the key word is "walk." The purpose of this brief study is to reveal Paul's ideas regarding the characteristics of the Christian walk. It is commonly believed that police officers are known by their feet! It is absolutely certain that Christians are known by their walk.

CHRISTIANS SHOULD WALK WORTHILY

"I therefore, the prisoner of the Lord, beseech you that ye walk worthy of the vocation wherewith ye are called" (Eph. 4:1). This is the first requirement of all who profess faith in Christ. The gospel of Christ supersedes all other teaching and presents the incomparable beauties of grace. Outcasts become the children of God, and hope is brought within the reach of every human being. The gospel brings new dignity to men and women; and fully conscious of this high and holy calling, Christians should adorn the doctrines preached. Their walk must be worthy of the Master.

CHRISTIANS SHOULD WALK DIFFERENTLY

"This I say therefore, and testify in the Lord, that ye henceforth walk not as other Gentiles walk" (Eph. 4:17). Conversion means the renunciation of former ideologies. A person becomes a follower of Christ because he has reached the place where he believes that Christ alone leads to reality. If he were completely satisfied with his former way of living, he would not become a Christian. His regeneration brings him into a new society of friends where new ideas are commonly shared. When he continues to walk in paths which he has already denounced, either his confession of faith was hypocritical or he has slipped again into the ways of sin.

CHRISTIANS SHOULD WALK AFFECTIONATELY

"Be ye therefore, followers of God, as dear children; and walk in love, as Christ also hath loved us" (Eph. 5:1-2). As the Lord loved us, so we must love. This rare plant cannot thrive where bitterness, fault-finding, and carnal criticism sour the soil. When discord ruins the church, when enmity separates brethren, the entire purpose of the Lord is hindered. John asked a very important question, "He that loveth not his brother whom he hath seen, how can he love God whom he hath not seen?" (1 John 4:20).

CHRISTIANS SHOULD WALK INTELLIGENTLY

"For ye were sometimes darkness, but now are ye light in the Lord: walk as children of light" (Eph. 5:8). It is very disconcerting to see an athlete floundering in a bog. Avoiding obvious difficulties, the runner strains every nerve in the supreme effort to reach the finish line. It is wiser to lose a minute avoiding trouble than to waste an hour overcoming it. Light means illumination and illumination means guidance. Finality, purpose, and decision are characteristics of the Christian pilgrimage. Hoboes may wander indecisively, but Christians walk!

CHRISTIANS SHOULD WALK CIRCUMSPECTLY

"See then that ye walk circumspectly, not as fools, but as wise" (Eph. 5:15). A deliberate walk is not, of necessity, a hurried walk. The Christian pilgrimage is a matter of direction, not speed. Sometimes it pays to make haste slowly! Imagine a cat hurrying over the broken glass on the top of a garden wall! Recognizing the dangers abounding in all directions, the wise animal slowly puts a foot here, another there, and proceeds with extreme care. Christians should learn this lesson.

CHRISTIANS SHOULD WALK COURAGEOUSLY

"Put on the whole armour of God . . . having on the breastplate of righteousness; and your feet shod with the preparation of the gospel of peace; above all, taking the shield of faith . . . the helmet of salvation . . . the sword of the spirit" (Eph. 6:11-17). Success in Christian warfare largely depends upon stability in Christian dedication. Great knowledge of the doctrines of Christ is negated unless those identical truths are demonstrated in daily experience. Some people stand on their heads, but God made us to stand on our feet. The Christian walk is the foundation of all spiritual realities. (Reprinted from the author's book, Bible *Treasures*, pp. 141-142.)

Homily No. 5

PAUL . . . Who Had Very Firm Convictions!

Paul was a preacher with deep convictions; this was made very evident in his Epistle to the Galatians. "I marvel that ye are so soon removed from him that called you into the grace of Christ unto another gospel: which is not another . . . but though we, or an angel from heaven, preach any other gospel unto you than that which we have preached unto you, let him be accursed. As we have said before, so say I now again, if any other man preach any other gospel unto you than that ye have received, let him be accursed" (Gal. 1:6-9). This was the strongest language Paul could have used, for actually he was saying that any other message would condemn the preacher eternally. To understand the details of Paul's faith, it is necessary to study his Letter to the Ephesians, for there, using the word "without," Paul clearly expressed what he believed.

WITHOUT CHRIST . . . "Without hope, and without God" (Eph. 2:12)

Paul reminded his readers what they once were. He had arrived in Ephesus to preach to people who worshiped the goddess Diana; he had stayed two years, and the grace of God had saved many souls. It was incomprehensible to the apostle that any who had heard the glorious message of Christ could ever deny their faith or lose their first love for Jesus. There were good, sincere citizens in Ephesus, and some of them might have been living exemplary lives. Yet Paul insisted that however good they were, they remained lost and without hope. Unless Jesus Christ, who claimed to be the only way to the true God, was accepted as Savior, no person in Ephesus or anywhere else could enter the kingdom of God. Paul maintained that good works were insufficient and that without Christ, people were in danger of eternal damnation.

We appear to have reached an age where this kind of preaching has vanished. It has become customary not to offend listeners; there is good in all people, so we have been told. And the duty of the church is to locate that good, encourage it, help people climb the ladder of morality, and help them find acceptance with a very understanding God. Paul would have argued furiously against such conclusions. He believed that people at their best were still lost, and vehemently said so.

WITHOUT BLAME BEFORE HIM IN LOVE (Eph. 1:4)

Paul reminded his readers that "we all had our conversation in times past in the lusts of our flesh, fulfilling the desires of the flesh and of the mind; and were by nature the children of wrath even as others. But God, who is rich in mercy, for his great love wherewith he loved us, even when we were dead in sins, hath quickened us together with Christ . . . that in the ages to come, he might shew the exceeding riches of his grace in his kindness toward us through Christ Jesus" (Eph. 2:3-7). With that end in view, Paul stated that every Christian should endeavor to cooperate with the Lord in striving to be "without blame." This suggested a victorious life when the power of indwelling sin was overcome and the Holy Spirit permitted to occupy every part of the human temple. This meant growth in grace.

WITHOUT BLEMISH . . . "a glorious church" (Eph. 5:27)

Someone has said, "Christianity is a life of new beginnings." Paul stressed that walking with the risen Christ led to higher and better accomplishments. Having rescued us from the power of sin, Christ will continue His work until the entire Church is perfected. Paul urged husbands to love their wives, and wives similarly to love and honor their husbands. Christian homes would then reflect the love of the Almighty. Discord, envy, strife, and bitterness should have no part in any heart or home. Each day should take believers closer to that glorious culmination when, without blemish, the Church will be presented faultless to the heavenly Bridegroom. The sanctity of marriage should never be forgotten. Divorce could never be a reflection of the love of Christ for His Church. Therefore, the Ephesians were reminded of the need to exercise love in every facet of family life, for only thus would the world be attracted to the ways of Christianity.

Unfortunately, something appears to have gone wrong with the modern church. The old ideals of family dedication in many instances have vanished; people get married in haste and repent at leisure. It can only be a cause for regret when marriages terminate because participants permit illegitimate interests. People who have responded to Christ should be without blame; only thus can the Church be perfected.

Homily No. 6

THE PRECIOUS BLOOD OF CHRIST. . . The Master Key (Col. 1:20)

Every New Testament preacher, and all New Testament writings made reference to the blood of Christ. The theme is a scarlet thread running through the entire length of evangelical theology. Early in the sacred writings, God revealed that life is in the blood (Gen. 9:4), and throughout the New Testament the blood of Christ was synonymous with the life of Christ. Consequently, the shed blood of the Lord referred to His sinless life outpoured at Calvary. One fact remains indisputable: the apostles and leaders of the New Testament Church believed that man's salvation was procured through the sacrifice of Christ.

THE BLOOD OF CHRIST MADE PEACE FOR SINNERS

"And, having made peace through the blood of his cross, by him, to reconcile all things unto himself" (Col. 1:20). Man was at war with God; a state of rebellion existed in the human soul. When divine justice demanded retribution, the Lord Jesus voluntarily identified Himself with guilty people and accepted full responsibility for their sins. He carried their guilt to Calvary and thereby made peace possible.

The righteousness of God was vindicated and a way opened whereby the war might be terminated.

THE BLOOD OF CHRIST BROUGHT PEOPLE INTO A NEW FELLOWSHIP

"That at that time, ye were without Christ, being aliens from the commonwealth of Israel, and strangers from the covenants of promise, having no hope, and without God in the world: but now in Christ Jesus, ye who sometimes were far off are made nigh by the blood of Christ" (Eph. 2:12-13). Through the reconciling work of the Savior, new harmony was created. Man-made barriers and racial discrimination were removed from the Christian church when masters and slaves sat together at the Lord's Table.

THE BLOOD OF CHRIST CLEANSED FROM SIN

"But if we walk in the light, as he is in the light, we have fellowship one with another, and the blood of Jesus Christ, his Son, cleanseth us from all sin" (1 John 1:7). Entrance into the fellowship of the Church did not guarantee immunity from sin. The Christian life meant conflict and ceaseless watchfulness against evil. John emphasized that the blood of Christ continued, effectively, to meet the need of sinners. Literally, the text reads, "goes on cleansing us."

THE BLOOD OF CHRIST ENABLED MAN TO ENTER INTO THE PRESENCE OF GOD

"Having therefore, brethren, boldness to enter into the holiest by the blood of Jesus, by a new and living way, which he hath consecrated for us" (Heb. 10:19-20). The Epistle to the Hebrews provides striking contrasts between the Old and New Covenants. Formerly, one man, the high priest, drew near to God on the Day of Atonement; other people were excluded from that place of communion. The Savior introduced a "better covenant," for through His death all people may enter into the presence of God and find grace to help in time of need. Here is progression of thought. Every man brought from the far country to enjoy the fellowship of saints is not only assured of perpetual cleansing, but he is also guaranteed "around the clock" access into the presence of the King of Kings.

THE BLOOD OF CHRIST OVERCAME SATAN

"And I heard a loud voice saying in heaven . . . the accuser of our brethren is cast down . . . and they overcame him by the blood of the Lamb, and by the word of their testimony; and they loved not their lives unto the death. Therefore rejoice ye heavens . . ." (Rev. 12:10–12). Here is a great mystery, here is glorious truth. The power of the precious blood of Christ was the greatest weapon ever used by Christians.

THE BLOOD OF CHRIST PROVIDED THE THEME FOR ETERNAL SONGS

"And they sung a new song, saying . . . Thou hast redeemed us to God by thy blood . . . and the number of them was ten thousand times ten thousand, and thousands of thousands . . ." (Rev. 5:9-12). Probably, many of the memories of earth will disappear amid eternal splendor, but the Cross of Christ will never be forgotten.

Precious, precious blood of Jesus;
Shed on Calvary.
Shed for rebels, shed for sinners;
Shed for me.

(Reprinted from the author's book, *Bible Treasures*, pp. 145-146).

Homily No. 7

THE CHIEF CORNERSTONE (Isa. 28:16; 1 Cor. 10:4)

The size and strength of cornerstones used in ancient buildings continue to amaze modern engineers. How the ancient builders placed those large blocks in exalted positions remains an inscrutable mystery. It is still possible to see some of these stones, for archaeologists have uncovered precious masterpieces. Some of the corner pieces used in Solomon's temple were more than thirty-eight feet long and exceeded a hundred tons in weight. It is not a cause for amazement that ancient buildings attracted the attention of the prophets. Isaiah, who saw Solomon's temple on many occasions, wrote, "Therefore, thus saith the Lord God, behold I lay in Zion for a foundation a stone, a tried stone, a precious cornerstone, a sure foundation . . ." (Isa. 28:16). Simon Peter, who lived centuries later quoted that scripture and likened it to the Savior (1 Peter 2:6). Paul, who wrote of a similar theme, said, "That Rock was Christ" (1 Cor. 10:4).

THE STONE THAT SUGGESTS

God said through His servant Isaiah, "Behold, I lay in Zion for a foundation a stone . . . " (Isa. 28:16). He did not create it; He did not prepare it! He took that which already existed and placed it where it could perform its divinely appointed mission. Isaiah evidently used the imag-ery of stones cut from the mountains and prepared by men for their position in the temple of Solomon. God spoke of another structure, a living temple, in which men and women would be living stones. The foundation of that building would be the Rock of Ages! He would not "come into being;" that is, He would not be prepared by human hands. He who had been from eternity would be "laid" in a new position to accomplish something never before attempted.

THE STONE THAT SUPPORTS

It was essential that huge stones be obtained for Israel's temple, for the weight to be supported was almost beyond estimation. Situated on the crest of a hill, the structure had to rest solidly on strong foundations, otherwise, it would have slid into the valley. The temple erected by King Solomon was threatened by time and circumstances and, ultimately, was destroyed forever. The spiritual temple of which the New Testament preachers spoke is a building which cannot be destroyed. The stone which the builders rejected became the headstone of the corner, and as Peter said, "he that believeth on him shall not be confounded" (1 Peter 2:6). Paul also referred to this dependable foundation when he wrote, "Other foundation can no man lay than that is laid, which is Jesus Christ" (1 Cor. 3:11).

THE STONE THAT SHELTERS

Ira D. Sankey made famous a song which expressed this idea.

The Lord's our Rock, in Him we hide;
A shelter in the time of storm.
Secure whatever ill betide,
A shelter in the time of storm.
Oh, Jesus is a Rock in a weary land:
A shelter in the time of storm.

Most people have known the experience of sheltering behind a cornerstone. Probably that was one of the reasons why Peter said Jesus was precious. A free translation of the scripture might be, "He that depends on Him shall not be disappointed."

THE STONE THAT STRENGTHENS

Writing to the church at Ephesus, Paul stated, "Now, therefore, ye are no more strangers and foreigners, but fellowcitizens with the saints, and of the household of God. And are built upon the foundation of the apostles and prophets, Jesus Christ himself being the chief cornerstone: in whom all the building fitly framed together groweth unto a holy temple in the Lord. In whom ye also are builded together for an habitation of God through the Spirit" (Eph. 2:19-22). Unity is the secret of strength; cracks in a wall are the forerunners of disaster. Paul expressed the unity of the Church when he wrote, "Where there is neither Greek nor Jew, circumcision nor uncircumcision, Barbarian, Scythian, bond nor free; but Christ is all, and in all" (Col. 3:11). A cornerstone unites walls in which stones are cemented together to make a complete structure. The true Church is completely dependent upon the Lord who created it. Without the cornerstone, there would be no building; without the Chief Cornerstone, there would be no Church. Christians owe everything to their Savior.

On Christ the solid Rock I stand,
All other ground is sinking sand.

(Reprinted from the author's book, *Bible Names of Christ*, pp. 39–40.)

Homily No. 8

CHRIST . . . The Builder (Matthew 16:18)

It is not difficult to understand why people called God, "The Supreme Architect." He was the Master Builder who supplied Moses with the intricate designs of the tabernacle and insisted that everything be done according to His master plan. Jehovah was always interested in bringing things into being, and it is written, "In the beginning God created the heaven and the earth" (Gen. 1:1). It was to be expected that John would attribute identical characteristics to Christ. The apostle wrote, "All things were made by him [The Word—Jesus] and without him was not anything made that was made" (John 1:3). Throughout the New Testament, Christ is represented as a builder, and certain things become obvious when the Scriptures are examined.

THE MASTER PLAN . . . To Suggest

A builder who operates without a plan encounters problems. His employees have nothing to study, and the building will be disappointing and confusing. When God created the human body, He considered what He was about to do, and afterward David said, "I will praise thee; for I am fearfully and wonderfully made: marvellous are thy works; and that my soul knoweth right well" (Ps. 139:14). Paul evidently believed his Lord had a preconceived plan and mentioned this in Ephesians 2:15: "to make in himself of twain one new man. . . ." Furthermore, the apostle indicated this plan had existed from eternal ages. He wrote, "He hath chosen us in him before the foundation of the world, that we should be holy and without blame before him in love" (Eph. 1:4). Writing of this master plan which remained unrevealed and unexplained throughout the ages, Paul wrote, "Which in other ages was not made known unto the sons of men, as it is now revealed unto his holy apostles and prophets by the Spirit" (Eph. 3:5). God's plan was very explicit, nothing was left to chance. When the Son of God came to earth, He came to put into operation that which had been decided in the eternal counsels of God. Peter said of the Lord, "Him, being delivered by the determinate counsel and foreknowledge of God, ye have taken and by wicked hands have crucified and slain" (Acts 2:23).

THE MATERIALS . . . Supplied

Plans are useless unless materials are forthcoming by which they can be put into operation. Paul believed that God desired all racial strife to cease, that people should live as brothers and sisters, and that all nations should be united in the fellowship of the family of God. Throughout centuries of human history, this appeared to be an impossibility, but the death and resurrection of Jesus performed miracles! The Lord announced to Peter His intention to build His Church, and later the apostle referred to the Christians as "lively [living] stones built up into a spiritual house" (see 1 Peter 2:5). Writing to the Ephesian church, Paul said, "In whom ye also are builded together for an habitation of God through the Spirit" (Eph. 2:22).

Evidently, the human race was filled with sinful blemishes and unfit for a place in God's temple. Christ came to reclaim, cleanse, and beautify lost stones and incorporate them into His Church. Without His intervention, guilty people would have been rejected eternally.

THE MEN . . . To Serve

Prior to the Lord's ascension to heaven, He said to the disciples, "In my Father's house are many mansions: if it were not so, I would have told you. I go to prepare a place for you" (John 14:2). This is the place in which Christ and His bride will reside forever. It is called the "New Jerusalem" (see Rev. 21:9-27). Knowing that He would be busy in heaven, the Lord sent the Holy Spirit to be the divine overseer in the erection of the Church on earth. Obviously, as with any building, workmen are necessary, and one of the greatest privileges ever given to men and women is that of helping in the erection of the true Church of Christ. For example, Paul described himself as "a wise masterbuilder" (1 Cor. 3:10) and indicated that others were also helping in the work of construction. The Lord Jesus Christ is building an edifice which will defy the ravages of time; it will last throughout eternity. Compared with the work of redemption, even the creation of the universe fades into insignificance. S. J. Stone was correct when he wrote:

The Church's one foundation
Is Jesus Christ her Lord.
She is His new creation
By water and the Word:
From Heaven He came and sought her
To be His holy Bride,
With His own blood He bought her,
And for her life, He died.

(Reprinted from the author's book, *Bible Names of Christ*, pp. 67-68).

The Third Chapter of Ephesians

THEME: *The Start and Substance of Paul's Ministry*
OUTLINE:

I. The Stimulation of His Words (Verse 1)
II. The Secret of His Wisdom (Verses 2-7)
III. The Strength of His Work (Verses 8-13)
IV. The Scope of His Wishes (Verses 14-19)
V. The Sincerity of His Worship (Verses 20-21)

THE STIMULATION OF HIS WORDS

Expository Notes on Paul's Description of Himself

For this cause I Paul, the prisoner of Jesus Christ for you Gentiles (v. 1).

THEME: *The Reason for Paul's Unique Call*
OUTLINE:

A. His Amazing Perception
B. His Abiding Presence
C. His Ample Protection
D. His Assured Purpose

HIS AMAZING PERCEPTION

It is interesting that Paul described himself as "the prisoner of Jesus Christ." Unfortunately, he was incarcerated on several occasions. He had been confined to the prison of Fort Antonia in Jerusalem (Acts 23:10) and to Herod's Praetorium in Caesarea (Acts 23:35). In addition, he was imprisoned twice in Rome, with a house-arrest of two years separating his confinements (Acts 28:30) during which he was probably chained to a Roman soldier, and such a situation suggests several things.

HIS ABIDING PRESENCE

The continuing nearness of the guard indicated Paul was a prisoner of Nero; the soldier was responsible for the safety of the apostle. If for any reason he escaped or was harmed, the Roman was answerable with his own life. When Paul claimed to be the prisoner of Jesus Christ, he insinuated that his real Captor had not left him. David declared, "The angel of the Lord encampeth round about them that fear him, and delivereth them" (Ps. 34:7). The Savior promised His disciples: "Go ye therefore and teach all nations . . . and lo, *I am with you always even unto the end of the world*" (Matt. 28:19-20). This glorious fact was demonstrated during two of the most crucial of Paul's experiences. When he was imprisoned in Jerusalem, "the Lord stood by him, and said, Be of good cheer, Paul: for as thou hast testified of me in Jerusalem, so must thou bear witness also at Rome" (Acts 23:11). When Paul was being taken to the imperial city, a storm threatened the safety of the vessel, but he said to his companions, "And now I exhort you to be of good cheer; for there shall be no loss of any man's life among you, but of the ship. For *there stood by me this night the angel of God*, whose I am, and whom I serve, saying, Fear not, Paul; thou must be brought before Caesar; and, lo, God hath given thee all them that sail with thee" (Acts 27:22-24). Probably, one of the apostle's greatest assets was his continuing faith in the abiding presence of his Lord.

HIS AMPLE PROTECTION

Prisoners were always chained to a guard. If one soldier was insufficient to guarantee safety, other men would have been assigned to the task of providing what was necessary. When Paul looked at the Roman, he probably smiled. It was helpful to have someone with whom to converse, but the apostle knew his future depended on the promises of God. The apostle was able to write to the Corinthians, "There hath no temptation taken you but such as is common to man: but God is faithful, who will not suffer you to be tempted above that ye are able; but will with the temptation also make a way to escape, that ye may be able to bear it" (1 Cor. 10:13). Whether Paul was in or out of prison, that promise helped to solve his problems. Evidently, he believed that God understood the difficulties confronting His servant. The Lord was able, under any circumstances, to give assistance in time of need. He could "make a way of escape." The words of David must have been precious during the extended periods of Paul's imprisonment. "For he shall give his angels charge over thee, to keep thee in all thy ways" (Ps. 91:11).

HIS ASSURED PURPOSE

"For this cause I, Paul, the prisoner of Jesus Christ *for you Gentiles*." Paul reminded his readers that they were indirectly the reason for his incarceration. Therefore, they should give special consideration to his message and be grateful that Paul had been sent to them. That the apostle was inspired to write his Epistles did not mean the removal of his natural instincts and expressions. The Holy Spirit used men *as they were*. Paul apparently had a habit of changing his thought-directions in a hurry! The first chapter began with a very long sentence which was not a sentence! Chapter 3 supplies another example of Paul's unique style of writing. He began with the remark "For this cause," but then his thoughts turned to other things. Verses 2-13 must be regarded as interpolations. At verse 14, Paul concluded what he commenced in verse 1, "For this cause I bow my knees unto the Father of our Lord Jesus Christ." Between verse 1—the commencement of his statement—and verse 14, the continuance of it, Paul introduced many things which, doubtless, were suggested by the statement "*for you Gentiles*." God especially ordained him to become a preacher to the Gentiles, and the apostle never forgot his commission. When he reminded the Lord that he was best suited to influence Jews, God interrupted him saying, "Depart: for I will send thee far hence unto the Gentiles" (see Acts 22:17-21). The Christians in Asia were reminded that Paul's teaching was God's message especially sent to them. Yet, when he wrote, "for you Gentiles," his thoughts turned in a new direction, a fact which introduces the next section of this chapter.

THE SECRET OF HIS WISDOM

Expository Notes on the Authenticity of Paul's Message

If ye have heard of the dispensation of the grace of God which is given me to you-ward how that by revelation he made known unto me the mystery; (as I wrote afore in few words, whereby, when ye read, ye may understand my knowledge in the mystery of Christ) which in other ages was not made known unto the sons of men, as it is now revealed unto his holy apostles and prophets by the Spirit; that the Gentiles should be fellowheirs, and of the same body, and partakers of his promise in Christ by the gospel: whereof I was made a minister,

according to the gift of the grace of God given unto me by the effectual working of his power (vv. 2-7).

THEME: *The Making of a Minister*
OUTLINE:

A. An Astonishing Manifestation (v. 2)
B. An Acknowledged Method (v. 3)
C. An Absolute Mystery (vv. 4-5)
D. An Amazing Message (v. 6)
E. An Anointed Minister (v. 7)

AN ASTONISHING MANIFESTATION

Expository Notes on the Special Grace Experienced by Paul

If ye have heard of the dispensation of the grace of God which is given me to you-ward (v. 2).

Some theologians see ambiguity in Paul's statement, "*If ye have heard* of the dispensation of the grace of God which is given me to you-ward." The apostle had been a pastor in the city of Ephesus and doubtless helped to establish assemblies in adjacent cities. Many years had passed since that time, and other Asians had heard the gospel. Some of the Christians remembered Paul's pastorate, and others heard from the elders those things accomplished during his ministry. Therefore, it must be recognized that some saints had firsthand knowledge of Paul's experiences; others heard about them, and perhaps, new converts remained uninformed about Paul's exploits. The Living Bible translates the passage: "No doubt, you already know that God has given me this special work of showing God's favor to you Gentiles, as I briefly mentioned before in one of my letters."

Paul assumed that most of his readers were aware of his miraculous conversion when the grace of God saved him outside the gate of Damascus. He who had been a persecutor of the Christians embraced their faith and was subsequently commissioned to become the apostle to the Gentiles. The apostle reminded his friends of those facts, for a recognition of the legitimacy of his call was essential to an understanding of the importance of his message. What he preached was imparted to him by the Holy Spirit, and to question his authority was unpardonable.

Within the Greek New Testament, the phrase "the dispensation of the grace of God," is *teen oikonomian tees charitos tou Theou*. This means "the *administration* of the grace of God." The dictionary states that the word *administration* means: "dispensation; a special plan; the arranging or ordering of events" as by a divine Providence. Many preachers believe that the biblical dispensations represented times when God introduced new methods in dealing with mankind. Explaining the word *oikonomian*, Dr. Thayer says, "It means the management of a household or of household affairs; specifically, the management, oversight, administration of other's property; the office of a manager or overseer; stewardship." (See Luke 16:2-4.) Considered in this setting, Paul's statement suggests new thoughts. During the unfolding of history, God had special arrangements with Adam, Noah, Abraham, Moses, and others by which He introduced new methods of revealing truth. Paul believed his name had been added to that important list; once again God had revealed astounding truth. The apostle claimed equality with the greatest names in Jewish history. What he taught was as important as the commandments given by Moses.

God had chosen him to be the overseer and manager of His estate, and had given to him complete authority to act on His behalf in matters relating to the extension of that estate. The Lord had conceived a plan whereby His holdings would be vastly extended, Gentile territory was to be included in the enlargement of God's domain, and the "management" of that work had been given to Paul. He had been ordained as a preacher to the Gentiles. The apostle emphasized this fact so that all Christians would be aware of God's purposes. If they had heard this earlier, it was to their advantage; if they had not, he was repeating what he had said "*afore in few words*."

AN ACKNOWLEDGED METHOD

Expository Notes on God's Special Revelation

How that by revelation he made known unto me the mystery (v. 3).

God was the source of His own message. Gifted people could explain and declare it, but until Jehovah made known His will, even the greatest theologians could only speculate regarding His thoughts. No one could overestimate the value of education; uninformed speakers advertised their stupidity. Even Elijah and Elisha knew the value of training and established "the school of the prophets." Yet, it is thought-provoking that the Old Testament prophets were not the product of theological institutions. Only two of the New Testament writers graduated from a college. Luke evidently came from a university, and

Paul was trained in the school of Gamaliel. The prophets became teachers in their own right, but they were primarily indebted to God, who was the source of their knowledge. Seminaries may prove to be invaluable, and skilled teachers can develop the inherent qualities of students. Non-trained individuals should never be critical of educational attainments; nevertheless, God's people learn most on their knees! The Lord continues to reveal truth, but some people unfortunately have poor understanding.

It is worthy of attention that early in his Christian experience, Paul was sent into the desert where he remained for a considerable period (Gal. 1:17-18). He had plenty of time during which to reflect and listen. When he returned, he referred to a message which he called "my gospel." It was an indication that he was about to present a new message inextricably woven into the fabric of his own life. He had something to impart which was unknown to his compatriots. God had given him a special revelation of truth hitherto unknown. The apostle believed that the opposition of the Pharisees was unjustified. They taught that Moses received a revelation on Mount Sinai, that Jonah was given a special assignment to Nineveh, and that the ministry of every other prophet began in the same way. Was Jehovah incompetent to continue what had been done in earlier ages? Had God "gone out of business"? Paul claimed that God continued to reveal truth of superlative value. "God, who at sundry times and in diverse manners spake in time past unto the fathers by the prophets hath in these last days spoken unto us by his Son . . . " (Hebrews 1:1-2). The Greek word translated "revelation" is *apokaluphin*, which, according to Thayer means: "an uncovering, a laying bare, making naked, a disclosure of truth, instruction, concerning divine things before unknown." Paul claimed that he had received a special revelation from heaven, but how it came to him, he did not say. Evidently, God had no difficulty in speaking, and His servant was an excellent listener.

AN ABSOLUTE MYSTERY

Expository Notes on the Change in God's Policy

. . . the mystery of Christ; which in other ages was not made known unto the sons of men, as it is now revealed unto his holy apostles and prophets by the Spirit (v. 5).

God was an expert Developer of projects! He began with nothing, and made the universe; with Adam and Eve, and made the human race; with Abraham, and created the Hebrew nation; with Moses, and produced the foundation for international legal systems. The Pharisees assumed there could be nothing new; God had spoken the final word! Upon that premise they built their legal structure and added traditions which became more important than the commandments of God. They surrounded themselves with restrictive impositions, and any man or movement opposed to those rules and principles invited criticism.

The idea that God might have additional truth to impart never occurred to the Pharisees, and it was at that point that Paul encountered bitter opposition. Converts from Judaism might have asked, "Why did God take so long to announce new doctrines? Why did He not tell us earlier?" To those questions there could be several answers:

1. God had no *gospel to preach* until Christ came to earth. There was no message of reconciliation, no means of securing international peace. The law enslaved men, sinners needed deliverance.
2. God had *very few people* through whom He could effectively work. Even if there existed a message to preach, a few isolated prophets, often separated by centuries, could not have evangelized the world.
3. God was *determined to honor His Son*. The time had not arrived for Christ to enter the world. Channels of communication between nations were inadequate; people traveled by camels. Even when the Savior did come, He never went more than 150 miles from His birthplace.
4. God is *omniscient*; He sees the end from the beginning. Even at his best, humanity, with limited understanding and defective vision, should never question the wisdom of the Almighty.

Those who live in darkness appreciate light; slaves dream of freedom; the oppressed look for deliverance. Maybe God had to wait until men learned how to appreciate His kindness. A premature preaching about the unity of Jews and Gentiles could have been unwise. The bigotry of the Hebrews and the ignorance of the Gentiles presented insurmountable obstacles to international harmony. What had been an inscrutable mystery was now revealed to "his holy apostles and prophets." The redeeming love of Christ supplied the message, converted men with a passionate desire to preach were being called, and the Romans had built highways which would be lines of communication to the ends of the earth.

AN AMAZING MESSAGE

Expository Notes on the Content of Paul's Message

That the Gentiles should be fellowheirs, and of the same body, and partakers of his promise in Christ by the gospel (v. 6).

Paul was correct when he said that this message had not been known unto the sons of men. Jonah, a Jewish prophet, had reluctantly preached to the people of Nineveh, and the city had been spared. Yet, Jonah never believed that such people would share privileges of the chosen race. Rahab, the harlot, exercised faith, and her deliverance initiated her into the family of God. She was an isolated example; the rest of her people perished (see Josh. 6). A company of Egyptians traveled with the Hebrews when they commenced the journey toward the Promised Land, but their presence promoted problems. Isaiah predicted the ultimate glory of Israel when he declared, "And the Gentiles shall come to thy light" (Isa. 60:3). Yet, more often than not, every prophet denounced the paganism of the Gentiles and predicted their doom. Had someone suggested that all nations would eventually become one, the idea would have been considered ludicrous. It would have seemed as outrageous as Moses and Pharaoh becoming brothers. The idea would have been rejected instantly. That might have been another reason why God refrained from announcing His intentions earlier.

That all should "become fellowheirs" suggests that God desired to bestow His wealth upon Jews and Gentiles alike; there would be no favoritism; all people would be equal in His sight. All nations could share His bounty and be "of the same body and partakers of his promise in Christ" (v. 6). The term "in Christ" remained at the center of divine planning. Without Him, God would have been hindered; without Him, we would have been lost.

AN ANOINTED MINISTER

Expository Notes on the Calling of Paul

Whereof I was made a minister . . . (v. 7).

Paul was proud of his calling and thrilled with his privilege. He had been converted, called, consecrated, and chosen for his special task. It was neither something he had coveted nor a task he had diligently sought. It was beyond comprehension that a murderer could become a minister, that a persecutor could be a preacher. True ordination comes from God. The hands of church elders may rest upon a candidate's head, but unless the touch of God be upon his spirit, even the most eloquent preacher cannot be an effective witness to the power of Christ's gospel. Paul was *made* a minister; he did not, and could not, make himself a minister. Few would deny that this calling is one of the greatest privileges bestowed upon men. It suggests dignity, sanctity, separation to a God-given task, self-sacrificing devotion to the highest and best principles in life, and an absence of things unworthy to occupy a minister's heart. If a man wilfully abandons those principles, he brands himself as being unworthy of his profession.

The Holy Spirit had anointed Paul, abundant grace had fallen upon his soul, and an effective work of God's Spirit was evident in his life. Without the grace of God, Paul was just another man! Without the effective power of the Spirit inspiring his words and actions, the preacher would have become an orator who said nothing of value. "*I was made a minister*" should be the exultant testimony of every person entering a pulpit.

THE STRENGTH OF HIS WORK

THEME: *Paul's Explanation of His Greatest Desires*
OUTLINE:

A. An Exuberant Preacher (v. 8)
B. An Expository Preaching (v. 9)
C. An Exciting Purpose (v. 10)
D. An Eternal Pattern (v. 11)
E. An Extreme Privilege (v. 12)
F. An Emphatic Plea (v. 13)

AN EXUBERANT PREACHER

Expository Notes on Paul's Assessment of Himself

Unto me, who am less than the least of all saints, is this grace given, that I should preach among the Gentiles the unsearchable riches of Christ (v. 8).

This verse expressed one of the most thought-provoking statements made by the apostle Paul; it revealed three vital features of his ministry: *holiness*, *humility*, and *happiness*. It is worthy of attention that he who had given so much to God considered himself to be the most unworthy Christian—"the least of all saints."

Paul Gave the Gospel to the World

The twelve apostles had been content to remain within the boundaries of Judaism and, apparently ignoring Christ's last command, did not go into "*all* the world" preaching the gospel. The man from Tarsus alone heard and accepted the call and challenge of paganism. During his lifetime, the apostle journeyed throughout the known world preaching the gospel to Gentiles. He endured hardships of the most cruel type when other men would have retreated before the attacks of enemies. Yet, Paul never flinched and at the end of his pilgrimage was able to say, "I have fought a good fight, I have finished my course, I have kept the faith: henceforth there is laid up for me a crown of righteousness, which the Lord, the righteous judge, shall give me at that day: and not to me only, but unto all them also that love his appearing" (2 Tim. 4:7-8). Throughout his illustrious ministry, Paul never turned back; he never quit. He did more in one year of his ministry than the other apostles accomplished in their lifetime. Yet, in spite of his achievements, he believed himself to be the "least of all saints." That conclusion, to say the least, was astonishing.

Paul Gave the Most of the New Testament to the Church

There are twenty-seven books in the New Testament, and possibly fourteen of these letters came from the pen of this apostle. He wrote two letters to the church in Corinth; two to the church in Thessalonica, and single letters to the Galatians, the Ephesians, the Philippians, the Colossians, Titus, and Philemon. He wrote two letters to Timothy, and he might have been the author of the letter to the Hebrews. As far as literary ability was concerned, no other author compared with him. John wrote five books, but even he could not equal the efforts of Paul. If the words of the other apostles helped to establish the Church, it was Paul whose counsel enabled the believers to endure the persecution which awaited them in unevangelized countries. If the efforts of the original twelve brought the Christian ship into existence, it was the wisdom and unerring guidance offered by Paul which enabled that vessel to sail through uncharted waters toward an eternal shore. Paul chastised and encouraged his readers, answered their questions and solved their problems, carried their burdens upon his heart and set an example which all should follow. He was never jealous of his contemporaries, never compromised his faith, and never denied his Lord. He was a prince among men, a light shining in the darkness, a beacon which encouraged others to press toward a successful conclusion of their earthly pilgrimage. Lesser men would have accepted the accolades of their associates, but Paul refused such honor, believing he was "the least of all saints."

Paul Gave His Life to the Cause of Christ

To read the accounts of Paul's experiences is to become aware of a man within whose heart was an irresistible urge. He was motivated by a single desire—to proclaim the gospel of Christ until speech and effort became impossible. When Paul sent his letter to the Christians in Rome, he said, "I am debtor both to the Greeks, and to the Barbarians; both to the wise, and to the unwise, so, as much as in me is, I am ready to preach the gospel to you that are at Rome also" (Rom. 1:14-15). Simon Peter unfortunately suffered a temporary relapse when he denied his Lord; all the apostles lived to be ashamed of the time when "they forsook him [Christ] and fled" (Mark 14:50). Demas left the apostle to fraternize with people who did not share his faith. Yet, Paul remained immovable. He resembled a peak against which storms unleashed their onslaught, but when the skies cleared and the elements abated, like a mountain of stone, Paul was still there. He never lost sight of his goal, he never denied his Lord, and although sometimes he became discouraged, with each new morning he found strength to serve His Lord fearlessly and faithfully. It may be said of him as was said of Enoch: "Before his translation he had this testimony, that *he pleased God*" (Heb. 11:5). He was indisputably holy, unquestionably humble, and unceasingly happy. These were the unchanging characteristics of his career, the sure evidence that he walked and talked with God. Yet, in spite of his distinguished service for Christ, he remained convinced that of all the saints he was the most undeserving. For us to appreciate this fact, we should consider the homily, "Paul . . . and His Faulty Grammar!" p. 168.

AN EXPOSITORY PREACHING

Expository Notes on the Purpose of Paul's Mission

And to make everyone see what is the fellowship of the mystery, which

from the beginning of the world hath been hid in God, who created all things by Jesus Christ (v. 9).

THEME: *The Unveiling of God's Greatest Masterpiece*
OUTLINE:

A. A Superb Mission . . . "*to make all men see*"
B. A Special Message . . . "*the fellowship of the mystery*"
C. A Selective Majesty . . . "*from the beginning . . . hid in God*"
D. A Sublime Medium . . . "*by Jesus Christ*"

A Superb Mission . . . "to make all men see"

"Unto me . . . is this grace given, that I should . . . make all men see . . . " (v. 9). The word translated "see" is *photisai*; within the New Testament, Thayer tells us, it was used in three ways: (a) "to enlighten, light up, illumine; (b) to bring to light, to render evident; and (c) to enlighten spiritually, to imbue with saving knowledge." It was always used in connection with the giving of light. Frank E. Gaebelein in *The Expositor's Bible Commentary*, on page 46 of volume two, states, "Paul was called to 'make plain' (*photisai*) to everyone, the outworking of the secret plan of God. He was to shed light on it, so that no one would be in the dark any more about it." He was to be a man directing a torchlight toward something long veiled in darkness. He resembled someone who had discovered an exquisite treasure in the depths of a cave, and he was now focusing light upon it so that his companions could view what otherwise would have been unseen. God had commissioned His servant to illuminate the most wonderful truth ever discovered by man. Paul evidently believed that his sermon should be an enlightening experience for listeners. Old Testament prophets were searchlights penetrating the obscurity of future ages. If the message of a preacher does not challenge darkness, he should never be in a pulpit.

A Special Message . . . "the fellowship of the mystery"

"And to make all men see what is the fellowship of the mystery" (v. 9a). When Paul wrote to the Colossians, he repeated his message. "Whereof I am made a minister, according to the dispensation of God which is given to me for you, to fulfil the word of God: even the mystery which hath been hid from ages and from generations, but now is made manifest to his saints; to whom God would make known what is the riches of the glory of this mystery among the Gentiles; which is Christ in you, the hope of glory" (Col. 1:25-27). The apostle used the word "mystery" seventeen times in his writings.

The Greek word translated "mystery" is *musteerion* which means "a hidden or secret thing; something not obvious to the understanding; a hidden purpose or counsel; a secret will" (Thayer). Paul used the word six times in the Epistle to the Ephesians (1:9; 3:3; 3:4; 3:9; 5:32; 6:19) and four times in the letter sent to the Colossians (1:26; 1:27; 2:2; 4:3). The gospel revealed through Christ was God's special surprise for mankind. He had *planned*, *prepared*, *preserved*, *perfected*, and *presented* it. It was the glorious news that He loved all men and desired to make possible the entry of all nations into His family. Even unlovely, unattractive people were appreciated by the Almighty, and through Christ the most degraded could lean on the bosom of God. To Jews this was unwelcome, it was a stumbling block. To the Greeks it was foolishness, but to every Christian it was the most wonderful message ever proclaimed. God's revealed mystery made possible the words of the poet who wrote:

Jesus included me;
Yes, He included me:
When the Lord said, "Whosoever"
He included me.

A Selective Majesty . . . "from the beginning . . . hid in God"

" . . . the mystery which from the beginning hath been hid in God" (v. 9b). Evidently Paul wanted to teach that the Church, in which all nations would be united as a common family, was a carefully guarded secret which had been kept from eternal ages. He repeatedly emphasized that this was not an afterthought in the mind of the Almighty. To Paul's Hebrew readers, it must have been difficult to appreciate why God secretly planned such an innovation when, throughout the ages, His law demanded that Israel be an undefiled nation.

Most of the prohibitions of Jewish practice had been made by the rulers of the nation, but the fact remained that fraternization with heathen nations had been condemned, and that disobedience brought guilt upon offenders. Israel believed in one God as opposed to the many gods of the heathens; they obeyed one law as opposed to the

Gentiles who had no commandments and did as they pleased. Why did Jehovah encourage Israel to be separated from Gentiles when, at the same time, He planned to incorporate those same people into His family? That was indisputably God's greatest secret, and it was inevitable that it would create consternation among Jews who tried to obey the commandments of Moses. Paul claimed that since Jehovah had decided to reveal a special truth, it was encumbent upon all people to listen and not argue. That the message was *new* did not infer it was wrong! That God had not revealed it earlier was His business, and finite man should not question the decisions of the Almighty.

A Sublime Medium . . . "by Jesus Christ"

". . . the mystery . . . hid in God, who created all things by Jesus Christ"(v. 9c). The words "by Jesus Christ" are not found in most of the early manuscripts and are considered by many authorities to be an appendage by a later copier of the Scriptures. Other scholars dispute this conclusion, stating that it harmonizes with statements made by Paul and contemporary writers. John, speaking of the eternal Word, declared: "All things were made by him; and without him was not anything made that was made" (John 1:3). Paul, writing to the Colossians, said of Christ, "who is the image of the invisible God, the firstborn of every creature; for by him were all things created, that are in heaven, and that are in earth, visible and invisible, whether they be thrones, or dominions, or principalities, or powers: all things were created by him, and for him: and he is before all things, and by him all things consist" (Col. 1:15-17).

However complex the revelation of the mystery might have been, Paul was far more fascinated by the amazing fact that He who made the plans had actually come to earth to accomplish what had been decided. The Lord Jesus had become the appointed Messenger of Jehovah, the One through whom God's truth would be explained. It was incomprehensible that any person should question or challenge what was being taught, for God was revealing superlative truth—the greatest news ever told to sinful men. The writer to the Hebrews stated, "God, who at sundry times and in divers manners spake in time past unto the fathers by the prophets, hath in these last days spoken unto us *by his Son*, whom he hath appointed heir of all things, by whom also he made the worlds" (Heb. 1:1-2). God had spoken; when people refused to listen, they exhibited stupidity.

AN EXCITING PURPOSE

Expository Notes on God's Purpose for the Church

To the intent that now unto the principalities and powers in heavenly places might be known by the church the manifold wisdom of God (v. 10).

THEME: *God's Demonstration of His Wisdom*
OUTLINE:

A. The Inevitable Will of God
B. The Inexhaustible Wisdom of God
C. The Instruction of the Watchers of God

This is a remarkable verse which has been translated in various ways. The Living Bible reads, "And his reason? To show to all the rulers in heaven how perfectly wise he is when all of his family—Jews and Gentiles alike are seen to be joined together in his church." Phillips' New Testament in Modern English reads, "The purpose is that all the angelic powers should now see the complex wisdom of God's plan being worked out through the church, in conformity to that timeless purpose which he centered in Christ Jesus, our Lord."

The Inevitable Will of God

Repeatedly, Paul emphasized the fact that what he taught was an explanation of things God had planned before time began. The words "to the intent" imply that throughout his association with man, God was working according to a master-plan. Problems arose to hinder the fulfillment of His desires, but the end was never in doubt. Neither men nor angels, principalities nor powers could defeat the purposes of the Almighty. It was inevitable that His will be fulfilled; no power in time or eternity could overthrow God's kingdom or prevent the ultimate triumph of His Son. Continuing storms threatened to drive God's vessel from its appointed course, but the ship inevitably would reach its designated harbor. Probably it was this conviction which inspired the apostle's statement: "And we know that all things work together for good to them that love God, to them who are the called according to his purpose" (Rom. 8:28). The poet expressed the unfailing purpose of God when he wrote:

God is working His purpose out:
As year succeeds to year.
God is working His purpose out,
And the time is drawing near.
Nearer and nearer draws the time,
The time that shall surely be,
When the earth shall be filled with the glory of God
As the waters cover the sea.

The Inexhaustible Wisdom of God

Paul spoke of "the *manifold* wisdom of God." The Greek word translated "manifold" is *polupoikilos*. Dr. Thayer states it denotes, "much-variegated; marked with a great variety of colors; of cloth, or a painting." Paul suggested "a many-sided wisdom" a complex manifestation of divine knowledge that beggared description. It was a diamond with many facets, each of which sparkled with resplendence which emanated from God. If Jehovah could be described as an artist, then His unerring wisdom produced a picture of eternal beauty in which many kinds of colorful attractions blended into a masterpiece of incalculable worth. If He were a manufacturer of fabric, then He designed and produced material which reflected the beauty of heaven and excelled the best that man could make. The wisdom of the Almighty had brought planets into being and created color, music, and everything lovely; but what He did within the hearts of redeemed men and women was His most scintillating achievement. When compared with Old Testament history, the project appeared to be impossible. Perhaps that was the reason why "the mystery" could not have been revealed at an earlier date. If the secret had been revealed prematurely, everyone would have ridiculed the message. When Christ eventually brought the Church into being, onlookers at least could see the miracle of grace, and although many of the Jews rejected the concept, others at least began to comprehend what had been hidden in the mind of God.

The Instruction of the Watchers of God

"To the intent that now unto the principalities and powers in heavenly places might be known by the church the manifold wisdom of God (v. 10)". It was evident that Paul's thoughts were focused on "heavenly places." God made His acts known among the people of earth, but He was primarily interested in displaying His omniscience to whoever might be watching from other worlds. That statement has attracted the attention of many scholars. Some believe that Paul was thinking of the rulers of earth, but that conclusion is incorrect. The watchers were said to be "in heavenly places," and that meant somewhere in space. There are two possibilities:

1. Writing of the revelation of the gospel message, Peter stated, "Unto whom it was revealed, that not unto themselves, but unto us they have preached the gospel unto you with the Holy Ghost sent down from heaven; *which things the angels desire to look into*" (1 Peter 1:12). The Lord's plan for His Church was a source of increasing interest to angelic hosts. They desired to know more of the salvation to be offered to undeserving sinners.

2. Later in the Epistle, Paul again mentioned principalities and powers, and indicated the followers of Christ would need to resist them. He said, "For we wrestle not against flesh and blood, but against principalities, against powers, against the rulers of the darkness of this world, against spiritual wickedness in high places" (Eph. 6:12). It might be possible to infer that the apostle was speaking of the wickedness existing in Caesar's household, but that could never exhaust the meaning of Paul's statement. Therefore, it must be concluded that Paul was citing a different incident when the Savior " . . . spoiled principalities and powers . . . and made a shew over them openly, triumphing over them in it" (Col. 2:15). The Book of Job describes an incident when Satan accused Job before the Almighty and suggested that his righteousness was shallow, something easily destroyed. If Satan disputed the decisions of God then, he perhaps said of God's plan for the Church, "It cannot be done. I will oppose your actions and enslave your people." Maybe God replied, "It can, and it will be done; and someday I will prove it to you." That promise was finally honored when, through the merit of Christ's sacrifice, the Lord Jesus overcame the powers of hell.

AN ETERNAL PATTERN

Expository Notes on the Eternal Purpose of God

According to the eternal purpose which he purposed in Christ Jesus our Lord (v. 11).

THEME: *The Eternal Purpose of God*
OUTLINE:

A. A Blameless Church (Eph. 1:4)
B. A Beautiful Church (Eph. 5:27)
C. A Beneficiary Church (Eph. 3:6)

This verse is but an echo of the great truth which constantly filled the mind of the apostle. Apparently, Paul was fascinated by the fact that all he taught could be traced to the everlasting foreknowledge and planning of his Heavenly Father. All that had happened—and was still happening—was the fulfillment of God's cherished dream and the ardent desire of His heart. Paul's message should have been accepted instantly and joyfully instead of being criticized and rejected. He had become the oracle of God, and however strange his message appeared to be, it was evident that what he said was the harbinger of peace and happiness. God had envisaged a world free from bigotry and enmity, and that glorious achievement was now within reach of repentant, believing people. Careful readers of this Epistle recognize that underneath every claim made by the apostle lay the profound truth of God's unerring plan for future ages. Foreseeing every detail, the Almighty arranged the destiny of believing people even before they were born.

A Blameless Church

> **According as he hath chosen us in him before the foundation of the world, that we should be holy and without blame before him in love (Eph. 1:4).**

To be without guilt might be an objective hard to reach, but to be without blame should be the goal for which all aspiring Christians strive. It represents the "higher ground" of Christian experience where conscious sinning becomes a thing of the past. Later in his letter (5:27) the apostle emphasized that this is the ultimate height to which we shall be lifted. He wrote, "That he might present it to himself a glorious church, not having spot, or wrinkle, or any such thing; but that it should be holy and without blemish." At the beginning of time, God saw the result of His creative power (see Gen. 1:10, 12, 18); at the end, He will view the completion of His project, and it will be perfect.

A Beautiful Church

. . . a glorious church not having spot, or wrinkle, or any such thing (Eph. 5:27).

Writing to the Thessalonians, Paul said; "When he shall come to be glorified in his saints and to be admired in all them that believe . . . " (2 Thess. 1:10). The glory of Christ will cover His Church with resplendence and charm, and, throughout eternity, the scintillating beauty of His bride will amaze all who will be privileged to see her. It has often been said that "beauty is only skin deep," and that is true. Many people have not been blessed with a beautiful face, and those who are wealthy spend great sums of money to obtain the services of plastic surgeons. Yet, when beauty of expression is the product of a wonderful personality, when a person is beautiful both inside and out, it represents a treasure not easily found.

We know that God appreciates lovely things, for He made waterfalls, flowers, music, blue skies, and innumerable other things. Since the Church is to be His finest work of art, it is impossible for human beings to comprehend the extent of His designs. God intends to make us like the Lord Jesus Christ. How He will succeed in accomplishing this feat seems impossible to grasp. Some saints who rejoice in the prospect of absolute perfection still believe God will have problems. The consciousness of inherent weakness is a cloud which blots out their sun of expectation. Nevertheless, that God will complete what He commenced is beyond doubt.

A Beneficiary Church

That the Gentiles should be fellowheirs, and of the same body, and partakers of his promise in Christ by the gospel (Eph. 3:6).

Paul taught that only God was capable of planning such a transformation. It was impossible amid the bigotry and bitterness of racism for any teacher to envisage a time when everyone would be one. The veiled foreshadowing of things yet to appear was seen everyday in the church. Masters and slaves, the wealthy and poor, the educated and illiterate enjoyed fellowship. An Ethiopian eunuch, a Roman centurion, and a woman of ill-fame all could sit with Mary, the mother of the Lord, and find happiness associating with each other. Pride of race and position were unknown within the early church. The Savior came "that he might reconcile both [Jews and Gentiles] unto God in one body by the cross, having slain the enmity thereby . . . now, therefore, ye are no more strangers and foreigners, but fellowcitizens with the saints, and of the household of God" (Eph. 2:16-19). Eternal wealth had come within reach of impoverished sinners. The hand of faith could grasp riches beyond comprehension. Christians had become the beneficiaries of the greatest Person in existence, and it was not a cause for amazement when Paul referred to "the unsearchable riches of Christ" (Eph. 3:8).

AN EXTREME PRIVILEGE

Expository Notes on the By-products of the Christian Faith

In whom we have boldness and access with confidence by the faith of him (v. 12).

THEME: *The Privileges of Faith in Christ*
OUTLINE:

A. Boldness . . . *The Concept of Courage*
B. Access . . . *The Cause of Communion*
C. Confidence . . . *The Certainty of Continuance*
D. Faith . . . *The Contact with Christ*

This brief statement made by Paul included four outstanding words; each one indicates a very valuable by-product of the grace of God. The apostle had the ability to express eternity in a few words; yet at other times his mind was so filled with the knowledge of God that he hardly knew how to cease writing. He began this chapter with a simple claim and then, as though he had temporarily forgotten his original intention, branched off in another direction. Before he completed his opening statement, twelve verses were inserted into his manuscript. As Paul approached the end of the interpolation, he summarized his doctrines, and, in one verse, used four glorious words: (1) boldness, (2) access, (3) confidence, and (4) faith.

Boldness . . . The Concept of Courage

"In whom [Christ] we have boldness. . . ." The Greek word translated "boldness" is *parreesin.* It comes from *parreesia,* which means "freedom in speaking; free and fearless, confidence, cheerful courage, boldness, assurance." The writer to the Hebrews used the same word in Hebrews 4:16: "Let us, therefore, come *boldly* unto the throne of grace." This was a concept almost unknown in the Old Testament era. When God descended to Mount Sinai, the people were told not to touch the mountain so that they would not perish. "And the Lord said unto Moses . . . and thou shalt set bounds unto the people round about, saying, Take heed to yourselves, that ye go not up into the mount, or touch the border of it: whosoever toucheth the mount shall be surely put to death. There shall not a hand touch it, but he shall surely be stoned, or shot through; whether it be beast or man, it shall not live" (Exod. 19:10-13). During later generations when the priestly administration was predominant in Israel, only the high priest was permitted to enter into the Holy of Holies to speak with God.

Access . . . The Cause of Communion

When Paul and his contemporaries announced that a way had been created by which any person, at any time, could draw near to the throne of grace, they proclaimed one of the most revolutionary messages of all time. Actually, they were implying that the office of high priest was no longer necessary. Christ had become the High Priest of His people. Offerings had been outlawed forever and sin removed from the souls of believers. Through the redemptive work of the Savior, the last barrier had been removed; terror had been obliterated, and nothing would ever again prevent sinners from kneeling before God.

Confidence . . . The Certainty of Continuance

"We have access . . . *with confidence*." It is possible to gain access to a building by stealth, but every moment threatens discovery and danger. To enter the presence of God with confidence is assurance that the right of entry will never be challenged. Perhaps this is best illustrated by the following incidents which happened some years ago.

The story has often been told of a little boy who looked through the railings guarding Buckingham Palace. He desired to see Queen Victoria, but a guard prevented the child from going beyond the gate. The child's tears expressed the desire of his heart when Prince Edward saw him. Taking the lad by the hand, the prince led him through the gate and into the royal apartments. When Queen Victoria heard of the boy's interest, she commanded that he should be washed and clothed with a new suit, and when she finally sent him home, the child seemed a prince in his own right.

I remember a night in New Zealand when a young woman had difficulty understanding how she could be accepted by God. At that time, the Queen of England, with her husband, was touring the land, and I reminded the young lady that the royal visitors were staying in Government House. I asked, "What would happen if you tried to get through a back window to see the Queen?" Her reply was explosive when she said, "I would be out on my neck!" "But, supposing the Duke of Edinburgh came out to say, 'So you desire to see the Queen and cannot! Young lady, do not worry. Come with me and I will take you to her.' What would happen then?" She replied, "He could get me in!"

She understood when I said that we would never gain admittance into the royal house of heaven, but that the Prince of Life came to seek us, and He said, "I am the way, the truth, and the life; no man cometh unto the Father, but by me." To follow Christ is to have access with boldness. (Taken in part from the author's book, *Bible Highways*, pp. 159-160.)

Faith . . . The Contact With Christ

" Access with confidence *by the faith of him*." The verse can be interpreted in two ways: (1) *Our* faith in Christ provides the confidence which banishes fear. (2) We have confidence through *His* faith—that when our faith weakens, the faith of the Savior will be sufficient to negate accusations made against us. This might have been in the mind of Christ when predicting Peter's forthcoming failure, He said, "But I have prayed for thee, that thy faith fail not: and when thou art converted, strengthen thy brethren" (Luke 22:32). The Revised Standard Version reads, "We have access and boldness through our faith in him." The Living Bible translates the passage, "Now we can come fearlessly right into God's presence, assured of His glad welcome when we come with Christ, and trust in him." Faith in the Savior's ability is an anchor which holds the soul even in the most frightening storms.

AN EMPHATIC PLEA

Expository Notes on Paul's Desires for the Converts

Wherefore, I desire that ye faint not at my tribulations for you, which is your glory (v. 13).

THEME: *Paul's Expressed Desires for His Friends*
OUTLINE:

A. Paul's Concern for His Friends
B. Paul's Contentment in His Faith
C. Paul's Confidence in His Future

Paul's Concern for His Friends

"Wherefore I desire that ye faint not." Paul was always concerned that he not become a burden to his friends. "And when I was present with you, and wanted [was in need], I was chargeable to no man, for that which was lacking to me, the brethren which came from Macedonia supplied: and in all things, I have kept myself from being burdensome unto you, and so will I keep myself" (2 Cor. 11:9). "Behold, the third time I am ready to come to you, and I will not be burdensome to you, for I seek not yours, but you" (2 Cor. 12:14). Paul was very independent; when he had no financial resources, he returned to his trade of tentmaking and so met his obligations (see Acts 18:3). He likened himself unto the father of children (2 Cor. 12:14) and, therefore, was concerned about the spiritual health of his family. Anything which caused them anxiety troubled the apostle; he worried about their becoming unduly burdened. The letter to the Ephesians was written from a prison when the apostle was afraid that his friends were excessively concerned about his welfare. Paul assured his readers that all was well; everything was proceeding according to the will of God.

Paul's Contentment in His Faith

Paul evidently believed what he taught, "And we know that all things work together for good to them that love God, to them who are the called according to his purpose" (Rom. 8:28). When he wrote "... my tribulations for you, *which is your glory*," he expressed the faith that his sufferings were being overruled to become a blessing to his friends in Asia. Therefore, instead of grieving for the apostle, they should look for an outpouring of divine blessing. Paul would have loved the following hymn:

God holds the key of all unknown,
And I am glad.
If other hands should hold the key,
Or if He trusted it to me,
I might be sad.

Paul's Confidence in His Future

It must be remembered that Paul was still a prisoner when he wrote this letter. He was awaiting execution. Had he recanted, he might have regained his freedom. Any personal concern was completely overshadowed by love for fellow-Christians. Writing to Timothy he stated: "For I am now ready to be offered, and the time of my departure is at hand" (2 Tim. 4:6). The word translated "departure," or "release," is *analuseos*, and its meaning is exciting. It is comprised of two words. *Luseo* is a verb meaning "to loose;" the prefix *ana* supplied an additional thought of "going on a journey." Many years ago, my father owned racing pigeons, and it was in connection with those birds that I first aroused his anger. As a small child I noticed that on the eve of a race, he would choose a bird which was either expecting her babies or was already feeding them. I stubbornly insisted that some other pigeon should be chosen and not the mother bird! I did not understand my father's motives and continued to argue until he forcefully encouraged me to leave!

Today, I am wiser. If it had been possible to speak to that bird when she awaited liberation at the start of the race, she would have said two things: (1) "I want to get out of this basket" and (2) "I want to go! I have babies in Wales, and as fast as I can regain my liberty, I shall be on my way home." Those thoughts were in the mind of the apostle. He was a bird imprisoned in a basket of flesh. His release was at hand, and he assured Timothy that as soon as he escaped, he would be on his way home. He wrote, "The time of my departure is at hand, henceforth there is laid up for me a crown of righteousness, which the Lord, the righteous judge, shall give me at that day: and not to me only, but unto all them also that love his appearing" (2 Tim. 4:6-8). His faith in Christ created a confidence which remained unshaken even when execution was at hand. His future was assured! The Christians in Asia should share that glorious confidence.

THE SCOPE OF HIS WISHES

THEME: *Paul's Five Desires for His Friends*
OUTLINE:

A. That They Might Be Strengthened (v. 16)
B. That They Might Be Indwelt (v. 17)
C. That They Might Be Rooted (v. 17)
D. That They Might Comprehend (vv. 18-19)
E. That They Might Be Filled (v. 19)

Expository Notes on Paul's Continuance of His Opening Statement

For this cause I bow my knees unto the Father of our Lord Jesus Christ, of whom the whole family in heaven and earth is named (v. 14).

The third chapter of this letter began with the words: "for this cause," and this was followed by Paul's digression, in which his mind apparently wandered to other facts. When he had expressed his thoughts, he returned to his original statement to complete what was in his mind at the beginning. "For this cause, I bow my knees unto the Father of our Lord Jesus Christ." The additional material between verse one and verse fourteen concerned God's purposes in and for the church, and, therefore, the five desires expressed in Paul's prayer for the saints related to "for this cause."

The apostle desired his friends in Asia to be strengthened in their ability to conform to the will of God. He wrote, "For this cause, *I bow my knees* unto the Father." During the history of the church, it was customary for men to stand and with uplifted, outstretched hands pray to God. When they agonized before the Almighty, they prostrated themselves, falling to their knees and allowing their bodies to lean forward until their heads touched the ground. Thus they expressed their anxiety, trust, and utter dependence upon God for what they earnestly desired. This form of prayer still prevails in the Middle East, where, at specific times, Arabs fall on their faces before Allah. The term "I bow my knees unto the Father" indicated a form of prostration and followed the pattern set by the Lord in the Garden of Gethsemane. Luke wrote of the Savior, "And he was withdrawn from them about a stone's cast, and *kneeled down*, and prayed" (Luke 22:41).

It is significant that the family of God is said to be in heaven and earth. Paul, in Ephesians 1:10, used the same kind of expression, that all things *in heaven and earth* would be joined and consummated in Christ. There has been much discussion of the interpretation of Paul's words, "*the whole family* in heaven and earth." Does the term refer to the redeemed people, some of whom have already gone to heaven and some who remain on earth? Does it include angels who, by creation, are also said to be the sons of God? There are scriptures which might be quoted to support either of these interpretations. For example, Paul mentioned the saints who sleep and stated that these will come with Christ at His appearing (see 1 Thess. 4:14-16). The poet expressed this when he wrote:

Let saints on earth unite to sing
With those to glory gone;
For all the servants of our King,
In earth and heaven, are one.
One family; we dwell in Him
One Church; above, beneath.
Though now divided by the stream,
The narrow stream of death.

Interpreting this scripture, the commentators Jamieson, Fausset, and Brown state: "In New Testament Greek, the translation is justifiable, *'all the family,'* or *'the whole family;'* which accords with Scripture views, that angels and men, the saints militant, and those with God, are one holy family joined under the one Father, in Christ, the mediator between heaven and earth. Hence *angels* are termed *our brethren* (Rev. 19:10), and *sons of God* by creation, as we are [sons of God] by adoption (Job 38:7). The church is one part of the grand family, or kingdom, which comprehends, besides men, the higher spiritual world where the archetype, to the realization of which redeemed man is now tending, is already realized." (Quoted from the *Bethany Parallel Commentary of the New Testament*, p. 1142.)

THAT THEY MIGHT BE STRENGTHENED

Expository Notes on the First Petition in Paul's Prayer

For this cause I bow my knees unto the Father . . . that he would grant you, according to the riches of his glory, to be strengthened with might by his Spirit in the inner man (vv. 14, 16).

OUTLINE:

A. The Source of Strength . . . "*the riches of his glory*"
B. The Secret of Strength . . . "*strengthened . . . by his Spirit*"
C. The Safety of Strength . . . "*He is able to keep . . .*"

The Living Bible translates the verse, "That out of his glorious, unlimited resources he will give you the mighty inner strengthening of his Holy Spirit." The Jerusalem Bible has a slightly different emphasis. "Out of his infinite glory may he give you the power through his Spirit *for your hidden self to grow strong*."

The Source of Strength . . . "the riches of his glory" (v. 16)

When Paul wrote to the Christians in Corinth, he expressed his belief that there were two natures in every believer. He said, "For though our outward man perish, yet the inward man is renewed day by day" (2 Cor. 4:16). Evidently, the outward man is the person who walks the streets, converses with people, and is recognized as a human being. That man begins existence at birth, lives his life among men, and finally succumbs to disease, accident, or age. The inner man is the spiritual entity within every redeemed soul. When God transmits eternal life, there begins within the body a life which transcends everything mortal. This new person has the capacity to commune with God, and to appreciate and comprehend spiritual things which baffle the mind of ordinary people. Paul declared, "Eye hath not seen, nor ear heard, neither have entered into the heart of man the things which God hath prepared for them that love him. *But God hath revealed them unto us by his Spirit*" (1 Cor. 2:9-10).

That *inner man* has to develop, grow, and mature just as the outer man does, but unlike the mortal body, the new life never dies. As food and exercise strengthen a human being, so there are things which fortify and help the Christian. Contrition, confession, and communion do this, but it is important to remember that the source from which spiritual supplies are obtained is the inexhaustible grace of God, which the apostle described as "the riches of his glory." God is able to supply the needs of all His people; His grace is a well which never runs dry! The abiding presence of Christ is the guarantee that in every emergency of life, God's grace enables people to triumph over adversity. It was this fact which enabled Paul to say to his fearful fellow travelers, "For there stood by me this night the Angel of God, whose I am, and whom I serve, saying, Fear not, Paul; thou must be brought before Caesar: and, lo, God hath given thee all them that sail with thee. Wherefore, sirs, be of good cheer: for I believe God, that it shall be even as it was told me" (Acts 27:23-25).

The Secret of Strength . . . "strengthened . . . by his Spirit" (v. 16)

The Christian should never forget that when he surrendered to Christ, he became a temple within which the Holy Spirit came to reside permanently. He is the divine Communicator through whom God imparts knowledge, wisdom, guidance, and strength. He is the equivalent of the unseen Captain who accompanied Joshua on his travels and assisted in every conflict (see Josh. 5:13-15). Paul stated, "There hath no temptation taken you but such as is common to man: but God is faithful, who will not suffer you to be tempted above that ye are able; but will with the temptation also make a way to escape, that ye may be able to bear it" (1 Cor. 10:13). When the Lord warned His followers of approaching adversities and threatening tribunals, He said, "But when they deliver you up, take no thought how or what ye shall speak: for it shall be given you in that same hour what ye shall speak. For it is not ye that speak, but the Spirit of your Father which speaketh in you" (Matt. 10:19-20). The Christian's greatest concern should be the preservation of the lines of communication between his soul and the Holy Spirit. United with Christ, he succeeds; alone, he fails.

The Safety of Strength . . . "He is able to keep you from falling" (v. 16)

Throughout the free world, it is generally agreed that the strength of the United States of America is the greatest guarantee of world peace. One shudders to think what might happen if Russia alone possessed nuclear bombs. Taskmasters with unlimited power cannot be deterred by helpless slaves. It is only possible to negotiate when nations have the capability to resist aggressors. Crude spears cannot match the striking power of tanks; bows and arrows would be helpless against exploding missiles. Paul reminded his readers that they were engaged in total warfare and that their enemies were formidable. When David fought Goliath, he would have been helpless without God. Divine strength was made perfect in the lad's weakness, and the giant was slain. Christians are apt to be weaker than David, and the powers of darkness infinitely greater than Goliath. With that thought in mind, Paul prayed for his friends. They needed to be strengthened with might in the inner man and, without a vital relationship with the Holy Spirit, such strengthening would be impossible. The believers in Asia had to be made aware of the challenge of world evangelism, a task which Paul had commenced. Many difficulties awaited the saints, but defeat would be impossible if, as Paul desired, they were strengthened with might in the inner man.

THAT THEY MIGHT BE INDWELT

Expository Notes on the Second Petition in Paul's Prayer

That Christ may dwell in your hearts by faith (v. 17).

OUTLINE:

A. A Special Miracle
B. A Splendid Message
C. A Simple Means

The word translated "dwell" is *katoikeesia.* It is derived from *katoikeo*, which means "to dwell" or "to settle." For example, God is said "to dwell" in His temple, "to be always present for worshipers" (Thayer). The term suggests permanency. God is not visiting His temple, but constantly residing within it. This truth is interesting, for throughout the New Testament the saints were said to be *in Christ.* The apostle now provides the other side of the picture by declaring that *Christ was in the saints.*

A Special Miracle

Dr. T. Croskery, writing in the *Pulpit Commentary* (*Ephesians*, vol. 20, p. 118), supplies the following thought-provoking paragraph:

> "The believer is regarded as a temple or house to be divinely inhabited. It is originally a house in ruins, to be restored as a beautiful temple of the Lord. Judging by the analogy of restoring a ruined house, *the first operation* is a cleansing out of the rubbish; *the second*, an opening of the windows to admit the pure air of heaven, and a kindling of a fire on the hearth; *the third* is a closing up of all the cracks or openings in the wall by which the wind or air finds access; and *the fourth* is the furnishing of the rooms with such articles of convenience as our taste and our means may enable us to procure." Developing his theme, Professor Croskery continues: "*First*, the application of the blood of Christ to 'the heart sprinkled from an evil conscience;' *second*, the opening of the windows of the understanding to displace the tainted atmosphere of man's thoughts, and the kindling of the fire of love Divine in the heart; *third*, the watchful closing up of those avenues in the soul through which sin so easily finds access; and *fourth*, the furnishing of the soul with the needed graces of the Spirit."

To make all this possible, God had to transform sinners, a change only accomplished through the redemptive work of Christ.

A Splendid Message

"That Christ may dwell in your hearts." The analogy of Christ residing within believers is also to be seen in Galatians 4:19, where Paul writes, "My little children, of whom I travail in birth again *until Christ be formed in you.*" The suggestions in the text are obvious. God performed a miracle within the womb of Mary when He transmitted, or implanted, life. That delightful maiden then nurtured the seed until in due course she was able to present the Savior to a world filled with need. Paul believed that it was the duty of every Christian to follow that pattern. God transmits to sinners eternal life when Christ comes to reside within men and women. Thereafter, every believer should nurture that living seed until once again the Lord Jesus Christ can be presented to a waiting world.

A Simple Means . . . "by faith"

Paul evidently believed faith to be the key that unlocked God's treasure house. Throughout the history of Israel, faith had always been subservient to works. What a man did was considered of more importance than anything he believed. The Mosaic law had been the foundation upon which all Hebrew jurisprudence rested, but the original pattern had been ruined by the addition of innumerable traditions which enslaved the nation. The essential dictates of God's commandments were almost lost in the maze of man-made regulations. Unfortunately, a Jew could be a good Hebrew and have little, if any, faith in his soul. Paul insisted that true faith was the only link between an all-sufficient God and helpless humanity. It was not surprising that the apostle used the term 138 times in writing his Epistles. The writer to the Hebrews stated, "But without faith it is impossible to please him: for he that cometh to God must believe that he is, and that he is a rewarder of them that diligently seek him" (Heb. 11:6). The hymnist expressed vital truth when he wrote:

> Only believe; only believe:
> All things are possible
> Only believe.

THAT THEY MIGHT BE ROOTED

Expository Notes on the Third Petition in Paul's Prayer

. . . that ye, being rooted and grounded in love (v. 17).

OUTLINE:

A. Deepening Faith . . . *Rooted*
B. Dependable Fellowship . . . *Grounded*
C. Delightful Fervor . . . *Love*

The translation supplied by The Living Bible is attractive. "And I pray that Christ will be more and more at home in your hearts, living within you as you trust in him. *May your roots go down deep into the soil of God's marvelous love.*" The apostle evidently used two images to express his desires: (1) A building resting on sure foundations and (2) a tree planted in fertile soil. If the first suggested stability, the second envisaged health, continuity, and fruitfulness. Paul believed the dwelling should be dependable and the plant nourished. Both house and plant should last!

Deepening Faith . . . Rooted

"That ye being rooted. . . ." Without healthy roots plants cannot survive. The psalmist said, "Blessed is the man . . . whose delight is in the law of the Lord . . . he shall be like a tree *planted by the rivers of water*, that bringeth forth his fruit in his season; his leaf also shall not wither; and whatsoever he doeth shall prosper" (Ps. 1:1-3). Isaiah predicted the future of the house of Judah by saying, "And the remnant that is escaped of the house of Judah shall again *take root downward and bear fruit upward*" (Isa. 37:31). Perhaps Paul had considered Christ's parable of the sower. "But he that received the seed into stony places, the same is he that heareth the word, and anon with joy receiveth it; *yet hath he not root in himself*, but dureth for a while; for when tribulation or persecution ariseth because of the word, by and by, he is offended" (Matt. 13:20-21). Paul earnestly desired that none of his friends, having put their hands to the plough, would ever look back and be considered unworthy of a place in the kingdom of Christ. Therefore, he urged them to let their roots go down into the depth of the love of Christ.

Dependable Fellowship . . . Grounded

"That ye being rooted *and grounded. . . .*" "Grounded" actually means "established." The young plant, having rooted itself, no longer needs the coddling care of a gardener. Babies, whether they be human or plants, need careful attention, for the least neglect might endanger their lives. A well-rooted plant does not fall prey to enemies; it draws from the earth the strength to overcome. Paul believed that Christians whose roots went deep into the love of Christ would draw from His abundance all that was needed to guarantee continuance in the faith. The Savior would support the soul, and the believer would acquire strength derived exclusively from God. Although the apostle continued to love those who had strayed from the paths of righteousness, he never condoned their backsliding and constantly warned converts of the dangers of stunted growth. If they were rooted and grounded in the faith, victory in the battle of life would be assured.

Delightful Fervor . . . Love

"That ye being rooted and grounded *in love.*" True love for Christ is the key that unlocks everything of value. Someone might understand God's commandments and admire Christ's example, yet never endeavor to follow those precepts. Onlookers may watch from the grandstands of life and even applaud those on the playing field, yet never take part in the contest. When love for the Redeemer fills and thrills the hearts of believers, they are constrained to forsake all and follow Christ. Love exhibits cooperation, dedication, affinity of purpose, and a continuing, deepening desire to please the object of that affection. When the Lord sent a message to the church in Ephesus, He was addressing the greatest fundamental church in existence. The people detested heresy and shunned inactivity. The assembly was the type that held meetings every night—a frequency that set records of Christian service seldom equalled by other churches. Yet the Lord said, "Nevertheless, I have somewhat against thee, because thou hast left thy first love" (Rev. 2:4). Theology without love is an expensive automobile without gasoline, a lamp without light, a body without life. The love of Christ is a continent of rich, fertile ground. To endeavor to be rooted in such soil is the most essential duty of the Christian.

THAT THEY MIGHT COMPREHEND

Expository Notes on the Fourth Petition in Paul's Prayer

That ye . . . may be able to comprehend with all saints what is the breadth, and length, and depth, and height; and to know the love of Christ, which passeth knowledge . . . (vv. 18-19).

OUTLINE:

A. The Embrace of Christ's Love
B. The Extent of Christ's Love
C. The Experience of Christ's Love

Once again The Living Bible supplies an attractive translation of Paul's writing. "And may you be able to feel and understand, as all God's children should, how long, how wide, how deep, and how high his love really is; and to experience this love for yourselves, though it is so great that you will never see the end of it, or fully know or understand it." The questions might be asked, "How is it possible to comprehend the incomprehensible? How can man grasp the infinite or measure the immeasurable?"

The Embrace of Christ's Love

"That ye may be able to comprehend *with all saints*" (v. 18a). The apostle was careful to mention that this unsurpassed treasure was within the reach of all saints. To know the love of Christ in its fulness is extensive and limitless; yet, even the youngest believer was capable of understanding and experiencing it. A man may not comprehend the immensity of the world's atmosphere, but he can breathe! The air which covers the earth may be found in New Guinea, the heart of Africa, and in a million other places; yet, without being in those areas, a human being can inhale that same air and live. The oceans of the world reach every shoreline of earth; yet, a man can bathe on his own beach without any comprehension of how far those oceans extend. Similarly, "the love of Christ" is as an ocean reaching earth's remotest end. Man may never be given the privilege of experiencing that love in distant parts of the world; yet, wherever he resides, he can experience its warmth. Christians may never completely know ALL the love of Christ, but they can share its wonder wherever they reside.

The Extent of Christ's Love

"... the breadth, and length, and depth, and height ..." (v. 18b). Paul's request bordered on the impossible. To measure anything it is necessary to know the limits of its extension. There must be points where measurement begins and ends. Since the love of Christ is eternal and limitless, there is no point at which man can begin measuring it. Professor W. G. Blaikie made a very interesting comment, "*Breadth* might denote the manifoldness of that provision; *length* its eternal duration; its *depth* might be represented by the profundity of Christ's humiliation; and its *height* by the loftiness of the condition to which His people are to be raised." (Quoted from *The Pulpit Commentary, Ephesians*, vol. 20, p. 109.) The love of Christ is the air we breathe, the energy we use, and the area of existence in which we live, move, and have our being. It is the glorious essence pervading every aspect of God's salvation. It is that far-reaching, all-embracing quality which, emanating from the heart of the Savior, reaches all nations. To experience its warmth is to know happiness; to be unaware of it is to be left wandering in a maze of sadness from which there is no escape.

The Experience of Christ's Love

"And *to know* the love of Christ ...." To know about the love of Christ is knowledge: a mental apprehension of a truth spoken by God. Knowledge can be academic: a fact accepted by the intellect, but never translated into triumphant living. "To *know*" the love of Christ daily is something which transforms life, thrills the soul, and supplies the strength which enables believers to overcome adversity. It is not confined to moments of exhilaration when souls are emotionally lifted to heights of blessedness. It is an experience which continues moment by moment, day by day, until the end of life's journey.

THAT THEY MIGHT BE FILLED

Expository Notes on the Fifth Petition in Paul's Prayer

... that ye might be filled with all the fulness of God (v. 19).

OUTLINE:

A. The Perfect Pattern
B. The Practical Plea
C. The Profound Possibility

This was the final desire expressed by Paul; it was the most profound of his requests. The apostle's letters were filled with expressions which supplied windows to his soul. To look through them and see Paul's yearnings was to obtain an unforgettable glimpse of his concern for his children in the faith. He desired many things for them, but above all else he wanted them to be like Christ.

The Perfect Pattern

It should never be forgotten that the fulness of God is seen best in the Lord Jesus Christ. Paul wrote to the Colossians, "For in him [Christ] dwelleth all the fulness of the Godhead bodily" (Col. 2:9). "For it pleased the Father that in him should all fulness dwell" (Col. 1:19). The Savior could not have been any greater than He was! He was complete; He was absolute perfection. Everything God was could be seen in Christ; all God wished to say was expressed by Jesus. His purity was unquestioned; his example unsullied. Controlled completely by the Holy Spirit, He provided for man a pattern by which to live, the strength to be all that was possible, and the unfailing promise to be present to minister to His people. It has already been emphasized that Christ was never filled with the Spirit—He was *always* full. It is only possible to fill vessels that are not full. The Savior was permanently full of the divine Spirit, and, consequently, the apostle was able to say, "For it pleased the Father that in him should all fulness dwell" (Col. 1:19). When Paul urged his readers to reach that high plateau of Christian living, he encouraged them to emulate every example given by Christ—to be like Jesus.

A Practical Plea

"If ye then be risen with Christ, seek those things which are above, where Christ sitteth on the right hand of God. Set your affection on things above, not on things on the earth" (Col. 3:1-2). Christians agree that Paul's desire for the saints was filled with merit; yet, some say that such holiness is beyond the reach of mortals. They believe, as did Studdart Kennedy, who wrote:

> There's summat that pulls us up;
> And summat that pulls us down;
> And the consequence is that we wobble
> Twixt muck and a golden crown.

Nevertheless, Paul's words were not above the possibility of fulfilment. Although man may be exceedingly weak, it is still possible for him to reach the goals set by Paul.

DOUGLAS BROWN'S BASKET

I was only a lad when Dr. Douglas Brown, the well-known Baptist minister, visited our valley in Wales. The power of his ministry attracted great crowds, and the largest churches were filled to capacity. The language of the great man was so simple that even children understood his sermons, and it was not a cause for amazement when scores of young people professed faith in the Lord Jesus Christ. I regret to say that after half a century, I have forgotten his themes, and cannot recall a single text used by the speaker. Yet, an illustration which he gave in speaking to Christians will remain fresh in my mind forever.

He described one of the meetings held in his own church, where he had been speaking about being filled with the Holy Spirit. Great grace had been upon the gathering, and the preacher realized that God had blessed the message. At the conclusion of the address, the pastor retired to his vestry, to be followed by a desperate young man who said, "Pastor, what is the use of telling me to be filled with the Spirit? It would be futile to fill me for—for—," and pointing to a wastepaper basket in the corner of the room, he added "for I am as full of cracks as that basket. If I were filled with the Spirit, I would immediately drain dry."

A brilliant flash of inspiration illumined the minister's mind, and he calmly replied, "You are as full of cracks as that basket! What if you are? My brother, if that basket—so filled with gaping holes—be lowered into the sea, it will be filled, *and it will remain full*. If it abides in the ocean, it cannot be emptied. The basket will only lose its content when it is lifted from the sea. Young man, cracks or no cracks, *if you abide in Christ* you will always be filled with the Spirit. If you are lifted from that hallowed position—if you cease to abide in Christ—you will soon be empty and powerless." I have never forgotten that illustration, and during my travels through the world, I often mentioned Douglas Brown's basket.

It is bewildering and annoying that the unity of the church has been torn to pieces, and, more often than not, by people whose holiness teachings seem to be far removed from reality and Bible standards. Some folk stress the necessity of signs and wonders, and unless a man has had a sensational and supernatural manifestation, his being filled with the Spirit is said to be impossible. There are others whose holiness exists only in their speech; their actions are mean, disappointing, and unChristlike. Yet, all these men and movements claim to be the elect of God, the apple of His eye, and the one and only hope for revival. I have met earnest Christians whose equilibrium in spiritual matters has been upset. They asked if they were wrong to stay in their churches when noisy orators across the street shout praises to God and curses on all other assemblies. I have been asked again and again, "Sir, what must I do to be filled with the Holy Spirit? Must I go to tarrying meetings? Must I fast for days? Must I speak with other tongues?" And each time I have thought of Douglas Brown's basket. The Lord Jesus said, "Abide in me," and therein may be found the secret of all blessedness. If my heart be clean, if I know that nothing evil lies between my Master and me, if I am certain my all is upon the altar, I need not worry.

Is there need to fast for days, to spend hours pleading for God's blessing, to mourn and weep and strain in order to be filled with the Holy Spirit? Must God be persuaded to do what He longs to do? Is He so unwilling that we must persuade Him to comply with our request? How stupid is this idea! The infilling with the Holy Spirit is our inheritance in Christ, and since God yearns to give of His fullness, let us consciously abide in the center of His will and go our way, knowing that in every thought, word, and deed, the indwelling Christ will fill and work through us to the fulfillment of His purpose." (Reprinted from the author's book, *Bible Windows*, pp. 93-94.)

A Profound Possibility

There is danger in persistently seeking for special gifts. It might be possible to spend time looking for something which God does not wish to bestow. It is much better to concentrate on surrendering to the GIVER than to desire something which occupies more of my attention than does He! When the Holy Spirit controls the believer in Christ, He directs the Christian's steps and in every emergency will give—even before He is asked—the tools necessary to do His work. God's hand is always open; we do not have to pry His fingers apart to obtain some cherished possession He is reluctant to give. Paul prayed that his friends would be filled with all the fullness of God because that was a glorious possibility. All they needed could be found in Christ; unfailing resources were as close as a bended knee.

THE SINCERITY OF HIS WORSHIP

Expository Notes on Paul's Famous Doxology

Now unto him that is able to do exceeding abundantly above all that we ask or think, according to the power that worketh in us, unto him be glory in the church by Christ Jesus throughout all ages, world without end. Amen (vv. 20-21).

THEME: *Paul's Ascription of Praise to God*
OUTLINE:
- A. An Unlimited Ability . . . "*He is able*"
- B. An Undeniable Ally . . . "*the power that worketh in us*"
- C. An Unending Anthem . . . "*throughout all ages; world without end*"

With this doxology, Paul concluded the first half of his Epistle. He was probably aware of the effect his exposition would have upon readers, for he had urged them to reach heights of human perfection. How impoverished aliens could sit with Christ in heavenly places appeared to be beyond comprehension. It was necessary, therefore, that the apostle finish with a message of encouragement. If believers were to succeed in climbing such unprecedented heights, they would need a reliable guide.

AN UNLIMITED ABILITY . . . "He is able"

The apostle's words command attention. He said, "Now unto him that is able to do *exceeding abundantly above all that we ask or think*" (3:20). If the Christians in Asia were apprehensive, they should look steadfastly toward Christ. The Savior was able to surpass anything imaginable. He had lifted them from the depth of degradation; He would lift them to the height of perfection. If they were excessively weak, His strength would be made perfect in their weakness. If they stayed near to His side, He would unerringly lead them to their eternal destination.

AN UNDENIABLE ALLY . . . "the power that worketh in us"

A dying man might hear of the ability of a doctor residing on the other side of the world, but that knowledge would be useless if circumstances necessitated his staying at home. Individuals might hear of the accomplishments of the Great Physician residing in heaven, but the news would be meaningless if sinners had no access to Him. One of the miracles of the gospel was that the Savior, through the person of the Holy Spirit, had come to live within His people. Christians did not have to place long distance telephone calls to heaven and hope that contact would be made with the Son of God. They only had to stretch forth the hand of faith and touch the hem of His garment! His power was already working in the believer. According to the measure of human participation, so the work would continue. What had been commenced would be completed. The Holy Spirit was working on behalf of believers, and the Lord Jesus Christ was interceding at God's right hand. Why then should saints be despondent?

AN UNENDING ANTHEM . . . "throughout all ages; world without end"

Paul's closing statement envisaged eternity. He began his Epistle with the fact that before time began, God planned to produce a people "holy and without blame before him in love" (1:4). He terminated his message with the fulfillment of God's dream. The Church had been safely escorted to her eternal home, and her scintillating righteousness would bring glory to God eternally. Many details concerning Heaven are still shrouded in mystery, but we know it will be filled with music. God will listen when "ten thousand times ten thousand, and thousands of thousands, say with a loud voice, worthy is the Lamb that was slain to receive power, and riches, and wisdom, and strength, and honor, and glory, and blessing" (Rev. 5:11-12). "And there shall be no night there; and they need no candle, neither light of the sun; for the Lord God giveth them light: and they shall reign forever and ever" (Rev. 22:5). Blessed are they who can say:

> And I shall see Him face to face,
> And tell the story saved by grace.

A SUMMARY OF THE THIRD CHAPTER

It must be remembered that when Paul began to write this letter, his soul was consumed with an intense desire to reveal to his friends the immensity of the message received from God. An understanding of the divine revelation would influence their knowledge and conduct. His Epistle might be described as two books in one. If the readers could KNOW and UNDERSTAND what God had revealed, their lives would be transformed; they would become living epistles seen, "known, and read" (2 Cor. 3:2).

A MESSAGE FROM A PRISON

Paul was incarcerated in a prison in Rome and had little, if any, hope of liberation. He had been confined for a time to what might be termed *house-arrest*, but whether or not this letter was written at that time or when he was confined to a prison cell, is a matter of conjecture. Paul's message was characterized by:

1. *His Great Vision.* He described himself as "the prisoner of the Lord." Paul never thought of himself as the prisoner of the Jews, the Romans, or even Nero, the Emperor. He was completely under the jurisdiction of Christ, the Son of God.
2. *His Glorious Virtue.* He never grumbled about his fate. He never permitted his soul to be filled with misgivings or criticism of any kind to poison his thoughts. Lesser men might have complained, but the apostle preferred to say, "I can do all things through Christ which strengtheneth me" (Phil. 4:13).
3. *His Gracious Victory.* When he wrote to Timothy to say, "For I am now ready to be offered, and the time of my departure is at hand," he displayed tranquillity hard to comprehend. He saw not his execution, but an entrance into the palace of the King of kings. He terminated his earthly journey triumphantly. The letters which he sent from his prison expressed true ecstasy. He was ready and waiting to go to heaven.

A MESSAGE FROM A PALACE

Although Paul was not a member of the original band of disciples, he, nevertheless, probably spent more time with his Lord than did any of the twelve disciples. His sojourn in Arabia provided an uninterrupted period during which he listened to his Master (see Gal. 1:17-18). He was the only student in God's academy and at the end of his stay, graduated with honor. When he began his lifework, it became evident he had excelled in three areas:

1. *He had obtained a royal decree.* He had received special instruction and had been authorized to impart his wisdom to other people. He had been divinely commissioned to be the official representative of the Almighty.
2. *He had been made aware of a redemptive determination.* A divine secret had been revealed to the apostle, and though its content was destined to astound the world, Paul could assure listeners that

acceptance into the family of God was a privilege to be bestowed upon even the most unworthy supplicants.

3. *He was able to make a remarkable disclosure.* There was no favoritism with God; in His sight all men were equal. He affirmed "that the Gentiles should be fellowheirs, and of the same body, and partakers of his promise in Christ by the gospel" (3:6). Paul claimed that this was a direct edict from the palace of the Eternal King (3:3).

A MESSAGE FROM A PASTOR

When Paul met the elders of the Ephesian church on the beach at Miletus (Acts 20:17), he knew that he would never see them again on earth. When he sent this letter to the saints in Asia, he realized it would be his final communication and he included some of his most innermost thoughts:

1. *His Prayer* . . . "I bow my knees" (v. 14). Paul had been apprehensive regarding the future of his friends and had warned them that grievous wolves would endanger their growth in grace (see Acts 20:29-30). He stated, "Brethren, I commend you to God, and to the word of his grace, which is able to build you up, and to give you an inheritance among all them which are sanctified" (Acts 20:32). Paul's prayer in this chapter must rank as one of his most important utterances.
2. *His Purpose* . . . "that ye might be strengthened." The spiritual welfare of his friends weighed heavily upon the apostle's soul. He believed that God's promises were always honored, and, therefore said, "I cease not to give thanks for you, making mention of you in my prayers" (Eph. 1:16). The progressive nature of the apostle's requests reveals the increasing depth of his desire for his friends. Paul not only believed in prayer—*he prayed*!
3. *His Praise* . . . "Unto him be glory." Paul, who was probably the greatest of all New Testament Christians, claimed to be "less than the least of all saints" (3:8). He thought only of advancing the cause of Christ and exalting "the name which is above every name" (Phil. 2:9). His success in ministering the gospel was explained to the Galatian believers, "I am crucified with Christ: nevertheless I live; yet not I, but Christ liveth in me: and the life which I now live in the flesh I live by the faith of the Son of God, who loved me, and gave himself for me" (Gal. 2:20).

4. *His Prediction* . . . "forever and ever." Paul never entertained doubt concerning the future of the Church. Believers would not only arrive safely at their eternal destination; but as a corporate body they would also be the means by which God would be glorified forever. The apostle earnestly desired his readers to be aware of these facts and, to that end, dedicated three chapters of his remarkable Epistle.

HOMILIES

Homily No. 9

GOD'S ANSWER TO A SKEPTICAL WORLD

There is an interesting contrast in the gospel story. We are told that the people looked at the dying Savior and exclaimed, "Let him now come down from the cross, and we will believe him" (Matt. 27:42). Yet, that order was reversed when Christ spoke to Martha in Bethany. He said, "If thou wouldest believe, thou shouldest see the glory of God" (John 11:40). In the economy of God, faith foreruns vision, for it is "the substance of things hoped for, the evidence of things not seen" (Heb. 11:1). The infidel declares that no tangible evidence can be found to prove the reality of God; yet, the humblest Christian constantly discovers facts, the existence of which is denied by people whose hearts are barren of faith.

THE LORD JESUS CHRIST IS ABLE TO SAVE (Heb. 7:25)

"Wherefore he is able also to save them to the uttermost that come unto God by him, seeing he ever liveth to make intercession for them." The Christians of the early church were tested by great persecution. Some of the best Roman governors were the fiercest enemies, for, since they believed that denial of their pagan gods would bring disaster upon the empire, they used all means at their disposal to annihilate the new movement. Christians were fed to hungry lions and even burnt at the stake. Such opposition shook the faith of the people, and many were tempted to return to their former beliefs. The Jewish converts encountered difficulty, for the temple life had ceased, and the daily offering was no longer placed upon the altar. Caught between the cessation of the old system of worship and the unparalleled persecution of the new, the weaklings of the church faltered and questioned their leaders. The writer of the Epistle to the Hebrews explained that the living Christ superseded all acts of priesthood and now lived at God's right hand to make intercession for His people. The *greatest evidence* to support this fact was His ability to save. Every miracle constituted a challenge to agnosticism, and every transformed life an indication of Christ's power.

THE LORD JESUS CHRIST IS ABLE TO KEEP (2 Tim. 1:12)

" . . . for I know whom I have believed, and am persuaded that he is able to keep that which I have committed unto him against that day." This represented one of the most triumphant declarations of Pauline doctrines. When Timothy visited his great leader to sit with him in the prison cell, many questions filled the mind of the younger man. There at his side was the indomitable Paul, who could say, "Of the Jews, five times received I forty stripes save one. Thrice was I beaten with rods, once was I stoned, thrice I suffered shipwreck, a night and a day I have been in the deep" (2 Cor. 11:24-25). Other people had long since slipped back into error, yet, this brave apostle had persistently continued along his appointed course. Nothing had been permitted to prevent his following Christ, and now at the end of his journey, he was able to say, "Henceforth there is laid up for me a crown of righteousness" (2 Tim. 4:8). The secret of Paul's continuance lay in the keeping power of his Lord. He said, "He is able to keep," and his life-story endorsed his statement.

THE LORD JESUS CHRIST IS ABLE TO DO THE IMPOSSIBLE (Eph. 3:20)

"Now unto him that is able to do exceeding abundantly above all that we ask or think, according to the power that worketh in us." This is a superlative verse and is all the more remarkable because it was addressed to the church at Ephesus. The assembly in that city of Asia had been born in travail. The heathen worshipers of Diana had striven to overthrow the church, and even Paul had been in danger of losing his life. In an amazing fashion the power of God had triumphed over all opposition, and under the leadership of their beloved minister, the church continued to grow and had witnessed many miracles. Then Paul declared, "He is able to do far greater things." He can do more than the wildest imaginations would consider possible—"exceeding abundantly above all you can ask or think." There were times when Paul revealed a daring disregard for the laws of grammar. He mixed superlatives in the most bewildering fashion, for language seemed utterly inadequate to express the wonder of his message. (Homily reprinted from the author's book, *Bible Pinnacles*, pp. 159-160.)

Homily No. 10

PAUL . . . and His Faulty Grammar!

Sometimes, when I preach the gospel, I refer to Paul's text, "Unto me, who am less than the least of all saints, is this grace given, that I should preach among the Gentiles the unsearchable riches of Christ" (Eph. 3:8). This statement takes me back in thought to my student days in Wales where, years ago, I had a most formidable English teacher. With untiring persistence, she instilled into the minds of her students the principles of English grammar, and it was no cause for amazement when she became increasingly unpopular. I have often said that I would like to listen to a debate between my old teacher and the apostle Paul. Undoubtedly, she would reprove him for the careless way in which he handled superlatives. Perhaps he would retaliate by telling her that she had much to learn! "Unto me, who am *less than the least*. . . ." It is not possible to be less than the least! No man can be lower than the lowest, for if he be lower than the lowest, then the lowest is *not* the lowest—*he* is the lowest! At least, that is what my teacher would have said. This text is one of three which clearly indicate the remarkable progress made by Paul as he neared his journey's end.

PAUL . . . An Apostle by the Will of God

"Paul, an apostle, (not of men, neither by man, but by Jesus Christ, and God the Father, who raised him from the dead)" (Gal. 1:1). There existed within the early church, men who denied the authority of Paul and insisted that because he had not been one of the original twelve disciples, he was not an apostle and, therefore, had no authority to introduce new doctrines into the church. The legalistic Pharisees, some of whom embraced Christianity, opposed the entry of uncircumcised Gentiles into the fellowship of the church, and their insinuations brought from the apostle his denunciations. He wrote to the Galatians as follows: "But though we, or an angel from heaven, preach any other gospel unto you than that which we have preached unto you, let him be accursed" (Gal. 1:8-9). Paul was relentless in making this statement, so adamant that he repeated himself, "As we said before, so say I now again. If any man preach any other gospel unto you than that ye have received, let him be accursed." Paul affirmed that he superseded any preaching angel and exceeded that of any other apostle or layman who contradicted what had been given to him by God. Would it be correct to say that he was energized by righteous indignation? Was his claim based on youthful pride? Was he so convinced of the inspiration of his message that nothing in time or eternity could change his convictions in regard to the authenticity of his mission and the accuracy of his message? If we may use modern terminology, Paul was declaring war on his opponents by exclaiming, "If you do not believe what I teach, then you deserve the damnation which awaits you." No evangelical teacher would challenge his statement nor criticize his conclusion. Nevertheless, it must be recognized that those words were spoken by a very proud custodian of the faith. Paul was indisputably a very great man, but he had much to learn—about himself!

PAUL . . . The Least of the Christians

"Unto me, who am less than the least of all saints, is this grace given, that I should preach among the Gentiles the unsearchable riches of Christ" (Eph. 3:8). Years had elapsed since Paul wrote to the Galatians; he was now older and wiser. As he sat within the prison in Rome, he had time to reflect, and his appreciation of theology was evidently tempered by the love filling his soul. He realized that the warmth and quality of church fellowship was equally as important as theological understanding. He believed that there were others who interpreted certain scriptures differently, and yet their love for Christ was deep and unquestionably sincere. Two verses stood out in bold relief within the letter to the Ephesians. Recognizing the varying opinions of his fellow Christians, Paul wrote, "And he gave some, apostles; and some, prophets; and some, evangelists; and some, pastors and teachers . . . for the edifying of the body of Christ: *till we all come in the unity of the faith*, and of the knowledge of the Son of God, unto a perfect man, unto the measure of the stature of the fulness of Christ" (Eph. 4:11-13). The second text provides a strange but delightful contrast. Paul wrote: "I, therefore, the prisoner of the Lord, beseech you . . . *to keep the unity of the Spirit* in the bond of peace" (Eph. 4:1-3). Young preachers are apt to condemn all whose viewpoint is different. Maturity has a strange effect upon vision. Old Christians look for affection, warmth, and dedication to the cause of Christ. Youthful speakers emphasize sound doctrine and often believe that they, alone, know what that is! It is better to love than argue, to smile than frown. Paul had grown older, he was about to meet his Lord, and doctrine was the least important of his problems. His intense dissatisfaction with himself made it increasingly difficult to criticize other believers. He had matured and had lost sight of his own importance. He was "the least of all saints."

PAUL . . . The Chief of Sinners!

The apostle wrote to Timothy to declare, "This is a faithful saying, and worthy of all acceptation, that Christ Jesus came into the world to save sinners; *of whom I am chief*" (1 Tim. 1:15). Paul's wisdom increased with his age: (a) an apostle, (b) the lowest saint, (c) the greatest sinner. The closer one gets to the light, the more easily one sees the dirt! Cornelius, Paul, Nicodemus, and a host of others would corroborate this statement. We are not saved by works so that no one is able to boast. Eternal life is the *gift* of God, but it is only given to those who know their need, to those who come humbly seeking from God's hand that which could never be received in any other way. Some of life's most important lessons are hard to understand. They present an anomaly in words! One is never as tall as when he falls on his face before his Maker. If he would find a way to reach the stars, he must first kneel! (See also the next homily, "Abraham . . . and a Bunch of Rogues!")

Homily No. 11

ABRAHAM . . . and a Bunch of Rogues!

Self-esteem is rarely found in the heart of a true man of God, for the more virtuous a saint becomes, the less satisfied he will be with himself. Increasing love for God means hatred of the self-life. The Bible has many examples of this fact.

ABRAHAM . . . "I am but dust and ashes" (Gen. 18:27)

Abraham was the friend of God and the greatest character in the ancient world. Divine secrets were shared with the illustrious patriarch, and in a sense unknown by ordinary man, he walked with God. Yet Abraham despised himself and became conscious of his shortcomings. He considered himself unworthy to commune with God, and said he was dust and ashes.

JOB . . . "Behold, I am vile" (Job 40:4)

We are left with no doubts as to the true greatness of this man. It is recorded that the Lord said of him: "There is none like him in the earth, a perfect and an upright man, one that feareth God, and escheweth evil" (Job 1:8). When Job's friends declared that he was a hypocrite and that secret sin had brought about his misfortunes, he maintained that his heart was clean before God. Yet, when he came face to face with his Maker, he whispered, "I am vile."

DAVID . . . "Behold, I was shapen in iniquity" (Ps. 51:5)

The psalmist of Israel was a man after God's own heart, and although certain indiscretions marred his fine record of devotion, his integrity and true consecration were always beyond question. Yet, this great man sadly shook his head and denied his own virtue. Psalm 51 is a heart-throb in which we hear sobs of anguish, cries of disappointment, and the moan of a man who feels he is a complete failure.

EZRA . . . "I blush to lift up my face" (Ezra 9:6)

Ezra was one of the greatest men of his generation. He held an honorable place among the spiritual aristocracy of the nation. His courageous example at a time when Israel needed spiritual leadership lifted the nation to new heights of achievement. He and Nehemiah were the greatest men of that era. Nevertheless, Ezra's confession claimed for him a place in "Rogues' Gallery." He said, "O my God, I am ashamed, and blush to lift up my face."

ISAIAH . . . "I am undone . . . I am a man of unclean lips" (Isaiah 6:5)

Isaiah was one of the major prophets who gave counsel and guidance to a stumbling nation and at the same time provided unerring information concerning the coming of the Messiah. He was a friend of the king, a father to the nation, and a trusted servant of the Most High; yet, of himself, he had nothing good to say.

SIMON PETER . . . "I am a sinful man" (Luke 5:8)

There was something delightfully human about Simon Peter, for at all times he was unquestionably honest. Sometimes strong emotions and fierce temptation upset his equilibrium, but within minutes the real man appeared again. He was a great Christian, an excellent preacher, and a brother beloved. Yet, all who read the New Testament realize how much Peter abhorred himself.

THE CENTURION . . . "I am not worthy" (Luke 7:6)

This Gentile soldier won a place among the great immortals. His spiritual perception enabled Christ to say, "I have not found so great faith, no, not in Israel." Although he was an officer in Caesar's army and occupied a position of great importance, he believed his home to be unworthy of a visit from the Carpenter of Nazareth.

PAUL . . . "the chief of sinners" (1 Tim. 1:15)

Paul was undoubtedly the greatest of all Christian missionaries. He was the first to look beyond the narrow bounds of Israel's horizons and with determination of purpose to take the gospel into the unreached world. His indomitable spirit and untiring energy took the gospel to millions of heathen, and with God's help, he established the Christian church. Yet, Paul claimed to be the greatest sinner in the world.

God has strange ways of estimating the greatness of people. Sometimes, the first are last, and the last first. Those who are great in their own estimation are far from the will of God, while others who are overwhelmed by a sense of unworthiness are ready for the Master's use. A bunch of rogues? No! They were some of God's greatest ladies and gentlemen! (Reprinted from the author's book, *Bible Treasures*, pp. 7-8.)

The Fourth Chapter of Ephesians

THEME: *How to Live the Christian Life*
OUTLINE:

I. Paul's Entreaty (Verses 1-3)
II. Paul's Exposition (Verses 4-16)
III. Paul's Exhortation (Verses 17-24)
IV. Paul's Explanation (Verses 25-32)

PAUL'S ENTREATY

Expository Notes on Paul's Appeal to the Asian Christians

I therefore, the prisoner of the Lord, beseech you that ye walk worthy of the vocation wherewith ye are called. With all lowliness and meekness, with long-suffering, forbearing one another in love; endeavouring to keep the unity of the Spirit in the bond of peace (vv. 1-3).

The apostle had now reached the half-way point in his letter, and, as he commenced to write this fourth chapter, he seemed to be a man sitting at the controls of a powerful spotlight. With unerring accuracy, he had directed his beam of light into eternal ages and brought into sight things never seen before. He uncovered secrets hidden in the mind of God, had explained the inscrutable mysteries of the Divine Family, and described their desire to create a holy people called the Church. Paul carefully traced the details of God's revelation leading to the appearance of Christ and explained how reconciliation was made through the Savior's death and resurrection.

Then he suddenly changed the direction of the beam until the light shone directly upon the Christians in Asia. They had already seen God as He had been and still was; now what they should be and what they should think and do were brought into bold relief. Their revelation of God was followed by their responsibility to Him. The key word of this half of the Epistle was "walk," and, as was seen in the earlier homily, "Paul . . . Who Walked Through Ephesians," p. 114 to reveal to his readers what was expected of them.

The apostle was aware that his friends might fail to reach the high standards of moral and spiritual excellence demanded by their faith. Gentiles believed in idols, but they did as they pleased. Christians professed to be the servants of Christ, whose commandments they obeyed. The conduct of the Christian should endorse, and not contradict, his testimony. The famous evangelist Gypsy Smith often sang a hymn which asked the question, "How shall the world know of Jesus if they cannot see Jesus in me?" Paul evidently had similar thoughts when, having expounded the riches of the revelation sent by God, he urged his friends to reach the ultimate in Christian achievement.

At first glance it appears that progressive analysis of this chapter is difficult. The words "therefore" and "wherefore" seem to demand attention; they indicate that upon the basis of conclusions, the writer made suggestions. These connecting words are found in verses 1, 8, 17, and 25. Those statements supplied the outline found at the commencement of this chapter. First, Paul made an appeal by writing, "I, *therefore*, the prisoner of the Lord, beseech you that ye walk worthy of the vocation wherewith ye are called." When he described the characteristics of that walk, he used five of the most expressive words in the Christian vocabulary.

LOWLINESS . . . The Product of Humility

The word translated "lowliness" is *tapeinophrosyne*; it means "humility." The Living Bible supplies a thought-provoking rendering. "I beg you—I, a prisoner here in jail for serving the Lord,—to live and act in a way worthy of those who have been chosen for such wonderful blessings as these. Be humble and gentle. Be patient with each other, making allowance for each other's faults because of your love." Frank E. Gaebelein says, "The word for humility occurs five times in Paul's writings, and only once elsewhere in the New Testament. In classical Greek, *tapeinos* is a derogatory term suggesting 'low-mindedness' and 'groveling servility.' The adjective was redeemed by the gospel to represent a distinctively Christian virtue, and this euphonious noun was coined to stand over against the admired high-mindedness of the heathen." (Quoted from *The Expositor's Bible Commentary*, vol. 2, p. 55.)

The term "humility" was associated with weakness by people in the ancient world. Men admired strength, aggression, and the will to dominate. A quiet disposition belonged to men who were slaves, who never retaliated. They were either ashamed or unable to resist dominant neighbors. Paul's gospel gave an entirely new meaning to the unpopular term. He insisted that true humility represented the attitude of one who was content to be a slave of the Lord, a consecrated man or woman who resembled the Savior. Elsewhere, the apostle wrote of the Lord, "Who, being in the form of God, thought it not robbery to be equal with God; but made himself of no reputation, and took upon him the form of a servant, and was made in the likeness of men" (Phil. 2:6-7). Self-abasement is an unmistakable product of humility. It should be recognized in the conduct of every child of God.

MEEKNESS . . . The Patience of Humility

The word translated "meekness" is *praoteetos*; it is not an easy word to interpret. W. E. Vine in his *Expository Dictionary of Old and New Testament Words*, vol. 2, p. 55, states, "It consists not in a person's outward behavior only; nor yet in his relations to his fellow-men. . . . Rather it is an inwrought grace of the soul, and the exercises of it are *first and chiefly toward God.* It is that temper of spirit in which we accept His dealings with us as good, and therefore *without disputing or resisting. . . .*" It reflects an attitude of complete trust. The man filled with meekness bows before his Maker assured that what God does is beyond question. The Lord Jesus said, "Blessed are the meek: for they shall inherit the earth" (Matt. 5:5).

The word "meek"... is a little-big word with many meanings. Therefore, it is necessary to proceed slowly as we seek to understand the third beatitude. Often the word is used to express spinelessness; a person with very little backbone! Obviously, such a meaning has no connection with the thought Jesus expressed. The Bible says, "Now the man Moses was very meek, above all the men which were upon the face of the earth" (Num. 12:3). Moses did not fit into the mold of the modern interpretation of the word "meek." He could be angry and was never susceptible to imposition. The patriarch was the greatest leader Israel ever had, he was a figure of towering strength, and the splendor of his personality struck terror into the hearts of sinful men. Yet, he was described as the "meekest man on earth."...

The Greek word used in the Lord's beatitude is *praeis*; it comes from *praotees* and has several usages. It was often used to express humility and an absence of anger. It expressed docility, gentleness of character, and sometimes mildness of speech. Probably its best usage can be found in that it described an animal that had been domesticated, such as a dog trained to respond to the command of its master or a horse which had been broken.

These illustrations may seem strange, but they provide word-pictures of meekness. A sinful man can be like an untamed animal, a biting dog, or a horse which throws its rider. Yet, when the grace of God transforms the sinner into a saint, turbulent passions are tamed and brought into submissiveness to the Lord. The man who formerly lived to please himself learns to respond when the Holy Spirit gently pulls on the reins! The angry soul which loved to snap and bite becomes the willing servant of its trainer. A dog will hunt, warn, protect, and do anything the master orders. Instead of being savage and unrestrained, the domesticated dog plays with children and is a delight to the entire family. To the ancient Greeks, this was "being gentle or meek." It denoted a person who had come into contact with a higher power, a dynamic which had transformed an untrustworthy animal into a beloved companion. (Taken from the author's commentary, *Matthew's Majestic Gospel*, pp. 95-96.)

LONGSUFFERING . . . The Persistence of Humility

Once again the Greek word used in the text commands attention. It is *makrothumia.* Consulting Dr. Thayer's *Lexicon*, we find that it means "to be of long spirit, not to lose heart, to persevere patiently and bravely, to be patient in bearing the offenses and injuries of others, to be mild and slow in avenging, slow to anger, slow to punish." William Barclay provides a beautiful illustration of the true meaning of this word. "It is often possible to see a puppy and a very large dog together. The puppy yaps at the big dog, worries him, bites him, and all the time, the big dog, who could annihilate the puppy with one snap of his teeth, bears the puppy's impertinence with a forbearing dignity. *Makrothumia* is the spirit which bears insult and injury without bitterness and without complaint. It is the spirit which can suffer unpleasant people with graciousness, and fools without irritation." (Quoted from *The Daily Bible Study Series*, *Galatians and Ephesians*, p. 139.)

Paul knew that his friends lived in a hostile world where people could be cruel, thoughtless, and irritating. If Christians were to remain calm in spite of insidious attacks made upon them, they would need "*makrothumia* grace." They would need to resemble huge rocks at the shoreline. Successive waves would beat upon them; continual pounding would sometimes bury them with spray. But when the threatening waves retreated, those rocks remain unaffected by the onslaught. The apostle knew that often the greatest problems were caused by small, irritating details; not by large, overwhelming difficulties. The ancient writer said that it is "the little foxes that spoil the vines" (Song of Sol. 2:15). Longsuffering should be watchful and careful. Since vines are hard to produce, they should never be damaged by neglect.

FORBEARING . . . The Protectiveness of Humility

"Forbearing one another in love." The Greek word *anecho* is a compounded word meaning "to hold, to hold up," hence "to endure." Paul suggested that since each Christian had faults of his own, understanding should provide patience to enable each man to endure the indiscretions of neighbors. Humility should govern his conduct and prevent his acting hastily to condemn others with similar problems. The best preventative of criticism is a realization of personal guilt. To watch a modern Simon Peter betraying the Lord is an incentive for condemnation and anger, but those who are aware of their own failures will hesitate before condemning others. The apostle linked forbearance with love (agape), one of the strongest words in Paul's vocabulary. Love begets pity, not criticism; help, not condemnation. It is very difficult to love the unlovely, but Paul knew of unfailing resources for every believer. He said, "The love of God is shed abroad in our hearts by the Holy Ghost . . . " (Rom. 5:5). The inflow of divine love rejuvenates the most desolate love-less soul. With it, a Christian can do anything; without it, he flounders amid the repeated failures of self-effort.

PEACE . . . The Provision of Humility

In the Amplified New Testament is an excellent rendering of the original text. "Be eager, and *strive earnestly* to guard and keep the harmony and oneness of [produced by] the spirit in the binding power of peace." The word translated "endeavoring" is interesting. Thayer says it means "active, diligent, earnest." It indicates a person who has singleness of purpose; he concentrates upon *bringing to a successful conclusion the task in hand.* Paul urged the Christian to preserve the unity of the Spirit. This unity was not man-made; it was the evidence of God's divine presence. Man's task was not to make it, but to avoid breaking or spoiling it. It was said that on the day of Pentecost, the believers "were all with one accord in one place." That situation was the prelude to the greatest spiritual awakening the world ever experienced. To dwell in that kind of atmosphere and enjoy the presence of the Holy Spirit was to be acquainted with true peace, an attribute of the living God. This was one of the secrets of New Testament blessing. When Christians learned to praise each other instead of searching for their faults, the working of God in the hearts of unbelievers was unhindered.

The Greek word translated "bond" is *sundesmo*, but it is different from another word found in Ephesians 6:20—*halusei,*—"a chain." Hence Thayer's explanation that the term used to describe "the bond" of peace means "the ligaments by which the members of the human body are united together." Paul's chain could be seen; it was an inanimate object, a source of annoyance and suffering. The bond of peace was something unseen but gloriously real. It was the hidden entity which united every part of the body of Christ. It was the cement in the building, the blood stream in the body, the experience of the love of God beyond comprehension. Knowing that growth and progress in an alien world would be difficult, Paul urged his readers to cling tenaciously to everything that was good. He wanted them to remain humble before God and His people, for only then would they "walk worthy of the vocation wherewith they had been called."

PAUL'S EXPOSITION

SECTION ONE

Expository Notes on the Sevenfold Oneness of the Christian Faith

There is one body, and one Spirit, even as ye are called in one hope of your calling; one Lord, one faith, one baptism, one God and Father of all, who is above all, and through all, and in you all (vv. 4-6).

THEME: *The Basic Features of Christianity*
OUTLINE:

A. One Body . . . *The Church (v. 4)*
B. One Spirit . . . *The Comforter (v. 4)*
C. One Hope . . . *The Challenge (v. 4)*
D. One Lord . . . *The Christ (v. 5)*
E. One Faith . . . *The Credentials (v. 5)*
F. One Baptism . . . *The Confession (v. 5)*
G. One God . . . *The Creator (v. 6)*

Seven is the perfect number within the Scriptures, and, therefore, Paul presented a perfect survey of all he believed. He urged Christians to preserve harmony within their ranks and thereafter endeavored to reveal that each facet of their doctrines provided an example of the truth he taught. The apostle divided his exposition into seven parts, and what he enunciated became guidelines for church theology.

ONE BODY . . . The Church (v. 4)

When the apostle wrote this letter, many churches were in existence. Seven were mentioned in the second and third chapters of the Book of Revelation, and others received letters written by Paul. Nevertheless, the apostle continued to speak of *ONE* CHURCH. There were twelve tribes in Israel, but they represented *ONE* NATION. People do not always agree on viewpoints and conclusions, but they are seldom greater than when they agree to disagree. The Church included people whose interpretations of doctrine were different. Christian leaders had various methods by which to extend the kingdom of Christ, but nothing should ever have been permitted to cause discord among brethren. People who asserted that they had a monopoly on wisdom invariably became dictators. Men of this type, should they belong to a minority, persist at any cost until they establish a new denomination over which they become dominant rulers. Throughout history, Christianity has suffered irreparable damage because arrogant teachers have assumed that they have had authority to condemn all others who disagreed with their doctrine.

There is only ONE TRUE CHURCH; it includes all who love the Savior; all whose souls have been cleansed by the precious blood of Christ. When any assembly refuses to acknowledge the sincerity of other believers, it ceases to be a church and becomes a debating society with a Christian name. Christ is the Head of His Church, but if that Church—or Body—is torn apart by discord, the Head no longer controls His Body. When legs and arms do not respond to the commands of the head, the entire human structure is in jeopardy. Paralysis prevents movement, and continual deterioration leads to death. Christians should protect the unity of the assembly as they do their lives.

ONE SPIRIT . . . The Comforter (v. 4)

John urged his readers to "try the spirits, whether they are of God; because many false prophets are gone out into the world" (1 John

4:1). Evidently he contrasted *the many evil spirits* with the one true Spirit of God. Prior to His departure from this world, the Lord said to His disciples, "It is expedient for you that I go away; for if I go not away, the Comforter will not come unto you; but if I depart, I will send him unto you. . . . Howbeit when he, the Spirit of truth, is come, he will guide you into all truth" (John 16:7,13). A body without a head is a decapitated corpse; the Church without its Head—Christ—is useless. A body has one owner—one inhabitant. There is ONE SPIRIT, and He resides within the Church. His voice alone should be heard and obeyed in every matter of church concern. When other voices are heard, the Christians should be alerted to danger. John would never have urged his readers to try the spirits if he had not been aware of their threat to the welfare of believers. Dissenting voices can sometimes be loud and eloquent; they can sometimes be low and enticing, but there exists an infallible rule by which the children of God can test the spirits. *The Holy Spirit never contradicts the Word of God*, for one of His primary tasks is the leading of believers into the truth. His hand never guides people into bondage; His suggestions never create confusion in an assembly; His influence never usurps authority; He glorifies Christ—not Himself. The Lord said, "For he shall not speak of himself; but whatsoever he shall hear, that shall he speak: and he will shew you things to come. He shall glorify me: for he shall receive of mine, and shall show it unto you" (John 16:13-14). Paul insisted that there was only ONE SPIRIT, who remained the unquestioned guide of God's people.

ONE HOPE . . . The Challenge (v. 4)

" . . . even as ye are called in one hope of your calling." As the wise men followed a star to the culmination of their journey to Bethlehem, so Christians have one hope to guide them to their Promised Land. Writing to the Colossians, Paul spoke of this great anticipation: "For the hope which is laid up for you in heaven, whereof ye heard before in the word of the truth of the gospel" (Col. 1:5). " . . . the hope of the gospel, which ye have heard" (Col. 1:23). Paul was more explicit when writing to the Corinthians, "If in this life only we have hope in Christ, we are of all men most miserable. But now is Christ risen from the dead, and become the firstfruits of them that slept" (1 Cor. 15:19–20).

Christians may differ in many ways, but they have one thing in common; they share the intense desire to reach their homeland. "But we are citizens of heaven" (Phillips' New Testament in Modern English translation of Phil. 3:2). This world is not the home of the Christian. The followers of the Savior emulate the example given by Abraham: "For he looked for a city which hath foundations, whose builder and maker is God" (Heb. 11:10). That is the predominant hope of every believer, and is the star which guides them to their eternal home. It is "the hope of our calling."

ONE LORD . . . The Christ (v. 5)

Without Christ, there is no Christianity, and that fact makes the Church and its message unique. Other religions have many deities as was evident when Paul testified on Mars Hill in Athens. Since the apostle had seen "an altar with this inscription, TO THE UNKNOWN GOD." he said, "Whom therefore ye ignorantly worship, him declare I unto you" (see Acts 17:22-23). Fearful lest they had omitted to mention any God, the Athenians built an extra altar to appease the anger of the unmentioned deity. Millions of Moslems believe that Jesus was another in a long line of prophets, the latest and greatest of which was Mohammed. The innumerable temples in India contain gods of all kinds, shapes, and sizes. I remember standing before an idol which had a cloth over its head. A priest explained that this was necessary, for if any man looked into its face, he would be instantly turned into stone!

The Christian faith stands alone in magnificent isolation—it has but ONE SAVIOR, *the Lord Jesus Christ.* When Simon Peter preached in Jerusalem, he said to the listening people: "This is the stone which was set at nought of you builders, which is become the head of the corner. Neither is there salvation in any other: for there is none other name under heaven given among men, whereby we must be saved" (Acts 4:11-12). This corroborated the words of Jesus, "I am the Way, the truth and the life: *no man cometh unto the Father but by me*" (John 14:6). The Savior had no rival no substitute, and no other message. He was the door into the everlasting kingdom of God; men entered by Him or remained outside forever.

ONE FAITH . . . The Credentials (v. 5)

The Christian faith, which challenged and revolutionized the world, was described as "the Way." Primarily, this had little to do with doctrinal interpretation; it referred to a type of living, to people whose philosophy concerned a highway to heaven. Saul of Tarsus was commissioned by the high priest of Israel to go to Damascus so that "if he found any of *this way*, whether they were men or women, he might bring them bound unto Jerusalem" (Acts 9:2). When Paul's life was threatened in Ephesus, it was said: "And the same time there arose no small stir about *that way*" (Acts 19:23). Perhaps, the name was associated with the words of Jesus: "I AM THE WAY . . . " (John 14:6). It became evident that, amid all the confusion of conflicting religions, there had emerged a new and a living highway to the heart of God, and all believers in Jesus were said to be followers of "that way." They possessed faith in the Redeemer and refused to obey any other leader. That "way" was not a church covenant or a table of constitutional requirements. It was a message which captured and subjugated their entire being. It was a fire within their souls; a beacon which encouraged daily walk toward an eternal destination. That faith was so strong that it enabled the Christian to sing when facing death in the arena; it ignored impossibilities, and it went forth to conquer a hostile world. When believers met in the streets, they did not enquire concerning church affiliations; they asked if they belonged to "*the way*." When the sign of the fish was seen on doorways, buildings, in markets or other places, viewers realized that brethren were at hand. That bond united strangers and made them brethren.

ONE BAPTISM . . . The Confession (v. 5)

The New Testament Church knew nothing of unbaptized believers. Secret disciples were few and far between, because all who professed faith in Christ confessed it publicly in the waters of baptism. The rite was the outward sign of a mystical union when intelligent people were baptized into one body. Writing to the Roman church, Paul said, "Know ye not, that so many of us as were baptized into Jesus Christ were baptized into his death? Therefore, we are buried with him by baptism into death, that like as Christ was raised up from the dead by the glory of the Father, even so we also should walk in newness of life" (Rom. 6:3-4). Whatever might be claimed to the contrary, the baptism practiced in New Testament churches was by immersion. It signified the DEATH, BURIAL, and RESURRECTION of the candidate.

During modern funerals, the undertaker, for some reason, sprinkles dirt on the casket, but that custom was not practiced by the leaders of the early church. When a man died, his body was interred in a tomb or buried in the ground. The surviving relatives did not sprinkle dirt on a casket! There was *one baptism* that represented the sincere confession of a believer who testified that his former way of living had terminated; he was beginning a new life in union with his resurrected Lord.

ONE GOD . . . The Creator (v. 6)

Never did any author express so much in such few words. Paul's description of the Almighty was the most comprehensive utterance ever made; it encompassed omnipotence, omnipresence, and omniscience; it described the indescribable! Paul wrote, "One God and Father of all, who is above all, and through all, and in you all." The word "all" appeared four times and supplied the following revelations of the Almighty:

1. *Abundant Affection*. "One God, the Father of all." To every Hebrew reader, that statement would have been blasphemous! The Jews taught that Jehovah was the Father of the chosen race; Gentiles were outcasts, dogs. To suggest that God had any more than a passing interest in heathens was heresy. Yet, Paul taught that God was the "Father of all." Did the apostle imply that since Jehovah created all things, He remained their Father—if only by creation? Was Paul suggesting that God was the Father of angels, human beings, and every living creature? Did the Savior have that thought in mind when He said, "Are not two sparrows sold for a farthing? and one of them shall not fall on the ground without your Father [knowing about it]" (Matt. 10:29). Paul evidently envisaged unlimited compassion. Jehovah was not the unrelenting taskmaster as had been described throughout the ages. Even Micah caught a glimpse of God's love when he wrote, "Who is a God like unto thee, that pardoneth iniquity, and passeth by the transgression of the remnant of his heritage? *He retaineth not his anger forever, because he delighteth in mercy*" (Micah 7:18). The ideas expressed by some Hebrew leaders were often repulsive, forbidding, and frightening. Jesus was the most refreshing teacher ever heard. He described God as a happy father who ran to throw his arms around the neck of a returning prodigal (see Luke 15:20).
2. *Absolute Authority*. "Who is above all." Paul prayed that his friends would know " . . . what is the exceeding greatness of his [Christ's] power to usward who believe, according to the working of his mighty power, which he wrought in Christ, when he raised him from the dead, and set him at his own right hand in the heavenly places, *far above all* principality, and power, and might, and dominion, and every name that is named, not only in this world,

but also in that which is to come" (Eph. 1:19-21). It is thrilling to know that Christ and His Father were equal in rank and position. He who stepped down from His eternal throne to be found in fashion as a man (Phil. 2:6-8) was lifted to occupy His exalted position when He was raised triumphantly from the dead. His eternal excellence was not a reward, but something He reclaimed. Christ occupied His throne from eternal ages, and His glory will never diminish. The Lord Jesus Christ has been exalted far above kings and potentates; He will never be dethroned. Yet, He will ultimately relinquish His high office to enjoy fellowship with His bride, the Church. "And when all things shall be subdued unto him, then shall the Son also himself be subject unto him that put all things under him, *that God may be all in all*" (1 Cor. 15:28).

3. *Amazing Activity.* " . . . and through all." This conception of the omnipresence of God was not new to the understanding of the human race. The psalmist exclaimed, "If I take the wings of the morning, and dwell in the uttermost parts of the sea, even there shall thy hand lead me, and thy right hand shall hold me" (Ps. 139:9-10). The predominant thought in the mind of David was that wherever he went, God could find him. Jehovah was the inescapable God, and it would be folly to try to evade His presence. Paul's exposition of truth went further. He saw the Almighty working throughout the world. The planet was not a machine functioning alone while its Maker was on an extended vacation. God was involved in every part of His creation. He understood each detail of the operation and could make "even the wrath of man to praise Him" (Ps. 76:10).

   This conception of truth brought to people a new appreciation of the Almighty. He was not a remote Deity living far from His world; He was not an isolated resident in outer space where people would never enjoy accessibility to Him. God was living and moving in every part of His creation. The snowdrop pushing through the soil in the spring of the year, the entrancing song of a lark in the sky, the playfulness of a kitten, and the cry of a newborn child supplied evidence to prove the life, wisdom, and interest of the Almighty could be detected at any time, in all places. Jehovah never slept! David exclaimed triumphantly, "My help cometh from the Lord, which made heaven and earth. He will not suffer thy foot to be moved: he that keepeth thee will not slumber. Behold, he that keepeth Israel shall neither slumber nor sleep" (Ps. 121:2).

4. *Abiding Accessibility.* " . . . and in you all." Perhaps this was the

most incomprehensible of all the miracles of grace. Throughout the Old Testament era there was only one religious center in Israel. God lived in the tabernacle and later in the temple built at Jerusalem. When men wished to approach their Maker, they traveled to the recognized place of worship, and for many people, such a pilgrimage was the highlight of their careers. Today, churches may be found in almost every village in the civilized world. Where idols are worshiped there are thousands of accessible temples. During the earlier history of man, God was believed to inhabit the heavens, and it was a staggering truth when Israel was told that the distant God intended to make His home among the tribes of Israel. Afterward, millions of pilgrims journeyed long distances to feel that they were closer to a God they would never see. When Paul announced that such a need to find God in only one place had terminated and that Christians had now become temples of the Almighty, it was difficult for people to comprehend the implications of the astounding message.

"And in you all" embraced every man, woman, and child within the Church of Christ. There would never be need to visit a distant shrine. The Christian soul had become a temple, and each listening believer could clearly hear the voice of the indwelling Holy Spirit. Paul wrote to the Corinthians to ask, "Know ye not that ye are the temple of God, and that the Spirit of God dwelleth in you?" (1 Cor. 3:16). The implication of this teaching was amazing.

Formerly, men journeyed great distances to be near to God; Paul explained the procedure had been reversed. God had traveled even farther to be *with* and *in* His people. This was the final illustration of the unity exhibited by God and His new message. Paul said, "There is one body, and one Spirit, . . . one hope of your calling: one Lord, one faith, one baptism, one God and Father. . . . " That unbroken unity should be exemplified in the conduct of believers. It was their compelling duty to "walk worthy of the vocation wherewith ye are called" (v. 1). Compared with this sevenfold revelation of the majestic splendor of God and His work, the homily, "Five Heads . . . With But a Single Thought" (p. 218), might be interesting and instructive.

SECTION TWO

Expository Notes on God's All-sufficient Grace

But unto every one of us is given grace according to the measure of

the gift of Christ. Wherefore he saith, when he ascended up on high, he led captivity captive, and gave gifts unto men. (Now that he ascended, what is it but what he also descended first into the lower parts of the earth? He that descended is the same also that ascended up far above all heavens, that he might fill all things.) And he gave some apostles; and some, prophets; and some, evangelists; and some, pastors and teachers (vv. 7-11).

THEME: *The Distribution of Royal Gifts*
OUTLINE:
A. The Amazing Grace
B. The Astonishing Gathering
C. The Assorted Gifts

The word "grace" was one of Paul's favorite expressions; he used it ninety times in writing his Epistles. What is "grace"? *The Encyclopedic Dictionary* supplies ten different ways in which the word might be used. Among them are: (1) the unmerited, but freely given love and favor of God toward man, (2) the divine influence operating in man to regenerate, sanctify, or strengthen him, (3) the state or condition of being pleasing and acceptable to God, and (4) any divinely inspired spiritual virtue or excellence.

Grace is one of the most attractive words in the Bible but is not easily defined. Grace is tenderness, mercy, pity, gentleness, love, favor, forgiveness, acceptability, and many other virtues expressed in one word. It indicates an outflow from the heart of God, a blessing for every person in the world. When the apostle looked at the Lord, he saw grace; when he considered unregenerate men, he spoke about grace. It is an eternal treasure shared by God with impoverished men and women.

THE AMAZING GRACE

"But unto every one of us is given grace according to the measure of the gift of Christ" (v. 7).

1. *Grace is Acceptable.* It is not the product of man's ingenuity; it is not acquired by a course of self-discipline. Grace is an attribute of God shared with us, an eternal jewel beyond the purchasing capabilities of human beings. Grace alone can conquer inherent enemies, which defy the best intentions of men. God is patient with irritating sinners, and that quality in human hearts produces identical effects. Grace is love in action, patience in endurance, and praise in a world of criticism.

2. *Grace is Adequate*. Believers in Christ are not identical; they have different needs and encounter varying problems. This amazing gift from God is a "measured" gift. Christ examines the difficulties confronting His followers and with great wisdom allocates exactly what He believes to be essential. When Paul wrote to the Philippians, he promised, "But my God shall supply all your need according to his riches in glory by Christ Jesus" (Phil. 4:19). Paul had experienced this blessing within his own ministry and was able to witness, "I can do all things through Christ which strengtheneth me" (Phil. 4:13). When Daniel was thrown into the lions' den, the grace of God closed the mouths of the dangerous animals. When the disciples were afraid of the waves which threatened to capsize their small boat, the same grace, through Christ, stilled the storm. When Paul and Silas were imprisoned in Philippi, grace enabled them to sing praises at midnight. The grace of God is sufficient for every man under any circumstances.
3. *Grace is Altruistic*. It is always an expression of kindness toward others. God's grace concerned human beings; our grace extends to all with whom we live. We can only give what we possess, and since this quality is seldom found in sinful hearts, it is encumbent upon all Christians to receive from God what they convey to neighbors. The disciples were able to feed the multitude when they received bread from their Master's hand. Peter and his companions were able to reach the Pentecostal multitude when they had been endowed with the power of the Holy Spirit. God never gives December grace in June and never supplies strength to climb a mountain when His children are walking on flat lands. "As thy days, so shall thy strength be" (Deut. 33:25). Christians should be channels connecting eternal reservoirs with the desert-like conditions of a dying world.

THE ASTONISHING GATHERING

"When he ascended up on high, he led captivity captive, and gave gifts unto men" (v. 8). Paul quoted from Psalm 68:18-19. "Thou hast ascended on high, thou hast led captivity captive, thou hast received gifts for men; yea, for the rebellious also, that the Lord God might dwell among them. Blessed be the Lord, who daily loadeth us with benefits, even the God of our salvation." These verses have interested theologians in all ages, and as a result, varying interpretations have been given.

1. Some writers believe this is a reference to the time when the ark of God was carried to Zion, when, in the days of festivity which followed the event, gifts were distributed among the people of God. They further state that it refers prophetically to the ascending Christ, who led the powers of darkness captive, demonstrating He had "spoiled principalities and powers, and made a shew over them openly, triumphing over them in it" (Col. 2:15).
2. Others believe that it referred to the occasions when ancient kings, returning from battle, led their captives to the hill of Zion, either to execute or pardon them. Neither of these suggestions is acceptable, for if that were the case, the triumph of Christ was incomplete. If He led the powers of evil captive, then some of them surely escaped; they are still with us!
3. I have always believed that when Christ led captivity captive, He was leading His Old Testament saints to their eternal home. The offerings of birds and bullocks had supplied *a covering* for sin, permitting God to continue associations with guilty people. With the exception of Enoch and Elijah, the ancient saints did not go from earth to heaven when they died. Christ spoke of hades and described how the unrighteous dead went to one section, and the righteous dead to another to await resurrection (see Luke 16:19-31). Simon Peter wrote, "For Christ also hath once suffered for sins, the just for the unjust, that he might bring us to God, being put to death in the flesh, but quickened by the Spirit; by which also he went and preached unto the spirits in prison; which sometimes were disobedient, when once the long-suffering of God waited in the days of Noah, while the ark was a preparing" (1 Peter 3:18-20).

It seems evident that after His death and prior to His resurrection, Christ "descended into the lowest parts of the earth" and proclaimed His triumph before fallen angels (see also Jude, v. 6). Although the Lord indicated that the righteous dead occupied their section of hades, Paul declared, " . . . whilst we are at home in the body, we are absent from the Lord. . . .we are confident, I say, and willing rather to be absent from the body, and to be present with the Lord" (2 Cor. 5:6-8). The apostle taught that death was the opening of the door through which we enter into the presence of the risen Lord. A way had been opened to permit the saints to follow the Lord "when he ascended up far above all heavens . . . " (v. 10). Christ was not a returning king leading his captives to execution. He was more like Abraham who rescued Lot from captivity and then escorted him triumphantly back to his homeland. The entry of God's saints into heaven must have been one of the most amazing events ever to happen. Millions of saints followed the Lord to the palace of the Almighty, and their arrival caused no confusion.

I shall never forget arriving at a well-known hotel in Los Angeles. I was a guest at an important convention, and I reached the hotel a few minutes after three hundred people had arrived to check into the building. We stood in long lines awaiting our turn at the reception desk, but there was no confusion. The ladies behind the counters were the embodiment of patience: nothing upset them. One after the other, travelers were despatched to their assigned rooms, and a multitude of bellboys carried innumerable suitcases. When Christ reached His heavenly home, he escorted millions of guests who arrived together. Perhaps angels served as guides, the necessary information had been supplied earlier, and nobody had any luggage!

THE ASSORTED GIFTS

"And he gave some, apostles; and some, prophets; and some, evangelists; and some, pastors and teachers" (v. 11). When David returned triumphantly from battle, it was customary for him to divide the spoils of war among his people. Gifts were distributed for valor, and the faithful who had remained at home were suitably rewarded (see 1 Sam. 30:24).

Pentecost supplied the irrefutable evidence that the ascended Lord was bestowing gifts upon His chosen servants. When the first tide of blessing had receded and when the church had been established, it became evident that gifted men had been appointed to assist the assembly in further conquests for their King. God appointed *apostles* . . . to preside; *prophets* . . . to predict; *evangelists* . . . to preach; *pastors* . . . to protect; and *teachers* . . . to persevere.

Apostles . . . to Preside

The word *apostolos* which is translated "apostle" means "a delegate, messenger, one sent forth with orders." According to Bishop Lightfoot, "the word occurs 79 times in the New Testament, of which 68 instances are by St. Luke and St. Paul." The statement "*one sent forth with orders*" described the ministry of the original twelve. When Judas betrayed his Lord, the remaining disciples cast lots and decided that Matthias should be his successor. There is reason to believe that they made a mistake. If there are only twelve designated apostles

(Rev. 21:14), a choice has to be made between Paul and Matthias, and the answer becomes obvious. It should be remembered that within the New Testament, other men proudly carried that title (see Acts 14:14). The term was ascribed to ordained messengers of Christ who were empowered to have jurisdiction within churches. They presided at specially convened councils and exercised authority in all matters of jurisprudence within the assemblies of Christ (see Acts 15:13).

When emergencies arose regarding theology, the apostles were expected to arbitrate between opposing parties. The decisions made on those occasions were recorded in the Scriptures, and the Bible became the reference book for all churches. There are no apostles in the church today. Denominations may have appointed elders, who refer to the words of the original leaders of the assemblies. Certain sections of the church claim to have apostles, but only unpardonable arrogance would associate such men with James, John, Peter, and Paul. God gave apostles when they were needed; what they decided will always supply guidelines for enquiring people.

Prophets . . . to Predict

The word *propheetees*, which has been translated "prophet," means "to speak forth; to speak out;" hence, "one who speaks forth." Believers have been taught this word refers to a person who proclaims the gospel of Christ, but such a description is misleading. Prophets continued to preach, but there were men within the New Testament church who possessed the ability to predict future events. Such men were often mentioned during the Old Testament era. Elijah, Elisha, Isaiah, and others definitely preached to Israel, but *they also foretold the future*. There were Christians who possessed the same ability. When Luke wrote the Acts of the Apostles, he described an event which took place in Caesarea. "And as we tarried there many days, there came down from Judaea a certain prophet, named Agabus. And when he was come unto us, he took Paul's girdle, and bound his own hands and feet, and said, Thus saith the Holy Ghost, so shall the Jews at Jerusalem bind the man that owneth this girdle, and shall deliver him into the hands of the Gentiles" (Acts 21:10-11). John was an apostle and a prophet; the Book of Revelation describes many of the things he predicted.

When God had something to say, He found a man to be His spokesman. A prophet repeated what he heard, and listeners were informed about future events. It must be emphasized that there are no prophets within the modern church. God has nothing *new* to say! His revelation was completed when He instructed John to write, "For I testify unto every man that heareth the prophecy of this book, *If any man shall add unto these things, God shall add unto him the plagues that are written in this book.* And if any man shall take away from the book of this prophecy, God shall take away his part out of the book of life, and out of the holy city, and from the things which are written in this book" (Rev. 22:18-19). Christians have the Bible, and all they need to know can be found within its pages. Those who substitute other material for the Word of God run the risk of losing their souls. There is a vast difference between a prophet and a student of prophecy. A prophet predicts the future; a student of prophecy studies what has already been uttered and tries to impart his knowledge to listeners. There are many charlatans who resort to questionable practices, especially to raise money from gullible people. It is possible to sound like a messenger of God and yet be a spokesman for Satan.

Evangelists . . . to Preach

The modern church has a multitude of elected officials, most of whom are dedicated to the cause of Christ. There are archbishops, bishops, elders, deacons, and others who have been appointed to administrative positions, but none of these can take the place of the evangelist. Pastors and teachers are among the most wonderful people in the world, but if we consider the words of Paul, the evangelist is indispensable. His task is the proclamation of the gospel. Basically, the New Testament evangelist had little if any time to be a pastor, although Paul remained in Ephesus for several years and doubtless became the pastor of his Ephesian flock. Simon Peter became a *fisher of men*; John became a *shepherd of the sheep*! Either ministry complements the other. When Peter was called by Christ, he was "casting a net into the sea" (Mark 1:16). When Jesus issued a similar invitation to James and John, they "were in their ship *mending their nets*" (Mark 1:19). Peter was "the fisherman" and on the day of Pentecost, demonstrated his God-given ability. James and John repaired the net so that Peter's fish could not escape! The duties of evangelists and pastors should be mutually dependent; both need each other, but it is a cause for great regret that the evangelists have almost disappeared from the western church. (See the homily, "The House of Mercy . . . on the Jericho Road," p. 220).

Pastors . . . to Protect

The word *poimenos*, which has been translated "pastors," means "a herdsman or shepherd; the presiding officer, manager, director of any Christian assembly." The word is translated "shepherd" in the Authorized Version of the Bible. The apostle Peter commanded, "Feed the flock of God which is among you, taking the oversight thereof, not by constraint, but willingly; not for filthy lucre, but of a ready mind" (1 Peter 5:2). The *evangelist* might be compared with a surgeon who moves hastily to save the life of a patient. The *pastor* resembles the family physician who may treat a sick person for several months, watching carefully the effects of administered medicine. A *surgeon* acts hastily but carefully; the *physician* moves slowly and patiently in attending to the needs of sick people. A *shepherd* never runs to green pasture; his sheep are never stampeded into searching for nourishment. David wrote, "The Lord is my shepherd; I shall not want. He maketh me *to lie down in green pastures: he leadeth me beside still waters*" (Ps. 23:1, 2). An evangelist visits God's sheep, the pastor stays with them. An evangelist may advise where the bread of life may be found, but the shepherd finds it and makes sure his sheep are adequately nourished. A true pastor may never become a world-wide traveler, but he is invaluable in the oversight of God's people. When danger threatens the flock, the shepherd confronts the enemy; when sheep are resting, the shepherd "never slumbers nor sleeps." David was a shepherd, and when he described to Saul his credentials for fighting the Philistine, he said, "Thy servant kept his father's sheep, and there came a lion, and a bear, and took a lamb out of the flock: and I went out after him, and smote him, and delivered it out of his mouth: and when he arose against me, I caught him by his beard, and smote him, and slew him. Thy servant slew both the lion and the bear: and this uncircumcised Philistine shall be as one of them, seeing he hath defied the armies of the living God" (1 Sam. 17:34-36).

The pastor of a church may not have to fight lions and bears, but there are dogs which snap and bite (Phil. 3:2) and wolves which threaten to destroy the congregation (see Acts 20:28-30).

Teachers . . . to Persevere

To some small degree, evangelists, pastors, and teachers exercise interchangeable ministries, but all have a distinctive talent for performing special tasks. The Greek word *didaskalos* signifies "one who is able to instruct." He is a dietician who finds the right food to keep the sheep strong; he is expert at separating weeds from grass! A teacher is one who superintends the growth of a kindergarten child until the student becomes a graduate. A teacher explains and, when understanding is hard to acquire, gives to students special consideration.

When I was a child, I was often taken to the village physician who seemed to know a little about everything. Doctors who specialized in various departments of medicine and surgery lived in the large cities, and often their fees were prohibitive. When I came to America, I discovered that "family doctors" were, for the most part, non-existent. Every physician had a specialty, and enquiries had to be made where to find a practitioner who handled my type of ailment. Pastors are like the old physicians; they are required to know something about everything. Their people look to them for help about all kinds of problems. The evangelists and teachers are more like the specialists. Often they have neither the patience nor the time to sit with weary people; what they do must be done quickly! The pastor, on the other hand, if he is worthy of his calling, visits and knows his sheep and loves his lambs, and they know and love him. Alas, this also seems to be a disappearing virtue. Most pastors only see their sheep on a Sunday morning. Any other contact must be made over the telephone, for the sheep and the shepherd occupy different spheres of life. This was never the practice in the early church. A pastor cannot know his flock if he never sees them!

SECTION THREE

Expository Notes on the Perfecting of Believers in Christ

For the perfecting of the saints, for the work of the ministry, for the edifying of the body of Christ: till we all come in the unity of the faith, and of the knowledge of the Son of God, unto a perfect man, unto the measure of the stature of the fulness of Christ (vv. 12-13).

THEME: *God's Ultimate Purpose for the Church*
OUTLINE:

A. A Specified Mission . . . "*the perfecting of the saints*"
B. A Strengthened Ministry . . . "*the work of the ministry*"
C. A Special Motive . . . "*the edifying of the body of Christ*"
D. A Sublime Maturity . . . "*a perfect man*"

A SPECIFIED MISSION . . . "the perfecting of the saints"

It should never be forgotten that the giving of "apostles, prophets, evangelists, pastors, and teachers" (v. 11) was part of God's plan for the perfection of His people. The ordination of talented leaders was a means to an end. Probably the key to the understanding of this scripture is found in the word which has been translated "perfecting." *Katartismon* means "to fit, sound, complete, to mend, to fit out, equip, put in order, arrange, adjust" (Thayer). This was the term used by Matthew to describe how James and John were in their ship "mending" their nets (Matt. 4:21). The same word was often used to describe *the setting of a bone in a broken limb.* Therefore, it must be concluded that when Paul referred to the perfecting of the Church, he was thinking of "setting in order" that which was broken or repairing something that had been damaged. A broken net or body cannot be perfect; it needs special attention from skilled people. A net is repaired by competent fishermen; a body needs the attention of a trained doctor. Within the church, the ordained men were qualified to repair anything damaged. Nothing less than the best was adequate for the Savior.

A STRENGTHENED MINISTRY . . . "the work of the ministry"

"For the work of the ministry" (v. 12b). The progressive sequence of thought in Paul's message is obvious. If the Christians were to catch others for Christ, their equipment would need to be in perfect repair. If they were to succeed in being active members of the body of Christ, they would need to be healthy. Broken legs could not walk, broken arms could not serve. The phrase *eis ergon diakonias* literally means "for work of the service." The Living Bible offers the translation, "Why is it that he gives us these special abilities to do certain things best? It is that *God's people will be equipped to do better work for him, building up the church.*" Three closely related words were used in the New Testament: *diakoneo*; *diakonia*, and *diakonos*. They related to people who devoted time and talent to the service of others. "A deacon, one who, by virtue of the office assigned him by the church, cares for the poor and has charge of and distributes the money collected for their use" (Thayer).

The sixth chapter of the Book of Acts supplies an interesting example of this need to strengthen the ministry. "And in those days, when the number of the disciples was multiplied, there arose a murmuring of the Grecians against the Hebrews, because their widows were neglected in the daily ministration. Then the twelve called the multitude of the disciples unto them, and said, It is not reason that we should leave the Word of God, and serve tables. Wherefore, brethren, look ye out among you seven men of honest report, full of the Holy Ghost and wisdom, whom we may appoint over this business. But we will give ourselves continually to prayer, and to the ministry of the word" (Acts 6:1-4). This was the first time the church recognized the need for adequate organization; it registered the beginning of a development destined to continue throughout the centuries. To satisfy the spiritual hunger of the converts, the apostles devoted their time to the study of the Scriptures. To guarantee the preservation of harmony, gifted men were chosen to handle problems within the assembly. Evidently, every official was expected to be a man of integrity and above reproach.

A SPECIAL MOTIVE . . . "the edifying of the body of Christ"

" . . . for the edifying of the body of Christ" (v. 12). The word translated "edifying" is *oikodomeen* which means "to build a house or other building; to build from the foundation; to build upon a foundation laid by others; to carry on instruction begun by others" (Thayer). All these interpretations fit into the pattern outlined by the apostle. The men especially ordained by God were commissioned to superintend and develop the spiritual understanding of the Christians. These believers were part of the temple of the living God; therefore the ministry of the teachers helped to complete the *True Sanctuary* which was erected on the foundation—Christ. Writing to the Corinthians, Paul stated, "As a wise masterbuilder, I have laid the foundation, and another buildeth thereon . . . for other foundation can no man lay than that is laid, which is Jesus Christ" (1 Cor. 3:10-11). Self-effacement, total dedication to the project in hand, and continued consecration were hallmarks of these inspired servants of God. They served Christ and His people with no thought of self-enrichment. They took little in return for their effort and gave all they possessed. Many of them died to further the cause to which they had committed themselves. That dedication established the Church and bequeathed to posterity an example all Christians should emulate.

A SUBLIME MATURITY . . . "a perfect man"

"Till we all come in the unity of the faith, and of the knowledge of the Son of God, unto a perfect man, unto the measure of the stature of the fulness of Christ" (v. 13). This was one of the most comprehensive utterances ever made by the apostle. It described the conclusion of the battle, the end of the race, the fulfillment of dreams, and the climax of everything attempted by God in the formation, growth, and purification of the Church. This statement may be subdivided into four sections:

1. The Unified Faith . . . "*the unity of the Faith*"
2. The Universal Fellowship . . . "*the knowledge of the Son of God*"
3. The Unique Faultlessness . . . "*a perfect man*"
4. The Unprecedented Fullness . . . "*the measure of the stature of the fulness of Christ*"

When Moses went up into Mount Nebo to view the promised land (Deut. 34:1), he was permitted to see a country which Israel was predestined to occupy. When Paul wrote this amazing verse, he resembled the patriarch; he was looking into a realm, the like of which had never been known on earth. It was God's land in which perfection would be absolute. Each of the above divisions is a continent awaiting exploration; every turn of the road reveals vistas of entrancing beauty.

The Unified Faith . . . "the unity of the faith"

There are two interpretations of this profound statement:

1. Some theologians believe that faith is here seen as a common entity, a belief in Jesus as the Son of God, and that Paul was thinking of people in all ages who would accept Christ as their Savior. They believe that all who were predestined to be saved would share a common faith in Christ. Thus would the unity of the faith be reached.
2. The Living Bible translates the verse: "Until finally, we all believe alike about our salvation, and about the Savior, God's Son, and all become full-grown in the Lord—yes, to the point of being filled full with Christ." The differences in interpretation will someday be eliminated, questions answered, problems solved, and denominational emphases will disappear when the existence of *one church* will be revealed.

How that will be accomplished is something too controversial to explain. How a Baptist will agree with Episcopalians about whether immersion or sprinkling is the correct method of confessing Christ remains confusing. How the silent Quakers will worship alongside the boisterous Pentecostals appears to be an inscrutable mystery. How the militant Protestants will cease arguing with Roman Catholics about the authority of the Pope is beyond comprehension. Somehow the Lord will remove the theological difficulties and, when He has finished, no person will turn to a neighbor, and say, "I told you so!" Perhaps theology will become a thing of the past as saints are enthralled by the resplendence of their Lord. Paul was correct when he wrote, "We shall all be changed!" (1 Cor. 15:51). When that is accomplished, the miracles in the New Testament will fade into insignificance, and ecstasy will be known throughout eternity. Then, believers will have reached *the unity of the faith.*

The Universal Fellowship . . . "the knowledge of the Son of God"

"Till we all come to the unity . . . of the knowledge of the Son of God" (v. 13). Here, Paul drew a line of demarcation between what Christians knew about Christ and what they will eventually know of Him. Faith is an idea, a concept in the mind, an acceptance of something spoken. Affinity of purpose as well as the mutual sharing of desires, aspirations, plans, and delights is infinitely greater than intellectual acquiescence; it becomes a spiritual warmth that permeates the soul. This expresses a process which continues until Christians are like their Lord. It is "*a growing up of the body*." Frank E. Gaebelein quotes from the writings of R. A. Knox, "A baby's head is unusually large in comparison with the rest of its body. As it develops, however, the body grows up into a due proportion with the head" (*St. Paul's Gospel*, p. 84).

When the apostle wrote the thirteenth chapter of his First Epistle to the Corinthians, he expounded on the virtues of love and eventually wrote, "For now we see through a glass, darkly; but then face to face: now I know in part; but then shall I know even as also I am known" (v. 12). Paul knew the direction in which he was traveling. Once again it must be admitted that it seemed to be beyond human understanding that the eternal kingdom would become the home of innumerable people exactly like Christ. John said, "Beloved, now are we the sons of God, and it doth not yet appear what we shall be: but we know that, when he shall appear, we shall be like him; for we shall see him as he is" (1 John 3:2). This glorious unity will not be confined to theological principles; it will relate to every part of our immortal beings. There will be no friction, no arguments, no problems. "And there shall be no night there; and they need no candle, neither light of the sun; for the Lord God giveth them light: and they shall reign forever and ever" (Rev. 22:5).

The Unique Faultlessness . . . "a perfect man"

"Till we all come . . . unto a perfect man" (v. 13). Since the failure of the first Adam, there has only been one perfect man—the Last Adam. It is, therefore, impossible to consider the definition of "the perfect man" without thinking of the Lord Jesus Christ. It is generally believed that perfection means to be without blemish. A perfect portrait would be without flaw and *incapable of improvement.* If it were possible to increase its charm and beauty, it would only be perfect *as far as it went*! If men could be without moral or spiritual blemish, they might be classified as perfect, but that would be incorrect. The Savior was without sin, but He was much more. *Christ was incapable of improvement.* All the fullness of God was in Him. If search had been made throughout myriads of worlds, it would have been impossible to find anyone surpassing Christ. He was not only without blemish; He embodied perfection in all its indescribable ramifications. Even the Heavenly Father could not find anything in Christ capable of improvement. *that* and only *that* is a portrait of a perfect man. It was no cause for amazement that Paul was fascinated with the revelation God had given. The Almighty intended to make believers not only what *they desired*; He intended to make them what *He desired*, and that seemed incomprehensible.

The Unprecedented Fullness. . . "the measure of the stature of the fulness of Christ"

"Till we all come . . . unto the measure of the stature of the fulness of Christ" (v. 13). Professor T. Crockery writes, "The end of spiritual growth cannot be seen in this life. The Bible nowhere represents the perfection of the Church as occurring in this life. It is to be without spot or wrinkle when the day of its glorious presentation comes. Thus the design of the Christian ministry is to labor for the perfection of the Church." (Quoted from *The Pulpit Commentary*, *Ephesians*, vol. 20, p. 165.) The Greek text is *eis andra teleion* and literally means "unto a man full-grown." Dr. Thayer states that *teleion* means "wanting nothing necessary to completeness, perfect; of men, full grown, adult, of full age; mature." The picture provided is not that of immature, incompetent children, but of an experienced man who provides an example for his neighbors.

This fact became evident when Paul mentioned "children tossed to and fro, and carried about with every wind of doctrine" (v. 14). The

Christians had been children; they were destined to become adults. When Paul wrote his Epistle, his readers were in the process of growing into maturity. To refer once again to the translation offered by The Living Bible, it states we shall "all become full-grown in the Lord—yes, to the point of being filled-full with Christ." That is a most interesting suggestion. Believers will be filled *full*; they will reach the point where improvement will be impossible! Christ may have much more to give and may need eternal ages to give samples of His bountiful provision. Yet, even in the hereafter, our capacity to receive might be strained to the utmost. We shall be immortal vessels connected to an inexhaustible reservoir. According to our capability to receive, so we shall receive. We shall be *filled-full* with Christ.

SECTION FOUR

Expository Notes on Paul's Appeal for Maturity

That we henceforth be no more children, tossed to and fro, and carried about with every wind of doctrine, by the sleight of men, and cunning craftiness, whereby they lie in wait to deceive; but speaking the truth in love, may grow up into him in all things, which is the head, even Christ; from whom the whole body fitly joined together, and compacted by that which every joint supplieth, according to the effectual working, in the measure of every part, making increase of the body unto the edifying of itself in love (vv. 14-16).

THEME: *Paul Urges His Children to "Grow Up"*
OUTLINE:

A. The Instability of Children
B. The Insidiousness of Critics
C. The Inimitability of Christ
D. The Indivisibility of the Church

"That we, henceforth, be no more children . . . carried about with every wind of doctrine" (v. 14a). The life in Christ begins with a new birth; it has always been recognized that young believers do not mature overnight. There has to be a growth period when every developing convert becomes a target for trouble-makers within and without the assembly. As lambs can be easy prey for predators, so young believers are endangered by the enemies of Christ.

THE INSTABILITY OF CHILDREN

The Living Bible translates the passage, "Then, we will no longer be like children changing our minds about what we believe, because someone has told us something different, or has cleverly lied to us, and made the lie sound like the truth." Throughout the entire history of the church, men of this type have troubled believers. When argumentative would-be leaders have endeavored to dominate the church, their plausible arguments have upset the equilibrium of young believers, and discord has ruined fellowship.

I remember a crusade in North Scotland. The meetings were far from what they might have been, for I was preaching in a church unsympathetic to evangelism. One night after the service, a young man came seeking guidance. His problems were very confusing, and I talked with him for two hours before the light of the gospel illumined his soul. I had great affection for that convert. When I returned twelve months later, I met this young Christian and was appalled by what I discovered. He vehemently refused to attend any of my meetings, and when I asked the reason for his attitude, he replied, "I could never go into that place again. Furthermore, I am shocked that you—with your light—would ever preach in that church. Why do you do it?" My answer was short and to the point. "I am looking for your cousins; last year, I found you; maybe others like you are waiting to hear about Christ." Scornfully he replied, "Well, go ahead, I will pray for you." I pointed to the North Sea and said, "There is a ship out there sinking with three hundred passengers. I am about to launch a life-boat to rescue them. Yet you stand on this pier, smoking your pipe and saying, 'I'll pray for you, brother.' Thank you, I do not desire your prayers, but it would help if you pulled on the oars to help the rescue attempt."

Unfortunately, that young believer had been influenced by a man whose arrogance was notorious throughout the locality. He was never wrong about anything! His eloquence had unfortunately destroyed the radiance and stability of a very attractive convert. Paul encountered such people on many occasions, and it was against their influence that he warned the converts in Asia. Lack of wisdom is synonymous with children. They need time to learn from their peers. No small child should ever tell a seasoned veteran what to do in a crisis!

THE INSIDIOUSNESS OF CRITICS

Paul never "pulled his punches." When he spoke of the people who troubled the churches, he described them as "men of deception and deceit." When the apostle addressed the elders on the beach near Ephesus, he said, "For I know this, that after my departing, shall grievous wolves enter in among you, not sparing the flock" (Acts 20:29). The early church was distressed when legalistic Pharisees insisted that compliance with the laws of Moses was essential to salvation. They taught that faith in Christ was meaningless unless the believing males submitted to the rite of circumcision. This teaching led to the first church council (see Acts 15).

To understand Paul's attitude, it is necessary to remember what he wrote concerning the authenticity of his own ministry. "But though we, or an angel from heaven, preach any other gospel unto you than that which we have preached unto you, let him be accursed." The apostle was so convinced of the reality of the vision given to him by the Lord, that anything which contradicted his message was condemned as unpardonable. Tolerance and liberalism were unknown in the ministry of Paul, and it might be beneficial if some of his characteristics were evident in the modern church. The apostle had no doctrinal "gray areas;" either men agreed with him or they disagreed; they were for him or against him. All Christians should be on guard against the corruptive influence of false doctrines.

THE INIMITABILITY OF CHRIST

"But speaking the truth in love, may grow up into him in all things, which is the head, even Christ" (v. 15a). There can be but one head to a body, and Christ alone is the Head of the Church. He is the Brain, the Energizer, the Organizer of His people. As the ark of the covenant went before Israel in their daily pilgrimage toward Canaan, as it was their guide and strength in times of peace and war, so the Savior accompanies His people into every phase of activity. He is the Center and Circumference of all effort, the Alpha and the Omega of church progress. With Him the church succeeds, without Him failure is inevitable.

"Speaking the truth" suggests integrity of purpose; to speak it in love is the guarantee of inner harmony along with the absence of malice, criticism, and evil intent. Love is always attractive, growth is desirable. Therefore, when intelligence and love are joined, the glory of the Christ becomes evident in the appearance and activity of the Christian. Growth suggests the ambition to grow up into Christ. It is an honest attempt to become pleasing to the Head of the Church.

THE INDIVISIBILITY OF THE CHURCH

"From whom [Christ] the whole body fitly joined together and compacted by that which every joint supplieth, according to the effectual working in the measure of every part, maketh increase of the body unto the edifying of itself in love" (v.16). Paul once again uses the figure of a body to impress upon his readers the essential unity of all its members. Muscles, sinews, joints, blood-vessels, nerves, limbs, veins, bones, and innumerable other features work in perfect unison when the body is "fitly joined together." Disease, age, or accident interferes with the normal functioning of a body. Healthy members exist for one purpose, to obey the head. This is the standard by which the efficiency of the Church must be judged. Each member has something to contribute to the whole; without that assistance other members may be hindered.

Dr. Eadie declares, "No member or ordinance is superfluous. The widow's mite was commended by Him who sat over against the treasury. Solomon built a temple; Joseph supplied a tomb. Mary, the mother gave birth to the Child, and the other Marys wrapped the corpse in spices. Lydia entertained the apostle, Phoebe carried an epistle of old. The princes and heroes went to the battle, and wise-hearted women did spin. While Joshua fought, Moses prayed. The snuffers and trays in the tabernacle were as necessary as the magnificent lampstand. . . . The result is that the church is built up, for love is the element of spiritual progress. That love fills the renewed nature." (Quoted from the *Pulpit Commentary, Ephesians*, vol. 20, p. 150.)

The conduct of the Christian should be a mirror in which the likeness of Christ can be seen. Paul wrote, "But that with all boldness, as always, Christ shall be magnified in my body, whether it be by life, or by death" (Phil. 1:20). Paul wished to be a magnifying glass! That idea is very suggestive. A magnifying glass does not make print any larger; neither does it make the eye stronger. The eye is able to see print more easily because the type seems to be larger. Nothing we can do will make Christ more wonderful, and probably nothing we can say will improve the eyesight of neighbors. Nevertheless, if we are what and where we should be, onlookers will be able to recognize the beauty of the Savior. They will see Him *in and through us*!

PAUL'S EXHORTATION

THEME: *Paul Urges His Readers to Be Worthy Christians*
OUTLINE:

A. A New Walk (vv. 17-19)
B. A New Wisdom (vv. 20-23)
C. A New Worthiness (v. 24)

SECTION ONE

Expository Notes on the Gentiles' Walk Without Christ

This I say therefore, and testify in the Lord, that ye henceforth walk not as other Gentiles walk, in the vanity of their mind, having the understanding darkened, being alienated from the life of God through the ignorance that is in them, because of the blindness of their heart: who being past feeling have given themselves over unto lasciviousness, to work all uncleanness with greediness (vv. 17-19).

It is worthy of attention that the apostle, having expounded the riches of God's grace, proceeded to appeal for consecration from his readers. Their increasing knowledge resulted in greater responsibility. The Savior said, "If ye *know these things*, happy are ye if ye *do them*" (John 13:17). Paul emphasized identical thoughts. The apostle had mentioned the greatness of the inheritance in Christ and explained what was meant by the riches of the grace of God. If his readers comprehended these truths, it was their duty to exemplify those facts in their conduct. The apostle John wrote, "He that saith he abideth in him ought himself also so to walk, even as he walked" (1 John 2:6).

When Paul appealed for a decisively different walk, he explained why this was necessary. There was nothing attractive nor good about the conduct of the heathen. The apostle believed that the Gentiles walked "in the vanity of their mind." The word translated "vanity" is *mataiototeeti*. It comes from *mataio* which means: "to make empty; vain; foolish; brought to folly in their thoughts." The heathens had perverted minds, and their thoughts influenced their conduct. They pleased themselves, and interference from others was fiercely resented. Christians endeavored to obey the indwelling Spirit of God; heathens controlled themselves. They had no Savior and recognized no laws except their own. The spiritual walk was expressed in holiness, gentleness, goodness, faith, mercy, and love for Christ. Gentile practices were different. Paul used some of the strongest words to describe things he desired Christians to shun.

He described the Gentiles as, "having the understanding darkened, being alienated from the life of God through the ignorance that is in them, because of the blindness of their heart" (v. 18). Some of the terms used were word-pictures. "*Porosis* denotes a hardening; a covering with a poros; a kind of stone indicating a process." (Quoted from *Vine's Expository Dictionary of Old and New Testament Words*, vol. 2, p. 194.) This word was used in the phrase "the *blindness* of their hearts." The apostle described people whose hearts had become stone; in other words, they had hearts that had become so irresponsible that "they were petrified" and without sensitivity. The *New English Bible* offers the translation, "Dead to all feeling; they have abandoned themselves to vice." Paul used another descriptive word *aselgeia*, which has been translated "lasciviousness." This was a potent word. Thayer says it means, "unbridled lust, excess, licentiousness; lasciviousness; wanton-ness; outrageousness; shamelessness; insolence." *Aselgeia* included all that was evil, and the fact that the Gentiles "had given themselves" over to such actions indicated they were undisturbed by their conduct. Paul also mentioned "uncleanness with greediness" (v. 19). The word used was *pleonexia* which meant, "avarice; a greedy desire to have more; covetousness" (Thayer). The *Englishman's Greek New Testament* translates the text, "...the working of uncleanness *with craving*." Paul's description suggests people entirely enslaved by lust; passion had become the chain by which they were bound. The heathen were unresponsive to the gospel; they had deliberately alienated themselves from virtue; "their hearts had been turned to stone." They were petrified, nothing could revive them!

Paul firmly believed that there would never be an affinity between such sinners and believers who professed faith in Christ. Therefore, he made his appeal, "This I say, therefore, and testify in the Lord, that ye henceforth walk not as other Gentiles walk." Writing to the Corinthians the apostle said, "Therefore, if any man be in Christ, he is a new creature: old things are passed away; behold, all things are become new" (2 Cor. 5:17).

SECTION TWO

Expository Notes on the Results of Christian Education

But ye have not so learned Christ; if so be that ye have heard him, and have been taught by him, as the truth is in Jesus. That ye put off concerning the former conversation the old man, which is corrupt

according to the deceitful lusts; and be renewed in the spirit of your mind (vv. 20-23).

THEME: *A New Wisdom*
OUTLINE:

A. A Great Responsibility . . . "*ye . . . have been taught by him*"
B. A Glorious Renunciation . . . "*put off . . . the old man*"
C. A Gracious Renewal . . . "*be renewed in the spirit of your mind*"

Paul emphasized the incontrovertible fact that heathenism and Christianity had nothing in common. They were diametrically opposed, and, therefore, the daily walk of the believer should be completely different from that of Gentile unbelievers. A Christian who observed heathen practices revealed that his conduct was questionable, his faith shallow, and his love for the Savior doubtful. The apostle said to his readers, "But ye have not so learned Christ." If we may express this in modern terms, he said, "You people know better than to live as heathens. You have heard the truth—the very truth as it is found in Jesus. Therefore, you should be worthy representatives of your Master."

A GREAT RESPONSIBILITY . . . "ye . . . have been taught by him"

" . . . ye have heard him, and have been taught by him" (v. 21). It is evident that the Christians in Asia had not heard Jesus preaching in Palestine. They were young in the faith and owed their conversion to the untiring efforts of Paul. Nevertheless, the apostle said that *they had heard Christ and had been taught by Him.* This meant that the Lord, through His Holy Spirit, inspired Paul's message. Unseen by mortal eyes, Christ, nevertheless, had been *in their midst.* "Now faith is the substance of things hoped for; the evidence of things not seen" (Heb. 11:1). The Lord had been their teacher; He taught the truth, but had they listened carefully? Had they understood what He said? Hence the translation offered by the Jerusalem Bible: "Now that is hardly the way you have learned from Christ, *unless you failed to hear Him properly* when you were taught the truth as it is in Jesus." Perhaps the listeners were not as attentive as they should have been; the message "went in through one ear and out through the other!" People who have never heard the truth may have an excuse for their conduct, but they who hear and understand the words of Christ are responsible for their reactions to His message. To be ignorant of God's commands, and then to sin, is deplorable. To know the will of God and disobey it, is unpardonable. The Ephesian Christians were aware of God's desires; their duty, therefore, was obvious. They were to renounce and forsake their former habits.

A GLORIOUS RENUNCIATION . . . "put off . . . the old man"

"That ye put off concerning the former conversation the old man, which is corrupt according to the deceitful lusts" (v. 22). The "putting off of the old man" called for a definite act. A man might hope aches and pains will vanish, but he cannot wear a coat and hope it will disappear! If a person wishes to remove a garment, action must implement his desire; *he must do what he decides*; no other can do it for him. The old life may trouble a Christian, but he, alone, can decide to renounce and forsake things he has learned to detest. Prayer is a waste of time if he continues to ask God to do what he himself should do.

"Then throw off your old evil nature—the *old you* that was a partner in your evil ways—rotten through and through, full of lust and sham" (The Living Bible). " . . . that leaving your former way of life, you must lay aside that old human nature, which, deluded by its lusts, is sinking toward death" (The New English Bible). Some theologians believe this to be a reference to the custom practiced at baptismal services. Prior to being baptized into the fellowship of Christ, the candidate took off his outer garment and, after immersion, put on a white robe indicative of the righteousness of Christ, which, by faith, he had just embraced.

Baptism was a representation of being buried with Christ. It was inconceivable that a Christian would make a confession of abandoning former practices, only to return to them as soon as it became possible. A dirty coat which could not be cleansed was ready for destruction. The "old man," who was corrupt in all his ways, was ready for abandonment. With strong hands and resolute purpose, the Christians were urged to seize and expel the old man, so that a new one could occupy the premises!

A GRACIOUS RENEWAL . . . "be renewed in the spirit of your mind"

"And be renewed in the spirit of your mind" (v. 23). It is interesting to know that Paul wrote identical messages to the churches at Ephesus and Colossae, and that the letters were delivered by the same courier. The apostle wrote to the Colossians, "Lie not one to another, seeing that ye have put off the old man with his deeds; and have put on the new man, which is *renewed in knowledge* after the image of him that created him" (Col. 3:9-10).

The word translated "renewed" is the Greek word *ananeousthai*. It is derived from *ananeo*. W. E. Vine has an illuminating paragraph which explains the term. "To renew, make young . . . to be renewed in the spirit of your mind. The renewal here mentioned is not that of the mind itself, in its natural powers of memory, judgment and perception, but *the spirit of the mind*, which under the controlling power of the Holy Spirit, directs its bent and energies God-ward in the enjoyment of fellowship with the Father, and with His Son, Jesus Christ, and of the fulfilment of the will of God" (*Expository Dictionary of Old and New Testament Words*, vol. 2, p. 278).

The mind is the Christian's battle-ground where fierce battles are fought. When evil thoughts are predominant and permitted to influence action and when illicit pictures are allowed to hang upon the walls of the imagination, the believer's spiritual health is in jeopardy. When Paul urged the saints to put on the helmet of salvation (Eph. 6:17), he indicated that unless the saint filled his mind with the Word of God, Satan would poison his thoughts and ruin his happiness. If evil infiltrates a person's thinking, sleepless nights follow; frustration, defeat, and guilt harass his spirit; and, finally, his soul is filled with despair. The only preventative of this tragedy is to have "a renewing of the mind." This, according to Vine's interpretation, is a thought-rejuvenation in which a mind is made *young again* by the Holy Spirit. Paul exhorted, "Let God fill your heads; let love fill your hearts, and permit the Holy Spirit to be your Mentor each moment of every day."

SECTION THREE

Expository Notes on the New Life in Christ

And that ye put on the new man, which after God is created in righteousness and true holiness (v. 24).

THEME: *A New Worthiness*
OUTLINE:

A. Something Provided . . . "*which after God is created*"
B. Something Pure . . . "*is created in righteousness*"
C. Something Proven . . . "*and true holiness*"

Evidently the "new man" was the exact opposite of the "old one," which had to be rejected and expelled. As the Christians were urged to put off the first one, they were asked to embrace and accept the replacement. The text, though short, expresses three vital features.

SOMETHING PROVIDED . . . "which after God is created"

" . . . which after God is created." Phillips' New Testament in Modern English reads, "Put on the fresh clothes of the new life which *were made by God's design for righteousness*, and the holiness which is no illusion." God was, and still is, the only Creator of this new life. He conceived the idea and, through the merit of His Son, offered it freely to all who desired to receive it. The "new man" resembled a coat which had been made at great expense and was being offered without cost. It had to be "put on" to cover what was beneath. Throughout the Scriptures, God's gifts were likened unto garments (see the homily, "Huldah . . . the Prophetess Who Pressed Suits!" p. 222). Christians were described as being "in Christ," and one of Paul's greatest ambitions was to "be found in him, not having mine own righteousness, which is of the law, but that which is through the faith of Christ, the righteousness which is of God by faith" (Phil. 3:9). God alone was the Author of eternal life, and Paul emphasized this fact throughout his ministry.

SOMETHING PURE . . . "is created in righteousness"

" . . . which after God, is created *in righteousness*." When God looked at His creation, He was pleased; it was good. When He saw the work of His Son in redemption, He beheld the best the universe had ever seen. It was not only good, it was superlatively marvelous. There was no blemish, and, consequently, what was offered to men was the ultimate in purity. Conceived in the council of the Godhead and perfected by the Prince of heaven, it was exquisitely beautiful. It was an expanding grace which expelled evil from the souls of redeemed sinners.

When I was a small child, I became aware of a strange phenomenon which had taken place near my home. Each autumn I watched the leaves gently floating to earth and realized that winter was approaching. Then I saw a strange tree which, apparently, did not wish to lose its leaves. Although the winds blew and the rain fell, the leaves clung tenaciously to the branches and remained there throughout the dreary months which followed. When spring approached, I was fascinated to see the leaves beginning to fall. A new life was slowly rising within the tree, and the grip of the old leaves was broken. Sometimes it is difficult to dethrone the "old man," who resists expulsion. The leaves of the old life seemingly cling to us; they apparently wish to stay forever. Nevertheless, when God's "spring of the year" comes and when His new life begins to permeate our being, the icy grip of winter is broken; a new warmth floods our being, and slowly but surely the dead leaves drop. That experience suggests an old tree putting on a "new man"—a new garment of beauty which is righteous, good, and satisfying.

SOMETHING PROVEN . . . "and true holiness"

" . . . *and true holiness.*" "The holiness which is no illusion" (Phillips,' The New Testament in Modern English). "In the New Testament, righteousness (*dikaiosynee*) often stands for the righteousness of those who are made right with God. It is not the usual word for holiness which appears here, *hagiosynee*, but another *hostotees* meaning 'free from contamination.' It occurs only here and in Luke 1:25" (*The Expositor's Bible Commentary*, vol. 11, p. 63). It is difficult to read about true holiness and forget that Paul also considered another type, a substitute for the true. Unfortunately, during the history of the church, many who proclaimed that they were holy were proved to be false. To be holy, people must be like Christ; a person who proclaims his own holiness is an empty barrel making a lot of noise! The purity of Christ was tested throughout His lifetime. The Lord "was in all points tempted like as we are, yet without sin" (Heb. 4:15). Paul was amazed when this wonderful reality was likened to a garment and offered by God to sinners.

PAUL'S EXPLANATION

THEME: *The Continuation of Paul's Advice to Christians*
OUTLINE:

A. The New Man's Carefulness (v. 25)
B. The New Man's Conscience (vv. 26-27)
C. The New Man's Concern (v. 28)
D. The New Man's Conversation (v. 29)
E. The New Man's Consecration (v. 30)
F. The New Man's Contentment (v. 31)
G. The New Man's Compassion (v. 32)

THE NEW MAN'S CAREFULNESS

Wherefore putting away lying, speak every man truth with his neighbor: for we are members one of another (v. 25).

Unfortunately, lying and many other forms of deception were commonplace when Paul sent his letters to the churches. The moneychangers in the temple were notorious for the way in which they ran their business. Corruption was taken for granted in Paul's generation, and deception was considered justified if it brought prosperity. Some citizens deliberately lied; others condoned evil by refusing to endorse truth. The commandment, "Thou shalt not bear false witness against thy neighbor" (Exod. 20:16) was part of an ancient ritual; it was remembered in the temple, but forgotten in the streets! When Paul urged his readers "to put off the old man," he meant that they should disgard everything associated with the old life. The fact that unbelievers told lies made it imperative that Christians should be truthful.

Any evidence of unreliability in the followers of Christ damaged their testimony. If listeners questioned the integrity of Christians, they were justified in challenging everything they uttered. Honesty was, and always must be, the hallmark of those who claim allegiance to the Savior. One moral lapse can cause irreparable damage to the cause of Christ. Elijah's ministry in Israel surpassed anything known, but when he fled from Jezebel, he lost his greatest opportunity. He would never again be able to urge people to place their trust in God; they would have laughed and replied, "Why did you not do that when Jezebel threatened you?" Elijah's work came to a premature end when God took him to heaven. A Christian has only to make one mistake, and his influence on unbelievers diminishes. Paul urged his friends to be continually reliable for only thus would they be worthy followers of the Lord Jesus.

THE NEW MAN'S CONSCIENCE

Be ye angry, and sin not: let not the sun go down on your wrath: neither give place to the devil (vv. 26-27).

This is an interesting text, but it is not easy to state exactly what Paul meant. There are varying possibilities regarding his message. There is a difference between righteous indignation and an emotional temper when an angry person utters irresponsible statements. When the Lord saw the hypocrites in the temple, He was filled with indignation and drove out the offenders, but He did not sin. When a man is confronted by unpardonable exploitation of the poor, when a person condemns actions which threaten the happiness and security of innocent people, his indignation is justified. Nevertheless, if that displeasure is permitted to poison the spirit of the protester, then he also becomes guilty; he has permitted evil to enter the temple of the Holy Spirit.

The Living Bible offers the translation, "If you are angry, don't sin by *nursing your grudge.* Don't let the sun go down with you still angry—get over it quickly; for when you are angry, you give a mighty foothold to the devil." It may be easy to extinguish a match, but if the initial flame continues to burn, it might destroy a community. Paul urged his friends to settle their differences quickly in order to preserve harmony within homes and churches.

The phrase "Neither give place to the devil" is interesting. The term "devil" is usually attributed to Satan. The word in the Greek Testament is *diabolos*, and William Barclay draws attention to the fact that it has a double meaning. Dr. Thayer agrees with that conclusion, stating that *diabolos* primarily means "prone to slander, slanderous; accusing falsely." The name was given to Satan because he was said to be "the accuser of the brethren;" that is, *he slanders people before God* (Rev. 12:10). Paul might have written, "Neither give place to the slanderer." The thought expressed is obvious. Christians were urged to speak the truth and shun lies, but, at the same time, they were not to encourage others to do what they avoided. A slanderous individual can ruin homes, churches, and even communities. As people should prevent the lighting of the match which causes a conflagration, so Christians should resist those who would destroy the fellowship of the assembly. Believers in the Savior should be watchful so that Satan will not "gain a footing" within the soul.

THE NEW MAN'S CONCERN

> **Let him that stole steal no more; but rather let him labor, working with his hands the thing which is good, that he may have to give to him that needeth (v. 28).**

This verse is a window through which it is possible to see the miracle of grace performed in the human heart. Among the impoverished people in the Middle East, thievery was a means of survival. What could not be begged had to be stolen, and this was particularly true where employment was hard to obtain. Paul was aware that many thieves had been won for Christ and, therefore, wrote to them stating that their old method of subsistence had to be shunned: "Let him that stole, steal no more." Former thieves should diligently seek employment and work hard to be able to help others with special needs. Work was never popular among thieves who were accustomed to obtaining things easily. The idea of working to help other people was foreign to the men and women of Paul's generation. Any workman who did this became an object of derision. Yet, this was to be part of the convert's testimony; it was the evidence that he was *in Christ*, that "old things had passed away and everything had become new."

I shall never forget a woman who was won for Christ in one of my services. She did not possess the best of reputations, but when she became a Christian, she was transformed into a beautiful young lady. One day she asked, "Pastor, do you have any sick or elderly ladies in your church? I cannot do much for Christ, for I work in a store all day. But when I finish in the evening, I could clean house or wash clothes for those older people." She was an example of what Paul desired for his friends.

THE NEW MAN'S CONVERSATION

Let no corrupt communication proceed out of your mouth, but that which is good to the use of edifying, that it may minister grace unto the hearers (v. 29).

It is interesting to note that the word "edifying" is used three times in this chapter (see verses 12, 16, and 29). The Greek word is *oikodomeen*, which means "the act of building; edifying; edification," that is, "the act of one who promotes another's growth in Christian wisdom, piety, holiness, and happiness" (Thayer). Paul suggested that the conversation of the Christian should contribute to the strengthening of the assembly. It is interesting to note that his threefold mention of the word seemed to suggest edification in "learning, love," and "language." The word *sapros* translated "corrupt" means, "rotten, putrid, unfit for use." Hence in general, "speech of poor quality, unfit for use."

Christians should be recognized by their speech. Any man who tells suggestive stories dishonors his Lord and disgraces his church. A believer who uses the language of his old life can hardly have "put off the old man." Every word used by the followers of Christ should arise from a dedicated soul. Writing to the Colossians, Paul stated, "Let your speech be alway with grace, seasoned with salt, that ye may know how ye ought to answer every man" (Col. 4:6). James also denounced a tongue out of control! "Even so, the tongue is a little member, and boasteth great things. Behold, how great a matter a little fire kindleth! And the tongue is a fire, a world of iniquity: so is the tongue among our members, that it defileth the whole body" (James 3:5-6).

THE NEW MAN'S CONSECRATION

And grieve not the holy Spirit of God, whereby ye are sealed unto the day of redemption (v. 30).

The Greek word translated "grieve" is *lupeite*. Thayer says it means "to make sorrowful." That infers the presence of someone capable of emotional reaction. It is impossible to grieve an inanimate object. It is possible to hurt or damage a plant or arouse the anger of an animal, but to cause remorse and intense sadness indicates a sensitive person is being hurt. Paul taught that believers in Christ were the temple of the Holy Spirit. God dwelt within the ancient tabernacle, and when the children of Israel obeyed Him, His glory appeared as a cloud and fire upon the sanctuary. The same God resides within the Christian, and when His will is obeyed, the resplendence of the Lord can be seen in the saint. Paul desired this to be a permanent feature of each of his friends. He insisted that sin could "make sorrowful" the Holy Spirit and cause unpleasant repercussions in every part of the believer's life. Consecration and contentment were to be inseparable in the church. The abiding happiness given by the Holy Spirit guaranteed His continued blessing upon the assembly and its members. If, for any reason, God was grieved, the tide of blessing would cease to flow. Paul believed that what people were *to* God superseded anything they did *for* God. Unhindered, undefiled worship should be the ultimate goal in the Christian's approach to the Almighty.

THE NEW MAN'S CONTENTMENT

Let all bitterness, and wrath, and anger, and clamor, and evil speaking, be put away from you, with all malice (v. 31).

The verse supplies a word-picture of a landlord expelling six undesirable tenants! Bitterness, wrath, anger, clamor, evil speaking, and malice were vicious people, a nucleus of agitators who could ruin a community. Bitterness is a slow-moving cancer of the mind. Wrath, anger, and clamor are the enemies of tranquillity and peace. They have no relationship with the command, "Be still, and know that I am God" (Ps. 46:10). Evil speaking and malice are constant associates. A carnal mind manufactures poison; evil speaking injects it into the veins of unsuspecting people. Restlessness succeeds composure; bias warps the mind; doubt and suspicion chill the warmth of fellowship. When Samson's foxes ran through the cornfields of Israel, they caused an inferno which destroyed the crops of impoverished farmers. When carnal people send fires of dissension through the assemblies of Christ, the work of years can be destroyed in moments, and the cause of Christ immeasurably hindered. To be content, the Christians were urged to expel these troublemakers. Paul seemed to say, "Get rid of the enemies before they cause trouble." "A fence on the top of a cliff is better than an ambulance at the bottom." "A stitch in time, saves nine."

THE NEW MAN'S COMPASSION

> **And be ye kind one to another, tenderhearted, forgiving one another, even as God for Christ's sake hath forgiven you (v. 32).**

Overflowing compassion is a refreshing rain falling upon the parched soil of human hearts. It is difficult for a starving man to refuse food from the hand of a friendly neighbor. Anger, malice, and backbiting injure people; love, kindness, and pity are the "balm of Gilead," soothing inflamed wounds. Churches filled with compassionate people are an oasis in a desert, a hospital near a battlefield, a rescue mission in the ghettos, a light in the darkness, a signpost pointing to better things!

"Even as God for Christ's sake hath forgiven you." Paul was wise in making this the standard by which Christians could measure and assess the value of their deeds. Believers have been commanded to love everybody, but a fine line of demarcation is frequently drawn between *loving* and *liking* people. Many years ago I expressed dislike for a troublesome person in my town. When a friend reminded me that I should love everybody, I replied, "I *do love* everybody, but some I *do not like*." John was probably the most affectionate leader in the early church, but he had problems with Demetrius (see 3 John, v. 9). Paul was opposed by Alexander the coppersmith (2 Tim. 4:14), and from time to time, all Christians experience difficulty in "liking" unlikeable people. It helps to remember that God loved us when we seemed to be unloveable! It is impossible to be critical of other people when we are overwhelmed with gratitude to God, who permitted enemies to become His children. Paul said, "What Christ did for you, do for others."

A SUMMARY OF THE FOURTH CHAPTER

OUTLINE:

A. The Organization of the Church (vv. 1-13)
B. The Obedience of the Christians (vv. 14-21)
C. The Obligation of the Converts (vv. 22-32)

All people who desire to become citizens of the United States of America are required to read books and attend instructional classes to be informed concerning the life about to begin. Students of architecture, medicine, construction, and other professions enroll in institutions to prepare for their future. Paul's letter to the Ephesians resembled a university, in which he was a professor. Throughout the first three chapters, he explained the profound mysteries and privileges of the life planned by God for His people. At the commencement of the fourth chapter, the students graduated, but then Paul proceeded to explain what was expected of them. At the conclusion of the chapter, he reviewed their progress, and three things became obvious.

THE ORGANIZATION OF THE CHURCH (vv. 1-13)

The Savior brought into being something new. The church had only been a concept in the mind of God. Occasionally, through His prophets, mention had been made of the project but the idea was unknown that the Almighty would create a fellowship in which all people would be equal. God had performed what had been planned, and within the church of Christ, citizens of all nations had become a unified fellowship. There was not another institution of its kind, and, therefore, to belong to God's family was a privilege of inestimable worth.

Paul indicated that the glory of the Lord's handiwork in the church was seen in a sevenfold unity: There was (1) One Structure—the church, (2) One Spirit—the Holy Spirit, (3) One Statement—the hope of the calling, (4) One Savior—the Lord Jesus Christ, (5) One Substance—the faith, (6) One Sign—baptism, and (7) One Sponsor—one God and Father. Having established the church, He installed the machinery to guarantee its functioning. He ordained chosen servants to manage His organization. Apostles, prophets, evangelists, pastors and teachers were all to occupy important positions so that the work of extending God's kingdom would be adequately supervised. Each man would play an important part in the cause of Christ, and within the structure, cooperation would be paramount. Paul explained that through this innovation, the world would hear the gospel of the grace of God.

THE OBEDIENCE OF THE CHRISTIANS (vv. 14-21)

The apostle compared the church and its members with a human body and its organs. A healthy body is served by responsive limbs. There is neither argument nor dissension; each member contributes to the whole. Thus it should be within a Christian assembly. Every member, however insignificant, has a part to play and a definite sphere of labor within which to operate. As Christians depended upon God, so He depended upon them. "We are laborers together with God" (1 Cor. 3:9).

Paul contrasted the old and new lifestyles and emphasized that Christians should never compromise with temptation. The life in Christ had nothing in common with unregenerate people. Christians should not walk as other Gentiles walked "in the vanity of their mind." The statement "But ye have not so learned Christ" indicated separate spheres of action. The converts had been "alienated from the life of God," but after learning of Christ, had been filled with the life of God. Having renounced sin, the believer had no excuse if he returned to embrace what had been condemned. Unless the Word of God cleansed the life of the Christian, his theological thoughts were only dead dogma. The life of the Christian may be governed by his thoughts; his walk before others signifies whether or not his faith is genuine.

THE OBLIGATION OF THE CONVERTS (vv. 22-32)

Christianity is more than an idea; it is a way of life! Inactive believers are in danger of religious paralysis. Limbs which are never used deteriorate and die. Therefore, Paul urged the converts in Asia to be active in self-denial and missionary endeavor. The apostle's message to his friends may be summarized under five headings: (1) Beware, (2) Be wise, (3) Be willing, (4) Be watchful, and (5) Be wonderful.

1. *Beware.* "Neither give place to the devil" (v. 27). Paul was aware

of Satan's opposition. He believed that the powers of darkness were a constant threat to the followers of Christ, and, therefore, all Christians had to be careful as they served the Savior. He urged his readers not to give Satan an opportunity to ruin their efforts. He wrote, "Let not the sun go down upon your wrath." Unless disagreements are settled quickly, molehills become mountains, grudges darken the horizons of the soul, and thoughts are defiled.

2. *Be Wise.* "Let him that stole, steal no more; but rather let him labor, working with his hands the thing which is good, *that he may have to give to him that needeth*" (v. 28). When former thieves shared their wages with impoverished people, evidence was supplied that their lives had been transformed; they were new creatures in Christ. To assist other people was an experience hitherto unknown. Jesus said, "Give and it shall be given unto you; good measure, pressed down, and shaken together, and running over, shall men give into your bosom" (Luke 6:38). God said, "For them that honor me, I will honor . . . " (1 Sam. 2:30). What is given to God cannot be lost. The Lord is no man's debtor, and as Paul indicated, the thief who labored to share his earnings with less fortunate people would discover a happiness which beggared description.
3. *Be Willing.* Paul said: "Let no corrupt communication proceed out of your mouth, but that which is good to the use of edifying, that it might minister grace unto the hearers" (v. 29). The speech of church members could either poison the minds of listeners or bring them closer to Christ. When the Lord raised the widow's son at Nain, it was said of the young man, "And he that was dead sat up and began to speak" (Luke 7:15). The testimony of that convert became a source of interest, and every family in the community had reason to praise God. Good, clean communications can uplift souls and thrill listeners, and Paul affirmed that the testimony of his friends should be wholesome, inspiring, and sanctified.
4. *Be Watchful.* "And grieve not the holy Spirit of God" (v. 30). The sensitivity of Christians should be carefully protected. Their conscience should be aligned with the indwelling Spirit of God. Anything displeasing to Him should be instantly renounced, and, thereafter, resolute action should correct mistakes and expel anything offensive. "To grieve" means to hurt, offend, or endanger a relationship. Paul stressed the importance of preventing displeasure to the Lord. Saints should be in constant harmony with the Holy Spirit. Cobwebs should never hang in a place meant to be filled with God's glory. The Bible has much to say about people who slept when they should have been watching. "Another parable put

he forth unto them, saying, The kingdom of heaven is likened unto a man which sowed good seed in his field. But while men slept, his enemy came and sowed tares among the wheat, and went his way" (Matt. 13:24-25). Joshua failed in his initial attempt to defeat the people of Ai because he took too much for granted, and unrevealed sin grieved the Captain of the Lord's host (see Josh. 5:13-15; 7:2–11).

5. *Be Wonderful.* "And be ye kind one to another, tenderhearted, forgiving one another, even as God for Christ's sake hath forgiven you" (v. 32). Paul contrasted the old and new lifestyles. Bitterness had given place to kindness; wrath and anger had been superseded by tenderness; malicious gossip had been removed by forgiveness. Old things had passed away, all things had become new. The glitter of a heathen temple was inferior to the beauty of a human heart filled with the resplendence of the Almighty.

Paul's vision reached far horizons! He had explained that God's purpose in Christ was to make "a glorious church, not having spot, or wrinkle, or any such thing, but that it should be holy and without blemish" (Eph. 5:27). He urged his readers to cooperate in the fulfillment of God's purposes. The assemblies had to be warm, attractive, understanding, and consecrated. Each church should be a lighthouse in a dark world, a beacon giving directions to those seeking a safe anchorage. If each Christian radiated loveliness, the will of the Father would be done, and the kingdom of Christ extended.

HOMILIES

Homily No. 12

FIVE HEADS . . .With but a Single Thought

It is far better to have one aim in life and to achieve an ambition, than to attempt innumerable things and miss them all! Centrality of purpose is always a commendable feature, and it is truly significant that five of the leading Bible characters excelled in this respect. When these are grouped together, we are provided with a sequence of thought which embraces the entire range of Christian experience.

"ONE THING THOU LACKEST" (Mark 10:21)

When the Lord Jesus told the rich young ruler to keep the

commandments, the earnest seeker replied, "Master, all these have I observed from my youth. Then Jesus beholding him, loved him, and said unto him, one thing thou lackest: go thy way, sell whatsoever thou hast, and give to the poor, and thou shalt have treasure in heaven: and come, take up the cross, and follow me. And he was sad at that saying, and went away grieved; for he had great possessions." This illustrious young man possessed everything except that which mattered most. His home was filled with valuables, while his soul remained poor. Life begins when individuals respond to the call of Christ and follow in the path of discipleship. No amount of money, no degree of popularity, no worldly honors can compensate for the loss of eternal treasure.

"ONE THING I KNOW" (John 9:25)

The street was filled with people; the religious leaders were protesting against the enthusiasm aroused by the latest miracle of Jesus. The people were fools swayed by every wind of doctrine! This was a storm in a teacup! "Then again called they the man that was blind, and said unto him: Give God the praise: we know that this man is a sinner. He answered and said, Whether he be a sinner or no, I know not; one thing I know, that, whereas I was blind, now I see." In contrast to the rich young ruler, this man was willing to sacrifice anything in order to follow Christ, and his unashamed testimony surely brought joy to the Savior's heart. Military leaders say that attack is often the best defense, a saying also true of spiritual warfare.

"ONE THING IS NEEDFUL" (Luke 10:42)

The charming home in Bethany had suddenly become a place of strain. The atmosphere was tense, and there seemed every likelihood of a disturbing quarrel. When twenty people were waiting for their meal, and many tasks demanded attention in the kitchen, "Mary sat at Jesus' feet, and heard his word." Martha's patience suddenly failed, and looking into the Lord's face, she said, "Dost thou not care that my sister hath left me to serve alone? bid her, therefore, that she help me. And Jesus answered . . . thou art careful and troubled about many things; but one thing is needful: and Mary hath chosen that good part, which shall not be taken away from her." Spiritual appetite is always an indication of a healthy soul. In any case, Mary would have been useless in the kitchen when her heart was in the parlor!

"ONE THING HAVE I DESIRED" (Ps. 27:4)

David's soul was a ship adrift on turbulent waters. Surging emotions played havoc with his peace of mind, and memories of moral lapses haunted him. He had reason to believe that "in his body dwelt no good thing;" he had been born in sin and shaped in iniquity; evil was ever present with him. His heart and his flesh cried out for the living God. Where could he find eternal security? Where could the yearnings of his soul be fully satisfied? When his eyes instinctively turned toward the sanctuary, he cried, "One thing have I desired of the Lord, that will I seek after; that I may dwell in the house of the Lord all the days of my life, to behold the beauty of the Lord, and to enquire in his temple." David might have been the elder brother of Mary of Bethany. They attended the same school — only he was in a higher grade. Of course, after all, he was a little older!

"ONE THING I DO" (Phil. 3:13)

It is fitting that Paul, the indomitable missionary, should provide the final link in this chain of spiritual desire. He had graduated in God's school and was determined to translate his lessons into ceaseless endeavor. He declared, "Brethren . . . this one thing I do, forgetting those things which are behind, and reaching forth unto those things which are before, I press toward the mark for the prize of the high calling of God in Christ Jesus." Paul never permitted interference with the realization of his greatest ambitions, and, ultimately, he was able to state, "I have finished my course . . . henceforth there is laid up for me a crown." To a traveler, one guiding star is better than a million comets which have no meaning. (Reprinted from the author's book, *Bible Treasures*, pp. 89-90.)

Homily No. 13

THE HOUSE OF MERCY . . . on the Jericho Road

Dear Mr. Inn-keeper,

It seems an awful shame that you should be hidden amid your surroundings. You are one of the most attractive personalities in the gospel story. Perhaps it seems a little unfortunate that you should be so closely associated with such a thrilling account, for it is your proximity to Another which rather places you in the shade. And yet, if you were anywhere else, you would be seen at a disadvantage. Did you build or buy that house on the Jericho road? Surely bravery and wisdom were united in your soul; your nearness to danger provided the opportunity for fame. We have looked at the desolate surroundings of that notorious highway between Jerusalem and Jericho and have visualized the dramatic scenes of the ambush arranged for the unwary traveler. And then quite suddenly, we saw you standing in the doorway of your famous home. You seemed a very nice fellow. What was the name of your hotel? Our eyesight is not too good at this distance, but it looks strangely like "The Sanctuary." Yes, that is a very nice name which fits admirably into the general pattern of things.

A WONDERFUL PURPOSE

Did you help the good Samaritan to carry in the unfortunate victim? We have often read how that wonderful friend "went to him, and bound up his wounds, pouring in oil and wine, and set him on his own beast, and brought him to an inn, and took care of him." Perhaps you had often witnessed such rescues and had become accustomed to these acts of grace. It would never surprise us if we heard that the good Samaritan was often found on that dangerous highway. Isn't it stupid how self-confident men ignore obvious warnings and walk calmly into trouble? Perhaps you recognized this and planned a hostel of help. It has just occurred to us to ask: Were you, by any chance, personally acquainted with the wonderful Samaritan? Were you his friend? He seemed perfectly assured that you would care for his patient and continue his work of healing.

A WONDERFUL PRIVILEGE

Isn't it strange how we sometimes overlook obvious facts? The good Samaritan would have been in difficulty had there been no inn to which he could take his convert—dear me, I'm sorry, Mr. Innkeeper; that's the trouble with evangelists, we always get our stories mixed up with our message. Now, what was I saying? Yes, I remember that your hospitable inn was "The Sanctuary" to which the poor patient was brought. There he was fed and nursed back to life. It was during his convalescent days that he found a new fellowship; there he saw love in action. Your home was like a glorious church built alongside the highway of life. It seemed providential that it should have been placed in that exact position. The good Samaritan knew its location and in the hour of need left his precious charge in your care. You helped him. My word, what a great privilege came to you that day!

A WONDERFUL PROMISE

Did you accompany this great man to the door on the morning of his departure? Were you sorry to see him leaving? Ah, but you surely knew he would return, for he said so, didn't he? What does the record say? "And on the morrow when he departed, he took out two pence, and gave them to the host, and said unto him, take care of him; and whatsoever thou spendest more, when I come again, I will repay thee." Our hearts would have been thrilled had we been present that morning. Then, Mr. Innkeeper, you went indoors and looked after that patient as if he had been your own brother. Well, he really was, wasn't he? You were pleased to notice his returning health. You shook his hand and rejoiced that you had been of service to him and his great friend. Oh, sir, what happened when the good Samaritan returned? Surely his eyes lit with pleasure when you told him about his convert—oh dear, there I go again. Never mind, you understand what I mean, don't you? Was he pleased? Did he say, "Well done, thou good and faithful servant: inasmuch as ye did it to him, ye have done it unto me?" Were you thrilled with your reward, Mr. Innkeeper. Now shall I tell you a secret? We are emulating your example, for all Christians have been placed in charge of a similar place of healing. Our Master called it "The Church." It belongs to Him, really, but we are privileged to nurse His patients. We are trying to do well, for when He returns we want to be unashamed before Him at His appearing. That's all. Goodbye, Mr. Innkeeper, and thank you very much. (Reprinted from the author's book, *Bible Treasures*, pp. 103-104.)

Homily No. 14

HULDAH . . . The Prophetess Who Pressed Suits!

A famous British clothing firm stated in their advertisement, "You can always tell a man by the way he is dressed." Some years ago, the appearance of their sandwich-board man in the streets of Glasgow caused a great deal of mirth. He patiently walked up and down the main streets proclaiming to everybody the virtue of being dressed by his employers, yet he himself was a hobo in rags. Huldah, the prophetess, was probably a very useful person to have in the royal palace. Her constant care of the royal wardrobe assured the king that his various uniforms were always ready for use. Every Christian has been presented with a similar wardrobe which demands constant attention. Huldah should be the example for every follower of Christ.

THE GARMENT OF SALVATION

"I will greatly rejoice in the Lord . . . for he hath clothed me with the garments of salvation, he hath covered me with a robe of righteousness" (Isa. 61:10). After their act of disobedience, Adam and Eve patiently made garments with which to clothe themselves, and as far as we are able to judge, they were very satisfied with their efforts. Yet, when the voice of God sounded in the garden, they fled, for they realized that in spite of their commendable efforts, they were still naked. The demoniac of Gadara furiously tore the clothing from his body, for in his unbalanced state of mind, he considered his appearance to be perfectly satisfactory. Yet when Christ expelled the indwelling demons, the man realized his great need and gladly accepted the garment which Christ offered. The most elementary gospel truth teaches that our best righteousness is as filthy rags; we are naked in the sight of God and need to be clothed with the garments of salvation.

THE GARMENT OF HOLINESS

" . . . and the holy garments for Aaron the priest, and the garments of his sons, to minister in the priest's office" (Exod. 31:10). Divine law required that he who entered within the veil to intercede on behalf of Israel should be clothed in consecrated vestments. He who would prevail in the secret place should be suitably arrayed to reveal the magnificence of his office. Thus are we introduced to the next item in the royal wardrobe. He who claims allegiance to Christ and professes His salvation, should be clothed in the garments of holiness; there is no one so disappointing as the one who fails to practice what he preaches. If the Savior is the object of our admiration, it logically follows that Christ's holiness should be our example.

THE GARMENT OF HUMILITY

" . . . be clothed with humility; for God resisteth the proud and giveth grace to the humble" (1 Peter 5:5). That the apostle Peter should give this advice to *the elders of the church* seems to suggest that if *they* needed to be humble, then the entire assembly needed the same grace. Holiness and humility are twin sisters; they belong together. There are people who advertise their holiness and at the same time strut around like peacocks. There are truly godly saints who proclaim to everybody, "I am the chief of sinners." Humility is the shy emanation of inward godliness. Spiritual pride is the evidence that one's head has outgrown one's heart, that one's holiness is but a reflection of self-esteem.

THE GARMENT OF PRAISE

". . . the garment of praise for the spirit of heaviness" (Isa. 61:3). This portion of Isaiah's prophecy was read by the Savior in the synagogue at Nazareth (Luke 4:16-22), and when He went on to say, "This day is the scripture fulfilled in your ears," He clearly demonstrated that He had come to give joy. One cannot walk with Christ and remain sad, for His message leads to happiness. At the conclusion of His ministry, the Lord said, "These things have I spoken unto you, that *your joy might be full.*" The Christian wardrobe contains a glorious selection of exquisite clothing, but this increases personal responsibility. Huldah's activities seem to say to us, "You can always tell a man by the way he is dressed!" All of this should remind us that "when we put on the new man," our continuing appearance should reflect the beauty of the Lord. (Reprinted from the author's book, *Bible Pinnacles*, pp. 55-56.)

The Fifth Chapter of Ephesians

THEME: *Paul's Continuing Advice to the Christians*
OUTLINE:

I. Pleasing God (Verses 1-2)
II. Provoking God (Verses 3-10)
III. Perceiving God (Verses 11-17)
IV. Praising God (Verses 18-21)
V. Portraying God (Verses 22-33)

PLEASING GOD

Expository Notes on Paul's Conception of the Christian Life

Be ye, therefore, followers of God, as dear children; and walk in love, as Christ also hath loved us, and hath given himself for us an offering and a sacrifice to God for a sweetsmelling savor (vv. 1-2).

These two verses belonged to the fourth chapter and provided the appeal for which earlier statements prepared readers. Some theologians believe the placing of the fifth chapter heading was a mistake; the sequence of thought would have been better preserved had the fourth chapter terminated with these verses. However, such an observation is one point of view; the apostle might have desired these words to be a launching pad for the requests to be made throughout the fifth chapter.

Paul's choice of words is thought-provoking. The usual word to describe the disciples of Christ was *matheetees*, which indicated a "pupil, student, or scholar." Such people were known as the followers of Christ because they followed their Teacher as He walked through the countryside. Ancient philosophers often adopted this procedure. Schools contained within buildings were rare. Professors walked through the fields, teaching as they went. The Savior did this almost every day of His ministry, and those who followed Him heard His parables and sermons. Consequently, they became known as the followers of Jesus. Paul used a different word in writing to the people of Asia. He wrote, "Be ye, therefore, *followers* of God, as dear children; and walk in love. . . ." *Mimeetai* means "imitators" and is closely related to *mimeomai* which, according to Thayer, means "an actor or mimic." Adam Clarke in his commentary reminds readers that the English word "mimic" was originally derived from this Greek term. A mimic is a person who listens and then endeavors to reproduce, identically, what was heard. An actor devotes his talent to reproduce a character he has studied. Paul was reminding his friends that being a Christian was infinitely more than following Christ. The students who walk with their Teacher should be replicas of their Teacher. When believers appear on the stage of life, viewers should be able to see the Lord. When Christians speak, listeners should distinctly hear the message of the Savior.

The phrase "as dear children" is a weak translation of *tekna agapeeta*—children beloved. "Agape" is the warmest and strongest word for love in the New Testament and this word was commonly used among all believers. Even their meals developed into "love feasts" when they broke bread in the presence of their risen Lord. As sons and daughters exhibit the features and characteristics of their parents, so the children of God should reveal on their countenance and in their actions the beauty of their Heavenly Father. Paul's words may be summarized under three headings: His *statement*, *standard*, and *sacrifice*. His initial appeal might be considered one of his most challenging utterances.

The apostle proceeded to set even higher standards, for he insisted the love of the Christian should be compared with the love of the Lord. The apostle John endorsed that statement when he wrote, "He that saith he abideth in him ought himself also so to walk, even as he walked" (1 John 2:6). When a believer's speech and actions are at variance, there is dissension within his soul. To believe in Christ is wonderful; to serve Him faithfully is even better; *to be like Him* is the best and highest plateau of Christian experience.

When the apostle referred to Christ as giving "himself for us an offering and a sacrifice to God for a sweetsmelling savor," he opened a window through which many things could be seen. The link with the Levitical priesthood was unmistakable; it conveyed the idea that a sacrifice offered in accordance with the command of God pleased the Almighty. The Hebrews believed that the aroma of the roasted sacrifice ascended to God and that it pleased Him to know His people were obedient. The sacrifice of Christ was of superlative importance. If the aroma of slain animals brought pleasure to Jehovah, then the sacrifice of the Lamb of God exceeded anything previously known. Upon this premise, Paul implied that the sacrificial actions of the believer would never pass unnoticed. God, who saw every sparrow falling to the ground, would see and appreciate everything His children did for Him. To please the Lord should be the continuing ambition of every Christian.

When I was in New Guinea, I mingled with stone-age people who had only recently been discovered. I watched their ancient dances, known as "sing-sings," and asked many questions concerning their indigenous faith. I have never forgotten what I was told. The natives believed the great spirit lived above their village and that he could be angry or kind to people. The people feared great storms that they believed were sent as judgments by that same spirit. To placate him and appease his anger, they killed a pig and then burnt the sacrifice. They said, "We must burn the pig, for it is the smell of the singed hair that ascends to the spirit to assure him we have truly made our offering."

I encountered a similar belief in Jordan. My guide, Abdullah, drew attention to the cottages and asked if I knew why the windows and doors were painted blue! He explained that the people believed evil spirits abode above the homes and that the color blue was a means of protection. I wondered at the time if this had any connection with the ancient Hebrews, who sprinkled the blood of sacrifices upon the doorposts and lintels of their homes. The people had inherited from antiquity the advisability of either placating or overcoming demons. Paul would have rejected such teaching but nevertheless believed that a triumphant life could be an aroma pleasing to God. (See the homily, "The True Christian . . . and How He May Be Recognized," p. 258.)

PROVOKING GOD

OUTLINE:

A. Clean Instead of Corrupt (vv. 3-5)
B. Concerned Instead of Careless (vv. 6-8)
C. Chaste Instead of Carnal (vv. 9-10)

Expository Notes on the Purity of the New Life in Christ

But fornication, and all uncleanness, or covetousness, let it not be once named among you, as becometh saints. Neither filthiness, nor foolish talking, nor jesting, which are not convenient, but rather giving of thanks (vv. 3-4).

CLEAN INSTEAD OF CORRUPT

I have walked down the mile-long marble street of ancient Ephesus and tried to recapture the atmosphere of the city familiar to Paul. Archaeological teams are now restoring some of the buildings to their former grandeur, but everywhere tourists can see evidence that the city of Asia was one of the most magnificent places in the world.

I shall never forget the guide who pointed to an ancient street sign, an inscription on the sidewalk of the main street, and, with a whimsical smile on his face, explained its message. Nearby had stood the great temple of Artemis, the virgin goddess of the chase and of the moon. The sign indicated the way to the temple and explained that the priestesses offered free prostitution to travelers. We know that the money given to those women was donated to the authorities for the maintenance of the temple. The words of Paul can only be appreciated when considered against this sordid background.

Prostitution is recognized as the oldest profession in the world, but many people frown upon its participants, believing they represent the worst in modern society. It is necessary to remember that such women were regarded highly by the citizens of Ephesus. The priestesses were not outcasts, but honored citizens willing to give themselves in the service of their goddess. The financial assistance offered to the temple won the approbation of the priests and pleased lustful men who accepted the services offered. Such prostitution was never condemned by the people of Asia, but accepted as a meritorious gesture by women who desired to support the religious life of the city.

The people to whom Paul wrote this letter had belonged to that kind of society, and their conversion to Christianity had revolutionized their conduct. The converts renounced their old way of living, and that amazed the onlookers. The unbelieving Ephesians could appreciate abstinence from excessive drinking and other forms of vice, but many found it difficult to understand why Christians condemned what was considered to be virtuous and essential. Religion was said to be the means by which the needs of humans could be satisfied. Worship of the goddess nourished the soul; the service of the priestesses satisfied the yearnings of the body. Why then should any person condemn and forsake what had always been considered necessary for worship? Nowhere is the line of demarcation more clearly seen between heathenism and Christianity than in these trenchant words of the apostle. Paul insisted that the old and new lives had nothing in common.

It is difficult to decide whether Paul mentioned different vices, or whether his three words related to one sin. Fornication (*porneia*) means illicit intercourse. It is closely related to *porneuo* which means to "prostitute one's self in the lust for another." A related word *pornee* means "a woman who sells her body for sexual uses; hence, a harlot who yields herself to defilement for the sake of gain" (Thayer).

The apostle's second word was *akathasia* which meant "the impurity of lustful, luxurious, profligate living." Was this the equivalent of *porneia* or was Paul's vision expanded to include other vices equally infamous?

The third word, covetousness (*pleonexia*) means "a greedy desire to have more; avarice." That there was a connection among all three forms of vice is evident. Man's incessant desire for increasing riches could deify wealth and make him a slave of desire.

All these features were seen daily in the city of Ephesus. Paul asserted that these sins were not even to be mentioned by the followers of the Savior. To speak of them introduced evil to the mind, and the contemplation of former vices could easily become a snare.

Continuing his denunciation of heathen practices, Paul mentioned filthiness, foolish talking, and jesting; and he emphasized that the tongue of the believer should be used to give thanks to God rather than to repeat questionable stories. The word for jesting is *eutrapelia* which means, "to turn; easily turning; nimble witted, pleasantry, humor, facetiousness," and in a bad sense, "low jesting" (Thayer). Apart from the transforming power of the grace of God, people seldom change. It is thought-provoking that professing Christians of the first century repeated stupid and sometimes questionable stories about sexual behavior. Paul considered such conversation to be unworthy of Christ and the church. The modern believer should learn from the apostle's message. When a professing Christian tells questionable stories or even laughs when another person does, he exhibits a thoughtless disregard for his influence upon unregenerate people. Compromise in such actions is deadly. Abstinence from every appearance of evil is indispensable if the convert is to become a dedicated follower of the Lord.

Expository Notes on Paul's Conclusions Concerning the Ungodly

For this we know, that no whoremonger, nor unclean person, nor covetous man, who is an idolater, hath any inheritance in the kingdom of Christ and of God (v. 5).

The apostle never compromised his message; a man was a disciple of Christ or he was a lost soul. In spite of any affiliation with a church, if a person was a sex-offender or was persistently unclean in any other form of life, he did not belong to the true Church of Christ. Paul's phraseology—"a covetous man who is an idolater"—was significant. The greedy soul who constantly grasped for increasing wealth was an idol worshiper, even if he never bowed before an image. Paul affirmed that if gaining riches was the predominant thought in a person's mind, material possessions had become his idol. The same truth might be applied in many ways. Anything which dethrones God in the souls of human beings becomes an idol. The classic example of this truth was supplied by the rich, young ruler who refused to abandon his wealth and social position to follow the Savior (see Matt. 19:21-24). Christians should beware of such enemies. Sport, ambition, companions, riches, popularity, and increasing desires for prohibited pleasure might easily endanger the spiritual health of God's children.

Paul emphasized the necessity of making a choice between righteousness and evil. Heaven was a destination to be reached; people who rejected the Lord's commandments had no inheritance in the kingdom of Christ. God's riches were immeasurable, but through His grace, it had become possible for redeemed sinners to share His wealth. Paul believed that the people who practiced evil had no part in God's provision. Professing to be wealthy, they remained eternally bankrupt. The Savior delivered an identical message when He said, "Not every one that saith unto me, Lord, Lord, shall enter into the kingdom of heaven; but he that doeth the will of my Father which is in heaven. Many will say unto me in that day, Lord, Lord, have we not prophesied in thy name, and in thy name have cast out devils? and in thy name done many wonderful works? And then will I profess unto them, I never knew you, depart from me, ye that work iniquity" (Matt. 7:21–23).

Expository Notes on Paul's Warning Against Persuasive Heretics

Let no man deceive you with vain words; for because of these things cometh the wrath of God upon the children of disobedience. Be not ye therefore partakers with them. For ye were sometimes darkness, but now are ye light in the Lord: walk as children of light (vv. 6-8).

CONCERNED INSTEAD OF CARELESS

Paul was aware of a new kind of challenge arising within the church. It came from the teachings of compromising men. When he wrote to the church in Rome, the apostle said, "What shall we say then? Shall we continue in sin, that grace may abound? God forbid. How shall we, that are dead to sin, live any longer therein?" (Rom. 6:1-2). Since there were opponents who denied that Paul was an apostle, it was to be expected they would contradict his teaching. They said that he was too rigid in his interpretations, that his doctrines were contrary to custom and common-sense. They reminded hearers that God's grace was sufficient to forgive any or all sins and emphasized that "he [God] retaineth not his anger forever, because *he delighteth in mercy*" (Mic. 7:18). They taught that since God was pleased to forgive erring people, it was permissible to commit sins to provide pleasure for the Almighty. The happiness provided for God justified the crime committed by anyone. What could be wrong with anything which made the Lord happy?

These pernicious teachings were used continuously as an excuse for immorality. William Barclay reminds us, "In his speech *Pro Caelio*, Cicero pleads, 'If there is anyone who thinks that young men should be absolutely forbidden to love courtesans, he is extremely severe. I am not able to deny the principle that he states. But he is at variance not only with the license of what our own age allows, but also with the customs and concessions of our ancestors. When indeed was this not done? When did anyone ever find fault with it? When was such permission denied? When was it when that which is now lawful was not lawful? The Greeks said that Solon was the first person to allow the introduction of prostitutes into Athens, and then the building of brothels; and with the profits of the new trade, a new temple was built to Aphrodite, the goddess of love. Nothing could show the Greek point of view better than the fact that they saw nothing wrong in building a temple to the gods with the proceeds of prostitution.'" (*The Daily Study Bible. Galatians and Ephesians*, pp. 161-162.)

The false teachers were very persuasive; their arguments undermined the faith of new converts. They said, "Since God made man, why did He place all the desire for love within the human breast? Need those yearnings to be denied? If God forbade intercourse between the sexes, why did He make such relationships possible? Could He not have made humans in a slightly different form?" Paul considered these teachers to be Satan's servants and denounced them as children of the devil.

The apostle insisted that there should never be compromise among the servants of Christ. At all times they had to be careful to avoid being ensnared by the enemy of souls. When they became careless, they would be soldiers without armor, and defeat in the battles of life would be inevitable.

Expository Notes on the Children of Light

(For the fruit of the Spirit is in all goodness and righteousness and truth;) proving what is acceptable unto the Lord (vv. 9-10).

CHASTE INSTEAD OF CARNAL

It is significant that Paul mentioned the "light" five times in verses 8 through 14 and contrasted it with the darkness seen in the teachers of heresy. They remained victims of superstition by doing "those things . . . done of them in secret" (Eph. 5:12). The Christians who received God's revelation would be known by their testimony and conduct; they would walk as children of light. The Lord would reveal His presence by producing "the fruit of the Spirit" in the lives of those who followed Him. The words "goodness, righteousness," and "truth" represented true Christianity and indicated all that was missing from alien faiths.

The practice and worship of idols did not require goodness and moral purity. Pagans were never required to be righteous. As long as they conformed to the laws of the temple, immorality was inconsequential. Purity was a word seldom if ever used. It was permissible to cheat and swindle others if the culprit contributed to the temple funds. Paul denounced these things, but his condemnation of such men aroused the anger of his enemies (see Acts 16:16-24). When he spoke about "proving what is acceptable unto the Lord," the contrast between the children of light and darkness became unmistakable. Christians were concerned with details "acceptable unto the Lord." Christ ruled their lives and dictated conduct. They were not their own! Unbelievers thought only of pleasing themselves; they did not belong to Christ. Furthermore, there was no half-way point! People either belonged to the Savior or they did not; no person was justified in becoming a mixture of both.

There is the story of a missionary who desperately needed to learn one of India's many languages. He sought the services of the greatest teacher but was refused. When he offered to pay whatever was required, the man said, "I do not wish to become a Christian." The missionary thereupon promised that if he would cooperate, Christianity would never be mentioned. The Indian calmly replied, "To teach you my language, I would have to spend many hours of every day in your presence, and no man could live with you *and not become a Christian.*"

PERCEIVING GOD

OUTLINE:

A. No Fellowship (v. 11)
B. No Fear (v. 11)
C. No Forgetting (vv. 12-14)
D. No Foolishness (vv. 15-17)

Expository Notes on the Awareness of the Children of Light

And have no fellowship with the unfruitful works of darkness, but rather reprove them. For it is a shame even to speak of those things which are done of them in secret. But all things that are reproved are made manifest by the light, for whatever doth make manifest is light. Wherefore he saith, Awake thou that sleepest, and arise from the dead, and Christ shall give thee light. See then that ye walk circumspectly, not as fools, but as wise, redeeming the time, because the days are evil. Wherefore, be ye not unwise, but understanding what the will of the Lord is (vv. 11-17).

NO FELLOWSHIP (v. 11)

The word translated "fellowship" came from a Greek root-word meaning "to come into communion or fellowship; to become a sharer; to be made a partner; to join one's self as an associate" (Thayer). It is significant that Paul was referring to "the unfruitful works of darkness" rather than to the *people who perpetrated them.* It was inevitable that Christians would come into contact with unbelievers, for every market place was a meeting place for all types of people. To avoid such daily contacts, every believer would have had to become a hermit! The apostle was speaking against any participation which his friends might have in the exploits of unscrupulous men who would do anything for gain.

The only justifiable contact Christians should have with unbelievers was that which provided an opportunity to testify about Christ. God's people were asked to be beyond reproach; they belonged to the Church—"the called-out ones." To participate in illegitimate moneymaking was defiling. To sell sacrificial necessities to heathens was to become as guilty as the idolaters. The same principle was expressed when Paul wrote to the church at Corinth, "Be ye not unequally yoked together with unbelievers: for what fellowship hath righteousness with unrighteousness? and what communion hath light with darkness? and what concord hath Christ with Belial? or what part hath he that believeth with an infidel? and what agreement hath the temple of God with idols? For ye are the temple of the living God; as God hath said, I will dwell in them, and walk in them; and I will be their God, and they shall be my people. Wherefore, come out from among them, and be ye separate, saith the Lord, and touch not the unclean thing, and I will receive you. And will be a Father unto you, and ye shall be my sons and daughters, saith the Lord Almighty" (2 Cor. 6:14-18).

NO FEAR (v. 11)

The Amplified New Testament translation of Ephesians 5:11, 12 is very interesting: "Take no part in, and have no fellowship with the fruitless deeds and enterprises of darkness, but instead [let your lives be so in contrast as to] expose and reprove, and convict them. For it is a shame even to speak of or mention the things that [such people] practice in secret." There were numerous cults and sects in the ancient world which became infamous through the ritualistic ceremonies performed in the secrecy of caves. Some writers such as Adam Clarke believe that the reference was to "the Eleusinian and Bacchalanian mysteries, which were performed in the night, and were known to be so impure and abominable, especially the latter, that the Roman senate banished them both from Rome and Italy." (Quoted from *The Bethany Parallel Commentary. Ephesians*, p. 1152.)

These often ruthless societies did not hesitate to execute those who denounced their teachings. Paul was aware of this danger, but urged his friends to be fearless in their condemnation of evil. The New Testament preachers never compromised with those secret societies. Paul never sacrificed honor for self-preservation. His faithfulness to Christ and His gospel brought him to Rome where he was ready to lay down his life for the Savior. The fear of unpleasant repercussions should never interfere with a Christian's faithfulness to Christ.

NO FORGETTING (vv. 12-14)

"Wherefore he saith, awake thou that sleepest, and arise from the dead, and Christ shall give thee light" (v. 14). This was one of the most provocative statements ever made by the apostle. It was not a quotation from any of the Old Testament writings and, therefore, some critics have suggested that Paul's memory was poor. Isaiah wrote, "Arise, shine, for thy light is come, and the glory of the Lord is risen upon thee" (Isa. 60:1). The same prophet wrote, "Thy dead men shall live, together with my dead body shall they arise. Awake and sing, ye that dwell in the dust: for thy dew is as the dew of herbs, and the earth shall cast out the dead" (Isa. 26:19). Paul was not quoting from these verses, and it became evident that since he was speaking of the revelation made possible through *the light*, he was referring to the gospel message—the divine revelation. Therefore, the "*he saith*" was indicative of the fact that since God had spoken through His Word, there was need for a general awakening. Many tasks awaited believers, and certain lessons had to be learned. People who continued to sleep remained inactive. Paul urged the saints to remember what they had heard, to accept the challenge which had been given, and to awaken from the lethargic trance into which some of them had fallen.

Some authors believe that Isaiah's words had been incorporated into a baptismal hymn used among the assemblies. They suggest that the apostle was quoting from its lines when he wrote these verses. This is speculative, but it is unlikely that Paul, filled with the Holy Spirit, would misquote the Word of God. His command to "awake . . . and arise from the dead" has been needed in every age. Soldiers who sleep on a battlefield may never awaken! Many years ago, I read a verse in an autograph album. I never forgot the message, for in those days after working hard all week long in a Welsh coal mine, I liked to stay in bed on Sunday mornings.

Get up, get up for Jesus
Ye soldiers of the Cross
A lazy Sunday morning
Means certain harm and loss.
The church bells call to worship,
In duty be not slack:
You cannot fight the good fight
By lying on your back.

NO FOOLISHNESS (vv. 15-17)

Evidently Paul believed that true wisdom was being informed as to the purpose of God in human hearts. A Christian who walked in the light was a student graduating from God's academy. Dr. G. Campbell Morgan, the illustrious British expositor, often gave an illustration about walking circumspectly. He described a beautiful flower garden surrounded by a high wall. Then he envisaged a cat walking carefully among the many pieces of broken glass embedded in the cement at the top of the wall. He would say, "That cat was surrounded by many dangers—many pieces of glass, but it never cut itself! It walked circumspectly." The followers of Christ have always been confronted by difficulties and dangers, but they who know the will of God step carefully! The old proverb which says, "Make haste slowly," offers excellent advice.

PRAISING GOD

THEME: *The Place of Music in Christian Worship*
OUTLINE:

A. The Source of Happiness (v. 18)
B. The Songs of Happiness (v. 19)
C. The Strength of Happiness (vv. 20-21)

Expository Notes on a Strange Contrast

And be not drunk with wine, wherein is excess, but be filled with the Spirit; speaking to yourselves in psalms and spiritual songs, singing and making melody in your heart to the Lord; giving thanks always for all things unto God and the Father in the name of our Lord Jesus Christ; submitting yourselves one to another in the fear of God (vv. 18-21).

Drunkenness was a familiar vice in ancient times; even Solomon issued a warning against it. "Look not thou upon the wine when it is red . . . at the last it biteth like a serpent, and stingeth like an adder" (Prov. 23:31-32). There is evidence that even in the New Testament assemblies, the temptation to drink excessively was great. Often water was unobtainable in Bible lands, but in places where grapes were plentiful, wine was inexpensive and easily obtained. When the apostles preached on the day of Pentecost, the crowds believed that the preachers' minds had been affected by excessive drinking (see Acts 2:12-15). Paul's warning against such behavior was understandable, but his next utterance was amazing.

THE SOURCE OF HAPPINESS (v. 18)

Today's English Version of the Bible offers a translation which covers every aspect of the text. "Do not get drunk with wine, which will only ruin you; instead, be filled with the Spirit." Paul went from one extreme to another. He might have said, "Be not drunk with wine, but be careful to drink moderately." That would have been a natural sequence of thought. Rather, the apostle indicated that being filled with the Holy Spirit would fill the soul with the same ecstasy evident on the day of Pentecost. A. Skevington Wood made these valuable comments: "The theological implications of 'be filled' *(plerousthe)* are crucial for a biblical doctrine of the Holy Spirit. The imperative makes it clear that this is a command for all Christians. The present tense rules out any once-for-all reception of the Spirit, but points to a continuous replenishment (literally, 'Go on being filled'). Nor does it appear that Paul is urging his readers to enter into a new experience. ('Up to now you have *not* been filled with the Spirit, but you must start to be so.') Rather he is inviting them to go on as they began. ('You have, of course, been filled with the Holy Spirit; keep on like that.') Finally, the verb is passive. ('Let yourselves be filled with the Spirit.') This is not a manufactured experience.... There may, therefore, be successive fillings of the Spirit; indeed, the Christian life should be an uninterrupted filling. What this verse will not substantiate is the claim that after becoming a Christian, a single, additional, definitive filling is essential for completion." (Quoted from *The Expositor's Bible Commentary*, vol. 11, p. 72.)

Having made his appeal to the saints in Asia, the apostle spoke of praise in Christian worship. The Holy Spirit would fill the believer's soul with great joy which could not be concealed. As the light of a new revelation shone from God's presence, so spiritual ecstasy would come from the overflowing happiness of God's people. Evidently, Paul could not appreciate miserable Christians! His best advertisement for the Savior was a radiant life. There was nothing wrong with sacred music. David had played the harp; the Tabernacle and Temple had choirs of Levites; and to sing, even in adversity, had been a triumphant testimony of the sustaining power of the Lord (see Acts 16:25).

THE SONGS OF HAPPINESS (v. 19)

"Speaking to yourselves in psalms and hymns, and spiritual songs, singing and making melody in your heart to the Lord" (v. 19). It is strange to discover churches where singing is unknown and musical instruments are forbidden. When I was a young evangelist, I was invited to speak in a church where musical instruments were never used. Frankly, I was confused by the church leaders who forbade the use of organs and pianos in the church. Yet in their homes, I saw all kinds of instruments. I questioned the policy of those adamant officials who said that anything made by human beings should never be used in worship. They sang psalms unaccompanied because they believed that David's words were inspired and given by God. Hymns were never sung.

Paul wrote about "speaking to yourselves in psalms and hymns." The word translated "speaking" was *lalountes*. It was derived from *laleo* which according to Thayer meant "to utter a voice, emit a sound, to speak, to utter articulate sounds, to use words in order to declare one's mind, and disclose one's thoughts." It was never suggested that such words could only be *spoken*! Sometimes, a thrilling anthem from a dedicated choir is more acceptable than a boring sermon! Perhaps the critics objected even in Paul's day. The apostle spoke about "psalms and hymns, and spiritual songs." He also mentioned "singing and making melody in your hearts." There have been occasions when preconceived ideas hindered the cause of God and ruined worship services. Surely, if eternity is to be filled with the songs of the redeemed, it cannot be wrong to practice on earth. Some of us need to!

THE STRENGTH OF HAPPINESS (vv. 20-21)

Enthusiastic singing can thrill souls, but it can also be a shallow emotional expression. The strength of abiding happiness is found in the bonds of love which promote worship. There is no greater discord than when the singers allow grievances among themselves. It was written of the early Christians that "they were all with one accord in one place" (Acts 2:1). When choir members fit into that pattern, their contribution to a service is immeasurable. Was that the reason why the apostle urged his friends, "Submitting yourselves one to another in the fear of God?" (Eph. 5:21). The word translated "submit" means "to subject oneself, to obey". Members of a choir listen to the instruction of their leader and are submissive with each contributing to the whole. The strength of the happiness which pervades Christian service is the bond of love uniting the hearts of God's people. When Christian workers become arrogant, selfish, and critical of others, the work of the church is hindered. John mentioned an important detail when he wrote, "If a man say, I love God, and hateth his brother, he is a liar, for he that loveth not his brother whom he hath seen, how can he love God whom he hath not seen?" (1 John 4:20).

PORTRAYING GOD

SECTION ONE

Expository Notes on Ancient and Modern Situations

Wives, submit yourselves unto your own husbands, as unto the Lord. For the husband is the head of the wife, even as Christ is the head of the church; and he is the Savior of the body. Therefore, as the church is subject unto Christ, so let the wives be to their own husbands in every thing (vv. 22-24).

THEME: *The Duties and Privileges of a Christian Wife*
OUTLINE:

A. Different Circumstances . . . *A Changed World*
B. Delightful Compulsion . . . *A Consecrated Woman*
C. Definite Consideration . . . *A Challenging Witness*

Some of the ladies who belong to militant liberation movements dislike Paul's statements. When I reminded one of them of a verse which the apostle had written, she vehemently replied, "Bah, who was Paul? He was just another man who did not know what he was talking about." That lady was not a true representative of her cause, and wiser women would never endorse her statement. When discussing the role of women in the early church, it is necessary to consider several things.

DIFFERENT CIRCUMSTANCES . . . A Changed World

It should always be remembered that Paul lived in a society completely different from that in which we live. Within the Roman empire a woman was unimportant. She had no authority in the home, and her chief duties were the preparing of food and bearing children. Men were predominant in every facet of family life and could do as they pleased. A Christian home where the husband and wife were united in loving fellowship was a concept unknown among the Romans. The elevation of ladies to a position of honor, respect, and dignity was a product of Christianity. Evidence to support this conclusion may still be seen in the non-Christian countries of the Middle East, where a woman is subservient to her husband in all things.

To appreciate and understand Paul's writings, one must remember that he was addressing those "who had been united in the Lord." The possibility exists that if he were writing to Christians of the twentieth century, he would lengthen his letter and widen the scope of his message. What would Paul say to a Christian widow confronted by the task of rearing her fatherless children? What would he say to a believing widower faced with a similar task? What would he say to an unmarried man or woman who had adopted an orphan and was endeavoring to raise the child in the nurture and admonition of the Lord? We might ask what the apostle would say to a Christian wife who suffered continual beatings from a brutal, drunken, unregenerate husband.

It is necessary to emphasize that Paul was not enunciating laws to govern marital relationships for all time. He was addressing Christian husbands and wives who desired to please the Savior. Romans and other pagan nations would not have understood what he was trying to teach. He spoke of marital relationships as being "in the Lord." His remarks were never meant to be binding upon Christian wives whose sinful husbands insisted on improper and blasphemous behavior. Modern readers must take into consideration the fact that Paul was offering advice to New Testament believers who were expected to live exemplary lives in an alien world. Christians had to be *united* in the bonds of Christian matrimony. There is reason to believe that if Paul lived in our modern world, his advice would be equally as inspired and effective in guiding troubled souls through the ever-increasing perils of distressing times.

To lift the apostle's words from their original setting and apply them to other irrelevant areas is unwise. Arrogant teachers expect unfortunate people to conform to ancient standards and to adhere to laws and requirements which Paul never mentioned. Every Christian, regardless of circumstances, should endeavor to be Christlike. It is essential when people have different opinions that they become cautious rather than critical. Men and women who are *in the Lord* quickly discover that it is easier to hear the still, small voice of the Holy Spirit than to appreciate the insistent, unsympathic demands of legalistic church officials. Paul's message was sent to Christian families and not to people who were strangers to God's grace.

DELIGHTFUL COMPULSION . . . A Consecrated Woman

"Wives, submit yourselves unto your own husbands as unto the Lord, for the husband is the head of the wife, even as Christ is the head of the church" (vv. 22-23). This was evidently not a command to all wives, in all nations, for all time. It was a direction regarding a standard of procedure to be practiced by *believing* women in every succeeding generation. If the marriage of two believers became what it was meant to be, every Christian home would have become a sanctuary in which the beauty of the Lord was reflected. This necessitated dedication by both participants, but Paul was content to speak to either party separately. The wife's reaction may be considered under three potent headings: her *vision*, *virtue*, and *value*.

1. *Her Vision.* An argumentative, interfering, provocative woman annoys her listeners and loses her friends. Christian women should never emulate her example. A woman who professes to be a follower of the Savior should revere her husband, believing him to be the Lord's representative within the home. She accepts his decisions, believing him to be the divinely appointed head of the family. Such submission does not suggest that she is to resemble a ventriloquist's doll, which only reacts to its owner's desires. A wife has much to contribute to the welfare of the family. Her cautious approach to any subject can be of superlative worth, especially if her spouse is as gentle as a bull in a china shop! Paul's advice related primarily to *attitude* rather than to *words and deeds*. To be submissive did not imply she was to resemble a muzzled ox! Mutual discussion is excellent at all times, for women are often wiser than men. A thoughtful husband is content to leave many details in the capable hands of his wife. Happy homes are built upon a foundation of mutual respect. During the New Testament era, when men's superiority was expected and practiced, dominant women were not tolerated. Within Christian assemblies they would have created tension, pain, and discord.
2. *Her Virtue.* There are few women in the world who believe their husbands are perfect, and even if they did, they would never admit it! To submit to their partners *in everything* would be exceedingly difficult. When they do so gladly and willingly, their obedience to the Lord's commandment becomes indisputable. Often, the longest way around is the shortest way home, and wives sometimes gain more by their apparent readiness to allow their husbands to have their own way! When the Christian wife submits to her husband *as unto Christ*, arguments will never be heard in the family, and tension disappears from marital relationships. To kneel in submission is often the quickest way to reach the stars! To deviate for a moment, a woman is more likely to gain what she desires when her man believes he is the "boss" of the family. Giving, we receive; surrendering, we acquire. That is an irrefutable law of life. That

action, devious as it may be, results in Christian growth. By obeying the will of God, she discovers how the Lord rewards obedience.

3. *Her Value.* Let it be admitted that if God had believed Adam could have remained self-sufficient, Eve would not have been created. A world without women would be a battlefield upon which men would die struggling for supremacy. A world of men would never know the laughter of children and the joy of being young. A masculine world would eventually become an international graveyard! Men may furnish a house, but only a woman's touch can make it a home. Males enjoy a sense of importance, but the luster of achievement is only made possible by women whose influence sometimes removes mountains.

   The value of women became evident during the Lord's ministry upon earth. Mary worshiped; Martha prepared meals; Dorcas made garments and helped impoverished neighbors. Priscilla helped her husband to instruct a young preacher named Apollos, Peter's wife's mother arose from her bed to minister to the Lord, and a devoted company of women ministered to the needs of Jesus. Paul commended Phoebe to the church in Rome by declaring, "Receive her in the Lord, as becometh saints, and that ye assist her in whatsoever business she hath need of you: for she hath been a succorer of many, and of myself also" (Rom. 16:2). A good woman is the best jewel outside of heaven, and fortunate is the husband whose wife qualifies to be among that number. Her devotedness to him is the guarantee that her obedience to God's command will continue throughout her lifetime and that her dedication will never diminish. Her attention to details will safeguard his interests. Her counsel, though sometimes rejected, will be invaluable to her husband whenever he pauses to think. When a man believes he knows everything, he has much to learn.

A DEFINITE CONSIDERATION . . . A Challenging Witness

The strength of a nation is never founded upon armaments and wealth, but upon dedicated, godly families. Solomon stated, "Righteousness exalteth a nation, but sin is a reproach to any people" (Prov. 14:34). Broken families produce embittered minds, wayward children, and a continuing threat to the prosperity of a nation. When divorce becomes prevalent and when married people hasten to dissolve their partnership for any reason, they exhibit a reckless disregard for the laws of Christ and proclaim their right to be self-directed. When professing Christians rush into divorces, they have no consideration for their testimony before unregenerate neighbors. The followers of Christ should set an example to be seen and admired by all people. Their lips and lives should be partners in evangelism; if either contradicts the other, their testimony is without value.

Unfortunately, young people hurry into unholy alliances and afterward, wonder why their marriages did not last. Paul insisted that this matter should have urgent priority in the thoughts of all Christians. Marriage was a reflection of Christ's union with His Church, and nothing should be permitted to interfere with the harmony of that relationship. To prevent such a catastrophe, every believer needed to be alert. To permit secret sin to remain within the human temple would be a prelude to disaster. If Christians expected the Lord to bless them, they should preserve the honor of His name. Throughout the Roman empire, the most effective witness for Christ was not the fiery sermons of the evangelist, but the sanctity of redeemed families, where neighbors saw Christianity in action. The followers of Jesus were living epistles seen and read of all men. Pagans could bow before idols and afterward leave unchanged. When Christians bowed before the Lord, they were never the same again, but became "new creatures in Christ."

SECTION TWO

Expository Notes on the Duties of Christian Husbands

Husbands, love your wives, even as Christ also loved the church, and gave himself for it; that he might sanctify and cleanse it with the washing of water by the word, that he might present it to himself a glorious church, not having spot or wrinkle, or any such thing; but that it should be holy and without blemish. So ought men to love their wives even as their own bodies (vv. 25-28).

THEME: *The Wandering Thoughts of Paul*
OUTLINE:

A. An Expected Virtue (v. 25)
B. An Enlarged Vision (v. 26)
C. An Eternal Victory (v. 27)

As there are always two sides to a picture, so there are two participants in every marriage. Paul, having spoken to the Christian wives, proceeded to address their husbands. Doubtless, there were men who gladly endorsed every word of the apostle's teaching. They believed that women should be subject to authority and, consequently, hardly allowed their partners to speak! It cannot be over-emphasized that Paul did not merely urge women to be in subjection to their husbands; he also commanded them to be obedient to their *Christlike husbands*. That important fact shed new light upon the wife's place within the family. A husband who expected and took everything, giving nothing in return, was a self-made deity who expected everybody to worship at his shrine.

AN EXPECTED VIRTUE

Paul said, "Husbands, love your wives, even as Christ also loved the church, and gave himself for it" (v. 25). To love is glorious; to love as did the Savior is even more wonderful. This great affection may be considered under three headings.

1. *Christ's Love Was Pure*. He was never selfish, and everything associated with His affection for the Church emanated from the heart of God. Much of what is now termed "love" may be described with less attractive words. Human emotions can be lustful and temporary. It has been said that good marriages are made in heaven, but it is very difficult to avoid the conclusion that many are arranged elsewhere. Many divorcees live to ask, "What went wrong with my marriage?" The Bible teaches that an elder should be the husband of one wife (see 1 Tim. 3:12), but when another woman is permitted to spoil that relationship, the marriage is endangered and Christ is dishonored. Paul insisted that an untainted affection based upon holiness should be the standard for all people. If the human heart is the temple of the Holy Spirit, no defilement should be permitted to remain in that sanctuary. When Nehemiah, the inspired servant of God, returned from his brief visit to Babylon, he discovered that Eliashib had permitted Tobiah to live within the temple courts. As a result of this action, the temple had to be cleansed from defilement (see Neh. 13:7-9). When Christians maintain the sanctity of their inmost beings, their conduct will be exemplary, and their love for God surpassing excellence. The Savior's love for the Church was of this quality, and according to the teaching of Paul, nothing less should be evident in the attitude of redeemed men toward their wives.
2. *Christ's Love Was Protective*. The Savior was never thoughtless! He possessed the ability to foresee the needs of His followers and made special provision whereby they could be protected from

embarrassment and danger. When Simon Peter was worried by the tax-gatherers, the Lord recognized the problem confronting His follower and sent him on a fishing expedition to obtain the necessary money (see Matt. 17:24-27). When Jesus saw the hungry crowd, He fed them. When the disciples returned from their preaching crusade, the Lord graciously led them to a resting place where they could relax (see Mark 6:31). When the storm threatened to capsize the small fishing boat, the Lord arrived in time to rescue his threatened disciples (see John 6:18-21). The Savior delighted in protecting His followers, and His great concern reflected the compassion that filled the heart of God. When Elijah needed nourishment, the Lord understood and arranged for the ravens to bring food for the prophet (see 1 Kings 17:4). When Jonah was flung into the raging sea, God arranged for a fish to catch and carry him to a beach. The Savior said that it was impossible for a sparrow to fall injured to the ground without His Father being aware of the fact. This thoughtful concern was characteristic of God's dealings with His creation. That same care was evident in the actions of Jesus, and Paul believed it should be evident in the loving attention given by husbands to their wives. When men exhibit tenderness, it is never difficult for the wife to be "subject unto her husband."

3. *Christ's Love Was Provisional.* Within modern society where expenses are great, it is often necessary for both husband and wife to find employment in order to pay their expenses. It was not always thus. Paul knew that women had their assigned tasks and that it was the husband's responsibility to provide for the needs of his family. Writing to the Thessalonians, the apostle said, "For even when we were with you, this we commanded you, that if any would not work, neither should he eat" (2 Thess. 3:10). Paul taught that to meet the need of the Church, the Savior gave all He possessed. "He loved the church *and gave himself* for it." The Lord knew that people needed to be reconciled to God, and to make that possible, He became their sacrificial Lamb. He also realized that they needed a representative—an attorney—to plead their case at the bar of divine justice, and He became their High Priest at the right hand of the Majesty on High. The Lord Jesus promised to supply the needs of His followers and thereby set an example for Christians. Paul insisted that husbands should emulate the Savior and become responsible for the needs of their families. When an adoring wife shared such loving attention, both the man and woman enjoyed the happiness of achievement. Satisfaction would replace sadness, triumph banish tension, delight outlaw disputes. Throughout the

pagan world, such homes would shine in the darkness. Heathens would see radiance emanating from Christian families and ask, "Where did such blessedness come from?" Paul's high standards remain applicable in the modern world.

AN ENLARGED VISION

"Husbands love your wives, even as Christ also loved the church, and gave himself for it; that he might sanctify and cleanse it with the washing of water by the word" (vv. 25-26). Readers are again reminded of the unmistakable and unique style of Paul's writing. His mind was filled with the glorious facts of God's revelation, and that explained why his thoughts suddenly wandered from the topic under discussion. This happened in the writing of the third chapter where he wrote, "For this cause, I, Paul, the prisoner of Jesus Christ for you Gentiles. . . ." Then, so to speak, his thoughts wandered for twelve verses before he repeated his initial statement, "for this cause." His style might be compared with a sandwich! Verses 1 and 13 could be the "bread of life" between which was the "meat of the Word." This method reappeared in the verses now under scrutiny. Paul began (v. 25) by commanding, "Husbands, love your wives." He repeated the statement in verse 28. "So ought men to love their wives as their own bodies." What the apostle wrote between those two verses was in very deed and truth the "meat" of God's bountiful provision.

AN ETERNAL VICTORY

"That he might present it to himself a glorious church" (v. 27a). In all probability this will be the greatest event in the history of the universe. When the Lord was about to die, He looked back to the earliest ages and recalled what was determined by His Father. Then, with an exultant cry of relief and joy, He exclaimed, "It is finished" (John 19:30). It must be remembered that that event was only the end of one phase of the divine plan; it led to a new beginning. Precious souls had to be won and initiated into the fellowship of the Church, and the gospel message preached to all nations.

Paul's magnificent vision spanned time to see the moment when the Lord will say again, "It is finished." The Church will be complete, the saints resplendent in their robes of righteousness, and the trials of earth only memories. From every nation redeemed souls will be present, and all thought will be centered on that indescribable event when the marriage of the Lamb fills heaven with glory. The Savior, who redeemed the Church to God "out of every kindred, and tongue, and people, and nation" (Rev. 5:9), will be ready to "present it to himself, a glorious church, not having spot, or wrinkle, or any such thing . . . without blemish" (Eph. 5:27). At that time, Christ's finished work will initiate another phase in the fulfillment of His plans. Then will commence the eternal age of the future when the Church " . . . shall see his face, and his name shall be in their foreheads. And there shall be no night there; and they need no candle, neither light of the sun; for the Lord God giveth them light; and they shall reign forever and ever" (Rev. 22:4-5). It will never again be necessary to announce, "It is finished," for what begins at the marriage of the Lamb will never end.

SECTION THREE

Expository Notes on the Amazing Love of Christ

Christ loved the church and gave himself for it. That he might sanctify and cleanse it with the washing of water by the word. That he might present it to himself a glorious church, not having spot, or wrinkle, or any such thing, but that it should be holy and without blemish (vv. 25–27).

THEME: *Additional Notes on Christ's Plan for the Church*
OUTLINE:

A. The Undeserved Compassion . . . "*Christ loved the church.*"
B. The Unique Cleansing . . . "*the washing of water by the word.*"
C. The Unprecedented Consummation . . . "*that he might present it to himself.*"

THE UNDESERVED COMPASSION . . . "Christ loved the church"

"Christ also loved the church, and gave himself for it" (v. 25). When Paul sent this letter to the believers in Asia, he referred to every aspect of church life. He mentioned relationships between families and positions of authority within the assemblies, but he repeatedly returned to the basis of his teaching. The center and circumference of

God's revelation was the Cross of Calvary, where the Lord was offered as one sacrifice of sins forever (see Heb. 10:12). The reconciliation of sinners through the death of Christ had been planned by God in eternal ages (Rev. 13:8), predicted by the prophets, and accomplished by the Lord Jesus Christ. The sacrificial death of the Son of God was the foundation upon which all the plans of God rested. Without Christ, there could be nothing of eternal value.

Paul had paused in his dictation; his amanuensis waited for the continuation of the letter; his quill was in his hand. The apostle's eyes were misty, his thoughts far away. Suddenly, with a sigh, he was speaking again. "Christ loved the church and gave himself for it," and in that one glorious statement, the apostle encompassed eternity and revealed the heart of God.

1. *It Was a Sacrificial Love.* To express it, the Lord, "Who, being in the form of God, thought it not robbery to be equal with God: [a thing to be grasped, desired, coveted] but made himself of no reputation, and took upon him the form of a servant, and was made in the likeness of men: and being found in fashion as a man, he humbled himself, and became obedient unto death, even the death of the cross . . . " (Phil. 2:6-8). Evangelical preachers delight in explaining what Christ came to embrace, but they sometimes forget to emphasize what He abandoned before He came. He had been the joy of angels, the ruler of innumerable worlds, the glory of eternity; but He left it all. He voluntarily vacated His throne of splendor to be cradled in the womb of a woman. The poet was correct when he wrote,

    Out of the ivory palaces,
    Into a world of woe:
    Only His great eternal love,
    Made my Savior go.

2. *It Was a Special Love.* Writing to the Christians in Rome, Paul explained, "For when we were yet without strength, in due time, Christ died for the ungodly. For scarcely for a righteous man will one die; yet peradventure for a good man some would even dare to die. But God commendeth his love toward us, in that, *while we were yet sinners*, Christ died for us" (Rom. 5:6-8). How is it possible to love the unlovable; to reach the unreachable? That kind of love belongs to a very special category. It is the love of God shed abroad in human hearts, which enables medical people to care for lepers in missionary hospitals and charming young ladies to abandon the joys of their homeland to help impoverished people in the

swamps and villages of undeveloped countries. It is wonderful to remember that Christ loved the Church, but it is even more thrilling to know that He cared for guilty sinners even before they qualified to become members of the family of God.

3. *It Was a Satisfying Love.* Could language express the happiness of the Lord when He saw gratitude shining in the eyes of a cleansed leper? Could orators describe the ecstasy in the Lord's soul when He saw the adoration of a parent clutching the child whom Jesus had delivered from disease and death? Would it be possible to measure the Lord's joy when a little child smiled into His face? People who know how to give are certain to receive "good measure, shaken together, pressed down, and running over" (Luke 6:38). That unchanging truth applied to the Savior and to all who emulated His example. It is always better to have an open hand than a fist. God made hands; unfortunately, fists are made by people.

THE UNIQUE CLEANSING . . . "the washing of water by the word"

1. *Something Contaminated.* Paul never compromised his message nor changed his style of preaching the Word of God. He saw people as sinners whose lives were contaminated by evil. Even though they were intellectually enlighted and socially reformed, they needed to be cleansed from their sin. Once, during a visit to Athens, he apparently deviated from his usual method of presenting the truth in order to reason with the philosophers on Mars Hill. Unfortunately, that appeared to be the only city in which he did not establish a church. His subsequent journey to Corinth provided time for reflection, and when he arrived at his new destination, he had made an important resolve. Later, he wrote to the Corinthians saying, "And I, brethren, when I came to you, came not with excellency of speech or of wisdom, declaring unto you the testimony of God. For I determined not to know anything among you, save Jesus Christ and him crucified" (1 Cor. 2:1-2). The apostle believed that men and women were lost sinners and that before they could become members of the true Church of God, they needed to be forgiven and cleansed of their contamination.

2. *Something Cleansed.* The New Testament described two types of cleansing. First, there was the cleansing supplied through the precious blood of Christ. That took place when a repentant sinner surrendered himself to the Savior and appropriated by faith what was accomplished on his behalf by the sacrificial death of the

Lamb of God. John explained, "But if we walk in the light, as he is in the light, we have fellowship one with another, and the blood of Jesus Christ, his Son [continues to cleanse] us from all sin" (1 John 1:7). That divine process transformed sinners into saints.

Secondly, there was the cleansing which came through the reception of the Word of God. It was "the washing of water by the word." The Lord said to His disciples, "Now ye are clean through the word which I have spoken unto you" (John 15:3). Some teachers believe that the mention of cleansing by water was a reference to baptism and that without conformity to that ordinance, salvation could never be obtained. If outward baptism were necessary for salvation, the thief and many other repentant sinners would be excluded from the kingdom of God. Baptism was an ordinance by which redeemed souls confessed their faith in Christ. The cleansing obtained by being *immersed in God's Word* was, and ever will be, the means by which saints become sanctified. As water flowing through a pipe inevitably cleans the inside of the pipe, so the Word of Truth flowing through the souls of men and women removes imperfections and maintains the standards of purity required by God.

3. *Something Consecrated.* Doubtless, all the vessels used in the temple were first washed and then dedicated and used only for God's service. Those vessels became the exclusive property of the Almighty. Paul evidently believed that our salvation would cause the ultimate in dedication, and for that reason he wrote, "What? know ye not that your body is the temple of the Holy Ghost which is in you, which ye have of God, and ye are not your own? For ye are bought with a price; therefore, glorify God in your body, and in your spirit, which are God's" (1 Cor. 6:19-20). Many people who never read the Word of God depend upon ministers and others for information regarding the Lord's desires. When the informant fails to do his duty, the future of the believer is in jeopardy. It is difficult for any Christian to attain to standards of moral and spiritual excellence when the Bible is neglected. If the Lord paid such a high price that the Church should be separated and sanctified, believers should never be satisfied with anything but the best service they can give to Christ.

THE UNPRECEDENTED CONSUMMATION . . . "that he might present it to himself"

"That he might present it to himself a glorious church, not having spot, or wrinkle, or any such thing; but that it should be holy and without blemish" (v. 27). When Paul uttered those memorable words, his vision swept beyond the barriers of time to embrace eternity. He saw clearly the day when, clothed in resplendent robes of righteousness, the Church, the Bride of Christ, would be eternally joined to the divine Bridegroom. Then, eternity would echo the praise of innumerable people who will sing a new song, "Thou wast slain, and hast redeemed us to God by thy blood out of every kindred, and tongue, and people, and nation" (Rev. 5:9). That scene of eternal magnificence almost defies description; it will be the most scintillating event in the history of the universe. By His infinite grace and power, the Lord will have gathered His people from remote jungle villages and crowded cities; from east, west, north, and south; from palaces and hovels; from people of all races, colors, and backgrounds. He will then make them into one precious entity as a bride, a companion, an increasing joy for Himself. "And they shall see his face, and his name shall be in their foreheads. And there shall be no night there; and they need no candle, neither light of the sun; for the Lord God giveth them light; and they shall reign forever and ever" (Rev. 22:4-5).

Suddenly, having permitted his thoughts to roam through time to the eternal ages, Paul returned to the theme with which he began his discourse. He said, "So ought men to love their wives as their own bodies" (v. 28). The apostle concluded his remarks by suggesting that if the Lord devoted so much time and energy to the welfare of His bride, husbands should never cease promoting the happiness of their spouses. This would be an infallible way of helping them to "submit in all things."

SECTION FOUR

Expository Notes on Self-preservation

He that loveth his wife loveth himself. For no man ever yet hated his own flesh; but nourisheth and cherisheth it, even as the Lord the church: for ye are members of his body, of his flesh, and of his bones. For this cause shall a man leave his father and mother, and shall be joined unto his wife, and they two shall be one flesh. This is a great mystery: but I speak concerning Christ and his church. Nevertheless let every one of you in particular so love his wife, even as himself; and the wife see that she reverence her husband (vv. 28-33).

THEME: *Paul's Summary of Marital Relationships*
OUTLINE:

A. An Inherent Desire (v. 29)
B. An Immense Declaration (v. 30)
C. An Important Departure (v. 31)
D. An Inspired Doctrine (v. 32)
E. An Individual Decision (v. 33)

AN INHERENT DESIRE

"For no man ever yet hateth his own flesh" (v. 29a).

At first glance it may appear that this conclusion is false; it is therefore necessary to understand what the apostle was attempting to explain. Cripples may detest their deformity, and overweight people may dislike their excess weight. Within the spiritual realm, defeated Christians may hate their flesh life and detest the consequences of striving against temptation. From some angles, many people may hate their flesh, an situation that Paul was not endeavoring to teach. Only mentally deranged people or unfortunate folk overwhelmed by circumstances or depression contemplate suicide. Healthy men and women value their bodies, for without them life would be impossible. When sickness threatens, such people seek the aid of doctors so that physical disaster may be avoided. Paul believed that life was precious and that every care should be taken to preserve it. The apostle applied the same truth to the body of Christ and affirmed that the Lord exercised the same loving care toward His followers. The health of the Church was of primary concern to the Savior, and, therefore, every Christian should share His concern to preserve the unity, health, and happiness of the assembly. No hand ever fought with a foot, and no knee ever became jealous of an ear. Similarly, no believer should ever be antagonistic toward another member of the body of Christ. All should be united by the bonds of Christ's redeeming love.

AN IMMENSE DECLARATION

Expository Notes on the Body of Christ

"For we are the members of his body; of his flesh, and of his bones" (v. 30).

This was one of the most profound statements ever made by the apostle. His triple message concerning the body, flesh, and bones of

Christ emphasized the dependence of the Lord and His Church, either one on the other. As the vine was dependent upon the branch to bear fruit, so the branch depended on the vine for support, sustenance, and security; either one without the other was helpless. It was easy to understand how believers relied upon the Lord, but difficult to appreciate His need for Christians. In some strange but wonderful way, Christ needs His Body. Alone and without dedicated followers to do His will, His dreams would never be realized.

Paul's conception of the divine revelation is startling. The body, flesh, and bones were all necessary if a person were to function satisfactorily. A body without bones would collapse. Bones without flesh would be a skeleton, and both bones and flesh would be abhorrent if they were not united in a healthy body. All were meant for each other. Paul declared that this was true within the body of Christ. The Lord and His people needed each other. Together they functioned successfully—apart they were helpless.

AN IMPORTANT DEPARTURE

Expository Notes on Total Commitment

"For this cause shall a man leave his father and mother, and shall be joined unto his wife, and they two shall be one flesh" (v. 31).

Sometimes economic pressure or domestic circumstances necessitate that newlyweds reside with their parents, but that procedure is basically not advisable. Each woman needs her own home, and since each one has her own ideas concerning procedure within the family, it is better for a young wife to be queen within her own castle, even if she has to learn by making mistakes. It is often necessary for a son to continue helping his parents, particularly if they are sick or elderly, but if a mother attempts to retain her place of superiority in the life of her married son, trouble becomes inevitable. God declared that the unity of a man and his wife must be maintained at any cost. Marriage is the commencement of a new life, and nothing should be permitted to interfere with the growth and independence of newly-married couples.

The same principles applied to Christ and His Church. When believers were joined to the Lord in spiritual matrimony, they pledged allegiance to Him and vowed to be faithful eternally. No earthly ties or former associations should interfere with that spiritual union. When a man forsakes his wife to live with another woman, he is not a good example of the faith he formerly embraced. When a Christian such as Demas (see 2 Tim. 4:10), becomes enamored by worldly attractions and proceeds to flirt with an alien world, it becomes evident he has gazed too long at transient things and too little at the altogether lovely One (see Song of Sol. 5:16).

AN INSPIRED DOCTRINE

Expository Notes on a Great Mystery

> **"This is a great mystery, but I speak concerning Christ and the church" (v. 32).**

Paul used the word *mystery* frequently throughout his letter (see 1:9; 3:3; 3:4; 3:9; and 5:32). He was proud that what had remained a secret from eternal ages had been revealed to him (3:9). The Hebrew people considered it to be inconceivable that the Gentiles should be allowed to share any of the blessings of the Almighty, but the apostle insisted that "the middle wall of partition" had been broken down (2:14), thus allowing those who were afar off to draw near unto God (2:18-19). The idea that Jehovah was exclusively the God of Israel had been replaced with a better concept. Christ had become the Head of the Church and was destined to become the heavenly Bridegroom to be wed to an international bride! The magnitude of this truth and the unfolding of this entrancing theme were sensational, and even Paul was amazed that outlawed Gentiles had been incorporated into the body of Christ. His exegesis concerning the body and its functions was only a method of communicating truth, and when he had expressed all that was on his mind, he sighed and seemed to say, "I know some of you might be amazed and confounded by my words. This is a great mystery, but I speak concerning Christ and the church."

AN INDIVIDUAL DECISION

Expository Notes on Paul's Final Appeal to Married Christians

> **"Nevertheless, let every one of you in particular so love his wife even as himself, and the wife see that she reverence her husband" (v. 33).**

When the courier, Tychicus, carried Paul's letters to the churches in Asia, it was to be expected that the apostle's advice would be repeated in all the assemblies. For example, he wrote to the Colossians, "Husbands love your wives, *and be not bitter against them*" (Col. 3:19). Tychicus, who was entrusted with the epistles, read those messages in all the churches on his route. Paul appeared to say, "Even if you do not understand the mystery of this new revelation, at least you will understand what I am saying concerning marriage. Let everyone of you love his wife. You do not need a theological training to understand that command. *Love your wives* and do not be bitter against them."

Sometimes, inadvertently or otherwise, things are said and done within families which are regrettable. Words spoken in anger are never sincere indications of what exists in the soul. Yet words that appear to be sharper than knives may cause, in moments, wounds that take a long time to heal. Molehills become mountains, grudges become festering sores, and marital bliss is shattered. It was this realization which made Paul write, "Let not the sun go down upon your wrath. Neither give place to the devil" (Eph. 4:26-27). The apostle seemed to say, "Do not give Satan an inch, for he might take a mile!" Furthermore, since Paul had written to married people, he concluded, "And the wife see that she reverence her husband." Peter emphasized the same truth as follows: "Likewise ye wives, be in subjection to your own husbands; that, if any obey not the word, they also may, without the word, be won by the conversation of the wives. . . . Likewise, ye husbands, dwell with them according to knowledge, giving honor unto the wife, as unto the weaker vessel, and as being heirs together of the grace of life; that your prayers be not hindered" (1 Peter 3:1,7). A loving Christian family is a showpiece in God's beautiful garden.

A SUMMARY OF THE FIFTH CHAPTER

Some of the greatest Roman emperors were the fiercest persecutors of the Christians. They believed that the new religion would anger the gods and bring judgments upon the empire. Christians were different; they refused to worship idols and would not offer sacrifices to them. They never conformed to heathen customs and would not compromise the teaching of Jesus. Under pressure, they would not obey their rulers and in extreme circumstances, preferred death with honor rather than accept a life of shame. They were burned at the stake in Caesar's gardens, fed to ravenous beasts, executed in the arena, and even skinned alive. Yet, they would neither recant their testimony nor renounce their faith in the Savior. They endured persecution and were tortured unmercifully, but they died with a song on their lips. Those believers were different from all other people.

THE CHRISTIAN'S HOLINESS (vv. 1-7)

Continuing his message in the fourth chapter of the Epistle, Paul set out to reveal, not what a Christian believed or knew, but *what he was*. Faith in the Lord Jesus had revolutionized his life and conduct; he had become one of the "called out" people. Every detail of his life suggested that "old things had passed away; all things [everything] are become new (see 2 Cor. 5:17). At the beginning of the fifth chapter, Paul explained why Christians were different in their *walk*, *witness*, and *worship*.

1. The Christians no longer walked as did unconverted people; their former delights had been renounced; the attraction of a sinful life had been abandoned. As children of light, believers walked in the light (v. 8).
2. The believer's testimony was unique in that it was consistently different from any other message. He did not waste time on senseless chatter (vv. 5, 6) or participate in sensual conversations. He redeemed the time and was a light shining in the darkness, for he lived among sinful people whose conduct was despicable (v. 12). The Christian emulated the Lord's example by living an exemplary life, thus endeavoring to be a child of God.
3. The Christian's method of worship confused heathens. Idolators worshiped man-made idols which could be seen, while the followers of Jesus worshiped an invisible God. The Romans and Athenians had many gods, while the Christians had one. The pagans tried to placate their idols by offering food and other gifts; the followers of Jesus endeavored to be like Him. The idols had never lived; the Savior would never die again.

THE CHRISTIAN'S HAPPINESS (vv. 18-21)

The Christians were known for their radiance; they sang even when ravenous beasts were about to tear them limb from limb. Perhaps they learned this from the Lord, who, on the eve of His crucifixion, sang with His disciples. His followers were desolate; premonitions of the end had devastated their serenity. Yet, Jesus, after He had celebrated the Passover and instituted the new feast, sang a hymn (see Matt. 26:30). His anthem preceded his agony. The Lord and His friends knew where they were going. In contrast, the Sadducees, who did not believe in a life beyond the grave, faced eternity with fear, dread, and gloom. Someone has said that such unbelief explained their name. They were "sad-u-cees"! If that were the case, the Christians should have been called "glad-u-cees"! Their radiant faces banished doubts. They believed that each day's journey took them closer to their eternal home. They sang in their meetings, homes, and hearts (see 5:19). Men who were drunk with wine often sang popular melodies. The followers of Christ, who were filled with the new wine of the Holy Spirit, expressed in song the happiness which thrilled their souls. Had they not done so, maybe the stones would have protested (see Luke 19:40).

THE CHRISTIAN'S HOPE (vv. 25-27)

John wrote, "Beloved, now are we the sons of God, and it doth not yet appear what we shall be, but we know that when he shall appear, we shall be like him; for we shall see him as he is" (1 John 3:2). Writing to the Colossians, Paul explained that the purpose of Christ was "to present you holy and unblameable and unreprovable in his sight" (Col. 1:22). The same glorious anticipation was evident in this section of the Ephesian Epistle. "That he might present it to himself, a glorious church, not having spot, or wrinkle, or any such thing; but that it should be holy and without blemish" (Eph. 5:27). The apostle John described the final details of this remarkable transformation when he wrote, "Let us be glad and rejoice, and give honor to him, for the marriage of the Lamb is come, and his wife hath made herself ready. And to her was granted that she should be arrayed in fine linen, clean and white: for the fine linen is the righteousness of saints" (Rev. 19:7-8). Paul had already explained to his readers that they had been quickened, that is, raised from the dead and made to sit with Him in the heavenly places. That was only the foreshadowing of the great day when the Church would be enthroned with the Bridegroom. This was the inspiration of every Christian enterprise and the thrill of every redeemed soul. Paul would have appreciated the poet's words:

> And, Lord, haste the day
> When my faith shall be sight
> The clouds be rolled back as a scroll.
> The trump shall resound,
> And the Lord shall descend,
> Even so; it is well with my soul.

THE CHRISTIAN'S HOME (vv. 28-33)

There were many religious homes in Israel, but perhaps the first Christian home belonged to the parents of John Mark. It was there the followers of Christ held their meetings (Acts 12:12). When the number of disciples increased and congregations could no longer be accommodated in houses, the church held services in that part of the temple known as Solomon's Porch. Then, as years passed and persecution drove the Christians from Jerusalem, it became necessary to meet wherever possible. Homes became sanctuaries where each meal became a love-feast and where the Lord was remembered in the breaking of the bread. Paul wrote to the Christians in Rome, "Greet Priscilla and Aquila, my helpers in Christ Jesus, who have for my life laid down their own necks; unto whom, not only I give thanks, but also the churches of the Gentiles. Likewise, *greet the church that is in their house*" (Rom. 16:3-5 and see Acts 20:7-11). Christian homes became a very important part of the expanding church. They were oases in a desert, sanctuaries on crowded thoroughfares. Neighbors knew of their existence, and all eyes were focused on the behavior of their owners. A Christian homestead became a lighthouse from which the gospel shone into the surrounding darkness. Paul believed that it was imperative that conduct in such homes be above reproach.

The advice given to the Christian families was invaluable. Both husband and wife were to reflect the beauty of the Savior; both should be devoted to each other. The man had to give thoughtful, loving care to his spouse, and in return she was required to be appreciative, respectful, and helpful. God and the neighbors expected the houses of Christians to be havens of rest for the weary. The apostle's message remains applicable today. Christians should be different from all other people, and this should be evident in their *holiness*, *happiness*, *hope*, and especially in their *homes*.

HOMILY

Study No. 15

THE TRUE CHRISTIAN . . . and How He May Be Recognized

I shall always remember the young woman in Wales who asked if I would answer a question. She prefaced her remarks with the statement that students in the University at Cardiff had been debating it every lunch hour for three weeks, and no answer had been forthcoming.

"Sir," she said, "What is a Christian?" Her expression suggested that she sought an argument and not information. During the moments which followed, Paul's words seemed to supply me with what was needed. He had described four word-pictures in the Epistle to the Ephesians which related to her problem.

A STUDENT . . . Decision (Mark 1:16-20)

Paul in Ephesians 5:1 said, "Be ye, therefore, followers of God, as dear children." The word suggested a student following a teacher walking along a country road. Originally there were few schools as we know them; philosophers strolled in the fields and streets, and all who wished to learn walked behind, gleaning words of wisdom as they fell from the teacher's lips. The Savior adopted the same method; He walked the dusty highways of Palestine, teaching as He went. The Greek word for disciples was *matheetees*, which meant a "learner, follower," or a "disciple." When the earliest followers of Christ left their occupations to become itinerant preachers, they indicated that (1) they believed Jesus had knowledge they needed to acquire, and that (2) they were anxious to stay near to Him so that whatever He said they would hear and hopefully remember. The same truths are evident with all who profess to become Christians.

A SLAVE . . . Devotion (Exod. 21:5-6)

"Be ye, therefore, followers of God, as dear children; and walk in love. . . . Not with eyeservice, as men-pleasers; but as the slaves of Christ . . . " (Eph. 5:1 and 6:6). The word translated "slaves" is *doulos*, which means "a bondslave." A bondslave was one who preferred to remain in the service of his master rather than to be liberated as a freeman. When the year of liberation arrived, all slaves were automatically released, but when a slave preferred to remain, he was required to stand at the door of his house, where the master would pierce his ear as a sign that, of his own volition, he had requested to stay. During years of service, such a slave obviously came to respect and love his master. Necessity made him a slave, but love made him a bondslave. This is probably the most obvious evidence in the growth of a Christian. He loves the Lord to such a degree that nothing in existence could compensate for his loss of joy should their fellowship cease.

A SOLDIER . . . Discipline (Eph. 6:10-18)

"Finally, my brethren . . . . Put on the whole armor of God, that ye may be able to stand against the wiles of the devil." One of the Bible's greatest illustrations of this truth is found in Genesis 14:14. When Lot was taken captive by heathen kings, Abraham took 318 bondslaves and went to rescue his nephew. It may be safely assumed that he had no fear of betrayal from his soldiers; they were trained in his own house—they were bondslaves. Paul spoke about another great battle—the conflict against the powers of darkness—and urged his readers to put on the whole armor of God. Taking his illustration from the uniform and weapons of Roman soldiers, he proceeded to mention protection for every part of the body, *except the back*! Probably Caesar believed that if his soldiers ever ran from danger, they deserved to die! Each man had a covering for his loins, his chest, his feet, and his head. A sword was to be in his hand, and thus prepared, either the Roman or the Christian was ready for battle. The followers of Christ were never promised an easy road to heaven. Life was a battlefield, and the Lord depended upon trusted bondslaves to win conflicts against evil.

A STATESMAN . . . Dignity (Eph. 6:20)

Paul asked the Ephesians to pray earnestly for him, when writing, "I am an ambassador in bonds." Political leaders are never chosen from among the inhabitants of skid row. More often than not, the finest graduates of the university are chosen for such high honors. They are to become the representatives of their country in a foreign land. An ambassador remembers he represents his homeland and acts accordingly. Paul was conscious of the fact that his citizenship was in heaven. His attitude, conduct, and speech always testified to that fact. He was God's representative in an alien world, and even his enemies should be able to see the evidence of his high calling. Paul was a man apart! He was certainly a true Christian, and all who would covet his success should emulate his example by becoming (1) a student of Christ, (2) a bondslave of Christ, (3) a soldier willing to live and die for his cause, and (4) one who would walk worthy of his high calling. These are the hallmarks of a true Christian. (Homily reprinted from the author's book, *Bible Gems*, pp. 105-106.)

The Sixth Chapter of Ephesians

THEME: *Paul's Final Exhortation to His Readers*
OUTLINE:

I. Christ in the Family (Verses 1-9)
II. Conquest in the Fight (Verses 10-20)
III. Concern in the Fellowship (Verses 21-24)

CHRIST IN THE FAMILY

SECTION ONE

Expository Notes on the Responsibility of Parents and Their Children

Children, obey your parents in the Lord: for this is right. Honor thy father and mother; which is the first commandment with promise; that it may be well with thee, and thou mayest live long on the earth. And, ye fathers provoke not your children to wrath; but bring them up in the nurture and admonition of the Lord (vv. 1-4).

Evidently, the opening verses of this message were the continuation of the preceding chapter. Paul believed in the sanctity of the home, and here he explained in detail the relationship which should exist between husbands and wives, children and parents, slaves and their masters. Although slavery is no longer legal among most of the nations of the earth, the principles enunciated by the apostle are still valid, and all people should accept the advice given by God's honored servant. The apostle explained in the preceding chapter the sanctity with which men and women should observe their matrimonial vows. Christian matrimony should be a mirror reflecting the union between Christ and His Church. For some inscrutable reason the compilers of the New Testament decided to place the chapter heading where it is, but Paul had much more to say regarding the Christian home. Children were the natural result of marriage. The birth of a baby increased the happiness of the parents, and the subsequent growth of the child became their responsibility. Apparently, the modern problem of teen-age behavior was also prevalent among the families of first-century Christians.

It might be significant that Paul first addressed his remarks to the children. It was not unusual for growing boys and girls to believe they knew everything! Only age and experience can blunt the edge of an inflated ego. Obedience is the first requirement in Christian development, and nothing should destroy the reverence with which the child views his parent. Maturing wisdom promotes understanding and fellowship. The relationship between the parent and child must always reflect the union between God and His children. As the Heavenly Father expects and deserves obedience from His family, human fathers are justified in expecting the same from their offspring. Paul wrote, "Children obey your parents in the Lord for this is right." It is important to consider the phrase "*in the Lord*." The child who honors and obeys his Christian father will himself become a trustworthy parent. The boy who adores his mother will probably become an ideal husband.

When Christian sons and daughters belong to unregenerate families, problems are inevitable. Children can hardly obey their parents if, by so doing, they violate their consciences. When a choice must be made, obedience to God should supersede subservience to non-Christian parents. This should not lead to defiant rebellion, but to a calm, humble explanation of Christian allegiance. A child who arrogantly defies his annoyed parent has no chance of winning his family. A son who wisely explains that to do anything sinful promotes unhappiness might succeed in influencing his unenlightened father. When children are Christlike, even annoying parents will ultimately desire to discover the secret of their continuing happiness. There may be exceptions to this rule, for the Savior said, "Think not that I am come to send peace on earth: I came not to send peace, but a sword. For I am come to set a man at variance against his father, and the daughter against her mother, and the daughter-in-law against her mother-in-law. And a man's foes shall be they of his own household" (Matt. 10:34-36). Nevertheless, the dedicated children in every family will reverence their parents, and to the best of their ability, they will emulate the example of Jesus of whom it was written, "And he went down with them, and came to Nazareth, and was subject unto them: but his mother kept all these sayings in her heart. And Jesus increased in wisdom and stature, and in favor with God and man" (Luke 2:51-52).

Continuing his message, Paul explained why the obedience of Christian children was self-rewarding. He wrote, "Honor thy father and mother; which is the first commandment *with promise*" (see Exod. 20:12). It was significant to Paul that all the preceding commandments were mandatory and binding upon every Hebrew.

The commandment relating to obedience was productive insomuch that it promised longevity to obedient sons and daughters. If evidence were needed to prove the veracity of God's promise, the behavior of modern youth would supply it. Young people who respect and honor the wishes of their parents do not get drunk or drive their automobiles at illegal speed thus jeopardizing their lives in an accident. Grateful, adoring children refrain from taking drugs and do not ruin their health or commit suicide. Respect for the wishes of Christian parents promotes sobriety, care, and self-control and finds fellowship in the company of like-minded people. Many young folk who die prematurely have only themselves to blame. The story of the prodigal son taught the principle that unwise behavior and undesirable company are found on highways which lead to shame and a pigpen! To live long a man needs to live right! To forget God and disgrace one's parents is an easy way of self-destruction.

No mention was ever made of Paul's children; many teachers believe he was either a widower without children or a man who had never married (see 1 Cor. 7:8). Nevertheless, it was certain that Paul was aware of the difficulties of raising a family, for he had stayed in many homes and was the confidant of innumerable parents. To render a balanced judgment, Paul offered advice to fathers. They were not to take unfair advantage of their respectful children or, in times of annoyance and passion, to "provoke the children to wrath." Mutual respect should be the unbreakable bond uniting families. The father's experience should be the unquestioned guidance by which developing adolescents should reach maturity. Discord, quarrels, and troublemakers should be regarded as unwelcome visitors in Christian households. Devoted families should exhibit peace, not passion. Neighbors would then recognize the excellence which results from knowing and loving the Savior.

SECTION TWO

Expository Notes on the Relationship Between Masters and Slaves

Servants, be obedient to them that are your masters according to the flesh, with fear and trembling, in singleness of your heart, as unto Christ. Not with eyeservice, as men-pleasers; but as the servants of Christ, doing the will of God from the heart. With goodwill doing service, as to the Lord and not to men: knowing that whatsoever good thing any man doeth, the same shall he receive of the Lord, whether

he be bond or free. And, ye masters, do the same things unto them, forbearing threatening: knowing that your Master also is in heaven; neither is there respect of persons with him (vv. 5-9).

It must be remembered that these words were written when slavery was legal. Men were permitted to own other people, and for a variety of reasons, any person could become a slave. The system was not always a violation of human rights. It was a custom which began in antiquity. Hebrews were permitted to have slaves, and the contract continued until the year of liberation in which each man regained his freedom. During the passing of the centuries, organizations arose to oppose the ancient custom, and today, except for a few non-Christian countries, the degrading practice of enslaving men has become illegal.

Yet, in spite of the international changes, Paul's message remains valid, and his proposals should be applied in all realms of employment. Employees are not slaves, and employers should never become arrogant overlords. Dissension, friction, and devastating strikes paralyze a nation. When an industrialist pays people to work for eight hours a day, he is justified in expecting them to give of their best for the specified amount of time. When workers do their utmost for their employer, he should recompense them with trust, favor, and rewards proportionate to his profits. No owner has the right to become wealthy at the expense of his impoverished workers. Greedy employees should never strike when the employer is doing his best to reward their labor. When differences of opinion arise, problems should be resolved at a table and not upon a battlefield! Workers and employers confronting each other should ask a question, "What would Jesus do in this situation?"

Probably one of the best examples of the master and slave problem is seen in Paul's letter to Philemon. Onesimus, the runaway slave had reached Rome and somewhere within the city had been influenced by the teaching of Paul. When the slave became a Christian, his broken vows had to be renewed; his obligations were unavoidable. Other men might have refused to return to the place from which they had come, but Onesimus realized that although God had forgiven his sins, he still had to make restitution for past indiscretions. Doubtless, the apostle encouraged the convert to return to his former master and, to expedite matters, wrote a letter to Philemon in which he expressed certain vital facts (see Philemon vv. 10-22). Paul's message was exceedingly eloquent and persuasive, and the recipient probably did far more than was legally required. The master had lost a slave but had regained a brother!

The dignity of mundane, mandatory obedience was never expressed more eloquently than when Paul described it "*as unto Christ.*" Washing dirty dishes can be an unrewarding chore, but when Martha recognized it to be a service for Christ, her kitchen became heaven! The great machines of the world would become motionless if oil did not supply the necessary lubrication. The greatest Christian orators would soon become ineffective if unknown saints did not intercede for them. The upkeep of the temple would have been impossible if insignificant widows with adoring souls had not placed their offerings in the treasury. All service is important when rendered to Christ. Paul was wise when he said that sacrificial service was always seen by a watching Heavenly Father. The apostle's final statement deserves attention. If men expect favor and forgiveness from God, they should be willing to give those same gifts to others. (See the homily, "Paul . . . Who Met a Runaway Slave," p. 286, and "The Unjust Steward . . . When Stinginess Ruined His Future," p. 288.)

CONQUEST IN THE FIGHT

THEME: *Preparing for Spiritual Warfare*
OUTLINE:

A. Recognizing the Enemy (vv. 10-12)
B. Regarding the Equipment (vv. 13-18)
C. Remembering the Evangelist (vv. 19-20)

Expository Notes on Spiritual Conflict

Finally, my brethren, be strong in the Lord and in the power of his might. Put on the whole armor of God, that ye may be able to stand against the wiles of the devil (vv. 10-11).

The apostle had no illusions about the difficulties of the Christian warfare against evil. He realized that Satan would resist every effort to extend the kingdom of Christ. As the evil one harassed the Savior, so would he oppose every believer who endeavored to obey the commandments of God. The crusade to overcome evil would become increasingly difficult, and Christian warriors should not expect tranquil days as they follow their Lord. They should remember they have been recruited into God's army, and their task is to expel the enemy from occupied territory. There would be attacks and counterattacks. The real victory had been won at Calvary, but the enemy would never willingly retreat. Satan would have to be driven from the lives of sinful people. Paul emphasized the need to be able "to stand against the wiles of the devil." He mentioned the necessity of maintaining their ground and of refusing to run away from any evil onslaught.

This was a matter of top priority; *Christians should never retreat.* The ancient command given by God to Moses had to be an insignia engraved upon their hearts. "Speak unto the children of Israel *that they go forward . . .* " (Exod. 14:15).

During the five and one half years I worked in the Southern Hemisphere, I became intensely interested in Australia and New Zealand. I was thrilled to learn about the emblems emblazoned on the Australian coat of arms. Stanley Morrison pointed out to me that pictured in it are two creatures: an emu, a large bird that cannot fly, and a kangaroo. He said they were chosen by the Australians for this honor because of one common characteristic—neither can move backward! If an emu with its big, three-toed feet tries to go backward, it will fall over. And the kangaroo is prevented from going backward by its long tail. As a result, they can only go forward, thus portraying the spirit of Australia. (Taken from *Our Daily Bread*, September 5, 1987. Published by the Radio Bible Class, Grand Rapids, Michigan.) This same coat of arms could also signify the spirit of advancing Christians. Paul's advice may be subdivided into four categories. Be strong, serious, steadfast, and suspicious.

BE STRONG

"Finally, my brethren, be strong in the Lord, and in the power of his might" (v. 10). The battlefield was not a place for weaklings; the firing line was never a sanctuary for the timid! God needed strong, determined warriors who would be faithful unto death, should such a result become necessary. There could never be retirement, surrender, or defeat. The assault against evil would be brought to a victorious conclusion, but not unless Christians conformed to certain standards of conduct.

The first requisite was a realization of their own weakness. They were completely inadequate to out-maneuver their crafty enemy. If they relied upon their own ability, defeat would be inevitable. Each Christian soldier had to "be strong *in the Lord*, and in the power of *His might*." The strength and power of God would be made perfect in the weakness of each combatant. As the Commander-in-Chief of the entire operation, the Lord would issue each command; His unerring wisdom would plan strategy for the entire operation. He would supply orders to be obeyed, uniforms to be worn, weapons to be used, and strength to make His army invincible.

The second requisite was concentration on the job in hand! There could never be a compromise with the enemy. To listen, even for a moment, to the seductive propaganda of the devil would undermine the confidence of the soldiers, paralyze their effectiveness, and bring disaster upon the campaign.

The third requisite was constant vigil. Any soldier who fought with closed eyes would see nothing, not even his own grave! When Paul wrote about the wiles of the devil, he implied that Satan excelled in craftiness, that his methods were devious, that his spies were everywhere, and that opposition could appear at the most unlikely moment. Christian watchfulness would protect against surprise attacks. To be forewarned would be to be forearmed.

BE SERIOUS

The conflict against evil would never be an occasional skirmish, but rather a desperate continuing battle—a fight to the finish. If Christian soldiers approached the battlefield in a light-hearted spirit of joviality, they would be early casualties. Spiritual warfare never provided picnic areas. Each soldier had to be careful about his future; he would need to "put on the whole armor of God." There had to be complete understanding of what lay ahead. Any undefended part of the warrior would be a target for enemy arrows.

BE STEADFAST

To advance would never be easy, counterattacks would be made, but retreat would be the prelude to disaster. "STAND" was the rallying word for hard-pressed defenders. Faithfulness would guarantee the ultimate triumph. Nights of testing would give way to the dawning of new days when victory would be within the grasp of God's inspired people. Nothing could defeat Christians except secret sin within their hearts. The classic example of this fact was seen when the triumphant and overconfident Israelites were defeated by the insignificant defenders of a small garrison at Ai. The Hebrews, who had seen the mighty walls of Jericho fall, were humiliated by a small company of determined men from the threatened city of Ai. Even Joshua was confounded when he cried, "Alas, O Lord God, wherefore hast thou at all brought this people over Jordan, to deliver us into the hands of the Amorites, to destroy us? Would to God we had been content and dwelt on the other side of Jordan. O Lord, what shall I say when Israel turneth their backs before their enemies?" (Josh. 7:7-8).

Subsequent repentance and the removal of their sin restored blessing to Israel, but it would have been infinitely better if Israel's conquest of Canaan had proceeded without interruption. Those identical principles applied to every reader of Paul's message. There was continuing need that every individual in God's army should be steadfast, for only then would victory be assured.

BE SUSPICIOUS

"... that ye may be able to stand against the wiles of the devil" (v. 11b). Satan, the chief enemy in spiritual warfare, was not an ignoramus! His antagonism dated back into eternity when he rebelled against God (see Isa. 14:12-13). The devil is not an inexperienced novice! He knows every conceivable tactic which endangers the Christian warrior. Paul described his methods as "wiles of the devil" and earlier in the Epistle (4:14) referred to "cunning craftiness." Satan loves to seduce God's people, and, therefore, Paul considered it necessary that all Christian soldiers remain on the alert against infiltrators. They should anticipate how and when an attack might be launched and be ready to offset the onslaught. To forestall the devil's plans and thwart his efforts would be the forerunner of victory.

The "wiles of the devil" might include the smiling face of a temptress, an action suggested by the failure of a respected church leader, an inordinate desire for material possessions, the promise of easy gains at the expense of diminishing convictions. Despondency, jealousy, covetousness, anger, resentment, and sometimes, even loneliness could be arrows used by Satan. He knows the moods and weaknesses of every opponent and can create circumstances in which Christians seldom, if ever, read the Scriptures. He may encourage ambitions so that denunciation of the sins of possible benefactors would seem outrageous. The devil is very crafty; he possesses ways by which to overcome his opposition. Realizing this, Paul urged his readers to put on the whole armor of God, an action made possible by the Savior. To be satisfied with just a part of what God supplied would be evidence of stupidity.

Expository Notes on the Extent of Satan's Empire

For we wrestle not against flesh and blood, but against principalities, against powers, against the rulers of the darkness of this world, against spiritual wickedness in high places (v. 12).

Throughout his ministry, Paul was opposed by many difficult and dangerous men who tried to destroy his influence and defeat his purposes. There were occasions when their interference would have enraged an ordinary preacher. Many Pharisees criticized Paul's doctrines, and professing Christians opposed his teaching, stating he was not an "authorized" apostle. Some professed converts proclaimed that he was inferior in eloquence to Apollos, and Satan used a soothsaying maiden to annoy him as he walked to a prayer meeting on the banks of a river (see Acts 16:13-18). Paul's indignation was justified, for the conduct of his opponents was disgusting and life-threatening. Yet, through all those times of stress and strain, he realized that his enemies were only dupes of Satan. He never forgot that his real foe was the devil. It might have seemed advantageous to destroy Satan's messengers, but the apostle knew that others would succeed them. When Satan was defeated, subsequent emissaries would be inoperative. It was this fact which compelled Paul to warn his readers. Their service for Christ would be challenged and threatened by all kinds of obstinate, unenlightened adversaries, but the Christian soldier should never forget that his greatest opponents were not people. Paul wrote, "We wrestle not against flesh and blood, but against principalities, against powers, against the rulers of the darkness of this world, against spiritual wickedness in high places."

These words have caused continuing debates throughout the history of the church. Liberal theologians have denied the existence of evil spirits and claimed that Paul was referring to Nero and other officials who disliked Paul's doctrines and tried to silence the new teacher forever. They believed that the enemies were emperors, rulers, and other men elected to high office. These authorities were the rulers of the darkness which encompassed the earth. Nero deliberately blinded his musicians so that they would be unable to see and describe the debauchery prevalent among his guests. The immorality which took place around the emperor's table was hideous, revolting, and without parallel in human history. Nevertheless, Nero and all others of his type were still "*flesh and blood,*" and Paul insisted that such people were not the chief enemies of God's people. Since all humans may be described in the same way, the conclusion is unavoidable that the headquarters of the evil rulers of darkness were not upon the earth but in the heavens. Christians should never hate their human enemies, but pity and love them. They should be seen through eyes filled with compassion.

Nevertheless, believers must never compromise with Satan, even though his promises may be very attractive. The fight against him must be continuous and strenuous. "We *wrestle*!" It is wise to remember that *Satan never retreats willingly*. He never vacates a human soul until the incoming power of God expels him. To nullify his efforts, the Christian needs every assistance possible. Paul knew this fact and proceeded to explain each detail of the protection supplied by his Commander-in-Chief. Properly clothed and suitably arrayed, the redeemed warrior may confidently proceed to the battlefield.

Wherefore take unto you the whole armor of God, that ye may be able to withstand in the evil day, and having done all, to stand.

Expository Notes on the Attitude of the Christian Soldier

Wherefore take unto you the whole armor of God, that ye may be able to withstand in the evil day, and having done all, to stand. Stand therefore, having your loins girt about with truth, and having on the breastplate of righteousness (vv. 13-14).

THEME: *Outfitting the Christian Soldier*
OUTLINE:

A. The Soldier's Discernment . . . *to See*
B. The Soldier's Desire . . . *to Serve*
C. The Soldier's Determination . . . *to Stand*

Paul began his description of the Christian's uniform and weapons with a characteristic statement about determination and courage. He wrote, "Wherefore take unto you the whole armor of God, that ye may be able to withstand in the evil day, and having done all, to stand." He had enunciated identical truth in verse 11, but apparently considered it necessary to repeat his statement. The Christian's task was not necessarily to advance, but to stand. He was not asked to win a battle, but to preserve that which had been won by the Savior. "The battle is not yours, but the Lord's" (see 2 Chron. 20:15). To be able to stand against the wiles of the devil would be their greatest achievement. Many immature believers become frightened by the immensity of enemy strength and consequently believe that they will never be able to resist temptation. It is dangerous to look too long at Satan. He has the hypnotic ability to paralyze souls and destroy their defenses. It is better to emulate the example given by David, who stated, "I will lift up mine eyes unto the hills, from whence cometh my help. My help cometh from the Lord, which made heaven and earth" (Ps. 121:1, 2). Since the Lord always goes before His people into danger, it may be safely assumed that His presence may be found between Satan and vulnerable souls. God's nearness is the guarantee of safety; He stands between His children and the enemy. When Christians deviate from their appointed place of duty and turn either to the right or left, they become easy targets for "the fiery darts of the wicked one."

When Roman soldiers were attacked by their enemies, they formed themselves into human squares with men facing in every direction. If a soldier fell, another one from inside the formation took the place of the fallen comrade. Their greatest duty at that time was not to advance but to stand. More often than not, the attacks of the enemies were defeated because defenders refused to retreat.

The apostle apparently had such a picture before his mind when he urged his friends to stand together. Each faithful Christian would support and strengthen his comrades, and the unified purpose of the entire company would guarantee victory. However, each soldier had to attend to his weapons. Carelessness was never seen in the attitude of experienced warriors. Paul expressed unsurpassed wisdom when he wrote, "And having done all, *to stand.*" Thoughts of a premature victory might encourage surging enthusiasm. Unwise combatants might be tempted to assume too much. Paul said, "Stand." Enthusiasm should never run away with one's brains! Even the roughest waves will break when they fall upon immovable rocks!

Expository Notes on the Christian's Dedication

Stand, therefore, having your loins girt about with truth (v. 14).

Roman soldiers wore skirts made of resistant leather straps which reached from the waist to the knees. Some might have considered this to be the least important piece of uniform. Battles were never won by skirts! A modern parallel of the ancient custom might be the kilts of the Scottish Highlanders. During World War I, these valiant Scotsmen so terrorized the Germans that the enemy referred to them as "the ladies from hell." However, it should be remembered that guns conquered the enemy, not the type of clothing worn by the soldiers. The same might be claimed for the ancient Romans. Their dress code only enhanced their appearance and had nothing to do with their performance upon the battlefield. When the apostle wrote of the "loins girt about with truth," he probably referred to the belt which encircled the waist and supported both the scabbard and sword.

Some people might question Paul's wisdom in placing the belt, or skirt, first among the requirements of Christian soldiers. Perhaps there was a veiled reference to the fact that what a man *is*, supersedes anything *he does*; his appearance should enhance the quality of his service. Paul indicated the necessity of being "*girt about with truth.*"

This was the insignia of his dedication to the task and his allegiance to the cause for which he was willing to die. A soldier without clothing would be shameful; a Christian without truth would be unworthy of his calling.

Expository Notes on the Breastplate of Righteousness

. . . and having on the breastplate of righteousness (v. 14).

This statement possibly indicated that Paul was aware of Isaiah's reference to Jehovah. "And he saw that there was no man, and wondered that there was no intercessor; therefore, his arm brought salvation unto him; and his righteousness, it sustained him. For he put on righteousness as a breastplate, and an helmet of salvation upon his head; and he put on the garments of vengeance for clothing, and was clad with zeal as a cloke" (Isa. 59:16-17). Evidently Paul wished to convey the thought that Christian soldiers should, in some measure, resemble God. The soldiers of the Middle Ages wore cumbersome suits of armor. The chest was completely covered by steel, so that the sword of an enemy had no chance to pierce the heart of the defender. The apostle believed that righteousness would be an impenetrable covering for the soul of the Christian. If he were all he should be, his soul would be enclosed by a protection that even the wiles of the devil could not overcome. That fact endorsed the earlier statement that what a man *is* supersedes anything he ever accomplishes. A man's life is more eloquent than his speech. The sanctity of the soul is to be preferred more than success in service.

Expository Notes on the Christian's Footwear

And your feet shod with the preparation of the gospel of peace (v. 15).

More often than not, slaves had no shoes. Free and wealthy people wore sandals, but soldiers needed something more substantial. Unprotected feet could lead to unpardonable failure! Without reliable support, activity was curtailed, advance extremely difficult, and even captains could become cripples! Paul realized that there was nothing outstandingly beautiful about feet which, in the East, were often dirty and repulsive. It was significant that Isaiah said, "How beautiful upon the mountains are the feet of him that bringeth good tidings, that publisheth peace; that bringeth good tidings of good, that publisheth salvation; that sayeth unto Zion, Thy God reigneth!" (Isa. 52:7). The reference to the feet suggested the approach of a messenger; someone was coming to speak about peace.

At first glance, the subject appeared to be incongruous, for Paul was writing of weapons of war! The question could have been asked, "How could any soldier armed for battle talk about peace?" Evidently Paul was emphasizing that the warfare was against the destroyer of souls; the purpose of the Christian crusade was to liberate slaves. The Christian soldier had a message to proclaim (see Luke 4:18-19). The Savior made peace through the blood of His cross and commissioned His followers to carry that message into all the world. Although they opposed the powers of evil, their chief objective would be the proclamation of the greatest message ever told.

Expository Notes on the Christian's Shield

Above all, taking the shield of faith, wherewith ye shall be able to quench all the fiery darts of the wicked (v. 16).

The shield and the sword belonged together. With one hand the Roman soldier held his shield as a means of defense; with the other hand he held a sword or lance as a way by which to attack the enemy. The "*above all*" may have signified the shield's preeminent position in that it covered the breastplate and skirt; on the other hand, it might have indicated it was the first part of the equipment to be attacked. When faith diminishes, doubt arises; when soldiers cease to trust their weapons, they discard them. Satan's primary objective is to attack the faith of the Christian. A little doubt, a sly insinuation, an unpleasant circumstance, increasing pain, an acute disappointment—all are arrows from Satan's bow. Paul declared, "We are laborers together *with* God," and the same truth applied to all believers engaged in spiritual battles. They were never asked to fight alone. As God was *in Christ* reconciling the world unto Himself (2 Cor. 5:19), so He will be *in us* claiming the world for Himself. It must always be remembered that Christians and their Lord stand together amid the problems of life. With Him, victory is assured; without Him, failure becomes inevitable.

A dart or a javelin is something which arrives suddenly! Either may do more damage in moments than can be repaired or healed in months. That is the reason why Paul urged his friends to "put on the whole armor of God." Each part of the body had to be protected—with the exception of the back! When Romans faced their enemies, their backs were out of sight! Caesar never provided protection for deserters! A dart that was not instantly removed could lead to fatal complications. It has often been said that it is impossible to prevent a bird from landing in a tree, but it is possible to prevent the bird from building a nest there. Experience teaches that Satan is a master marksman; he knows how to infiltrate a Christian's thoughts. It may be difficult, or even impossible, to stop his arrows, but instant action can prevent the poison from flowing through the veins of the believer.

The Greek word translated "shield" is *thyrion*; it comes from *thyra* which means "a door." It referred to the long, oblong protective shield which the Roman held in front of him as he fought against the enemy. Frank E. Goblin writes, "It consisted of two layers of wood glued together, covered with linen and hide, and bound with iron. Soldiers often fought side by side with a solid wall of shields. But even a single-handed combatant found himself sufficiently protected. After the siege of Dyrachium, Sceva counted no less than 220 darts sticking into his shield. . . . Only in this instance does Paul indicate the effect of a particular piece of armor. With such a shield the believer can extinguish all the incendiary devices flung by the devil. Herodotus described how cane darts tipped with tow, were dipped in pitch and then ignited. Octavius used such arrows against Antony's fleet at Actium, and they were not unknown in Old Testament times. The reference is not, as some have surmised, to poison darts producing fever. The Christian's shield effectively counteracts the danger of such diabolical missiles not merely by arresting or deflecting them, but by actually quenching the flames to prevent them from spreading" (*The Expositor's Bible Commentary*, vol. 2, p. 88).

Expository Notes on the Protection of the Mind

And take the helmet of salvation (v. 17)

Without the use of a limb, a determined soldier may continue to fight. A wound may hinder the defense, but not make resistance impossible. Yet, without his head, a warrior becomes motionless and dead. The battle for the mind is the most crucial of all the struggles of life. When a Christian is defeated by the wiles of the devil, it is the result of Satan's ability to infiltrate thought. The mind of a human being is like an ancient castle; it has secret passages and Satan unfortunately holds the key to every door. It is disconcerting how he can suddenly appear within the consciousness, and even believers can be appalled by the sinful thoughts suddenly flooding the mind. When those thoughts are permitted to remain, they fester, and soon the health of the soul is threatened. It seems there is a television set in every head, and the moment Satan turns it on, all kinds of detestable pictures appear on the built-in screen. When a Christian welcomes such sights, he loses his grip upon reality. When he continues to watch and think evil thoughts, his battle is lost, and the crusade for righteousness reaches a premature end. He becomes a slave to the desires of his carnal nature. It is, therefore, of utmost importance that the mind of the believer be constantly protected. Paul urged his readers "to take the helmet of salvation"—*and wear it*!

It cannot be overemphasized that, although the devil may produce unwholesome pictures in the mind of Christians, believers are never compelled to watch. It is within the capability of believers to refuse to listen to material which belongs to hell's propaganda programs. Lustful thoughts and evil desires are by-products of compromise. Solomon was correct when he said, "For as he thinketh in his heart, so is he" (Prov. 23:7). When the mind of the believer is filled with thoughts of God's amazing grace and when his soul is tuned to God's broadcasting station, it becomes increasingly difficult for any pirate-station to silence God's broadcast from heaven. Paul summarized, "Finally, brethren, whatsoever things are true, whatsoever things are honest, whatsoever things are just, whatsoever things are pure, whatsoever things are lovely, whatsoever things are of good report; if there be any virtue, and if there be any praise, *think on these things*" (Phil. 4:8).

Spiritual success is always dependent upon the battle of the mind. A displayed helmet may stimulate conversation in a home or a museum, but it will never save the life of an endangered soldier unless it is worn. Helmets were never designed to be revered, but rather for protection in combat.

Expository Notes on the Power of the Scriptures

. . . and the sword of the Spirit, which is the word of God (v. 17).

A sword is quite useless until it is used! It may be made of the finest steel and fashioned by a master craftsman, but without a swordsman, it remains useless. The Savior provided the famous examples of how the Word of God can defeat the enemy. When Satan tempted the Lord, Christ repulsed each attack with His shield of faith, and parried each thrust of the devil's insinuations by quoting the Word of God (see Luke 4:3-12). When the Lord became hungry, Satan suggested that Christ should attend to the satisfying of personal need. "And Jesus answered him, saying, it is written, that man shall not live by bread alone, but by every word of God" (Luke 4:4). When

Satan suggested an easy way of gaining the world, Jesus recognized the subtlety of the idea and replied, "Get thee behind me, Satan: for it is written, thou shalt worship the Lord thy God, and him only shalt thou serve" (Luke 4:8). When the evil one appeared to be religious and asked Jesus to exercise faith in God, the Savior replied, "Thou shalt not tempt the Lord thy God" (Luke 4:12). The Lord never argued with the devil; when He used the Word of Truth to offset temptation, His enemy was forced to retreat.

Every talented swordsman acquaints himself with his weapon; other swords may be useful, but none equals his own. No Christian should neglect the greatest tool God ever offered. Unless the Bible is read, believed, and, where possible, memorized, its effectiveness in the life of the believer is negligible. Churches have lost their effectiveness in the world because their faith in the Word of God has been undermined. Church history affirms that every time the assemblies were revitalized, there was a return to the proclamation of the Scriptures. The anointing of the Holy Spirit and the acceptance of the Word of Truth transformed ordinary men into prophets. Rejection of the truth of Scripture as well as a faith in material things changed preachers into soothsayers. A Christian warrior without his sword is a David without his pebbles! Such men become shadowboxers—they often work hard, but hit nothing!

Expository Notes on the Power of Prayer

Praying always with all prayer and supplication in the Spirit, and watching thereunto with all perseverance and supplication for all saints (v. 18).

If the aforementioned pieces of equipment may be considered invaluable to the warrior; then prayer is the breath he breathes, the life flowing through his veins, the secret of his actions and thought. Without prayer even the greatest of Christians remains ineffective and helpless. What, then, is prayer? The following message is an extract from the author's book, *This I Believe*.

I am firmly convinced that the overwhelming majority of Christians *do not know how to pray*. I am also convinced that of the rest, most of them, even if they know how to pray, are always in too great a hurry to practice what they know. Prayer is a telephone talk between the soul and heaven, and it would repay us to consider that only fools rush into a telephone booth, grab the receiver, start shouting, and then, having banged the receiver down, rush out again. There must always be an intelligent approach to a telephone conversation, for otherwise, a person talks only to himself. First, it is necessary to get through to the person with whom conversation is desired. Often this necessitates patience to await the assurance that a voice is answering. Then it becomes logical to say what has to be said. But that is not all that happens. The person at the other end of the wire also desires to speak, and the man making the call must intersperse his speaking with listening.

Telephone conversations are a two-way affair, and when they terminate, both parties have a clear understanding of the matter needing attention. Prayer is only *true prayer* when these same principles are applied. All Christians pray—that is, they ask for divine aid—but it is problematical how many linger to listen. When a few extra minutes in bed in the morning necessitates a last-minute dash for the train or bus; the long, exacting day makes them so tired that they breathe a fervent good-night to God and wearily slip into bed before they fall asleep on their knees! Periods of anxious prayer are only known when a doctor suggests a visit to the hospital, when trouble looms on the horizon, or when people are about to lose something they eagerly desire to retain. Then they besiege the throne of grace, asking for divine intervention. Afterward they go on vacation, blissfully forgetting that their heavenly Father would dearly love to see a little more of the people whose voices are heard only when the need becomes frightening. . . . It would bring revival to the church if every Christian shortened his prayer and devoted the other moments to listening. What would a business man think of a traveler who daily rushed into his office to say in one breath, "Goodmorningsiritsanicedayisn'tithopeyouarewellsirmustleavenow sirgoodbye!" He would gaze at the swinging door and issue orders that the maniac should be kept in the street ever afterward. But that is how some people act in regard to prayer. They rush unannounced into God's presence, blurt out their desires, and before the Lord can say a word, they are running to their cars. *That is not prayer*—unless men *make* time to pray, intercession will be squeezed out of the daily program.

Most business executives announce at times to their secretaries, "I am not to be disturbed for ten minutes. I have to make an important telephone call." Those same men could remain undisturbed when a call to heaven needs to be made, and if this became the normal procedure in the head office of the Christian business firm, the staff would recognize that Christianity had become an integral part of the organization to which they belonged. It has become the common practice for most Christian workers to have many irons in their fire!

Some of those irons could be removed forever and nothing would be lost. Some activities may not be necessary; they might even be hindrances. If Satan can keep us busy with unessentials, there will be less time for things which really matter.

One of the most vital features of prayer is that *it changes the one who prays*. Whether or not his immediate desires are granted is a matter of minor concern. There are occasions when prayers are not answered as we might desire, and the man on his knees may experience frustration and disappointment. Yet, the sublime and thrilling feature of the exercise is the quiet transformation that comes to the person who has truly communed with his heavenly Father. The growth of the soul is governed and directed, not by the disappearance of a man's problems, but by the way in which he confronts them. Probably Daniel prayed earnestly to be kept out of the lions' den—at least, that is what I would have done! Yet, God permitted the seeming catastrophe because He preferred to accompany Daniel into the den rather than leave him outside. Similarly, had the disciples not been permitted to go into the tempest, they would never have discovered the amazing power of Christ to still raging seas. Oftentimes, God can teach us far more in the storm than He ever could in the calm.

Therefore, it must be emphasized that of far more importance than any miracle wrought on my behalf through prayer is that other miracle wrought "within me" when I learn to say, "Thy will be done." Prayer takes the irritability out of the irritable soul. True prayer calms the ruffled and tired spirit. Quiet communion produces a soul not easily upset. Prayer makes big people, for a man is never larger than the thing which makes him angry. People become irritable because they have never discovered the secret of walking and talking with the Most High. Often the best cure for worry and stomach ulcers is an extended call to the King of kings.

It is possible to be evangelical and even evangelistic, yet to remain only a piece of reliable machinery. Prophets were never machines; they were living souls. Unless I can emulate their example, discover their secret, and possess their dynamic, my efforts will only resemble shadowboxing. With tremendous energy, I shall succeed in hitting nothing! Unless *I* am first changed, my message will never change others. I must pray until the glory of Christ thrills my soul.

Why should it be necessary to pray? Cannot God save souls whether we pray or not? Maybe He will and maybe He will not, but one fact remains irrefutable. If prayer changes us, then the very fact that we have prayed guarantees that God will have better instruments to use.

Our being made usable makes God's task a lot easier than it otherwise might be. I believe that prayer changes things; I believe prayer changes *the man who prays.*

Real prayer is not a marvelous display of oratory meant to impress a listening audience, nor is it an appeal for financial assistance when wealthy people are listening. Prayer is the outpouring of a worshiping soul, a confession before God of our deepest needs. I believe in prayer meetings. I do not believe young people can be effectively held for Christ and the church by feeding them socials, dances, card parties, and other questionable entertainments. A young man is never as great as when he kneels to pray. A young woman is never as graceful, charming, and lovely as when she bows in humble prayer. The Christian who does not love the prayer meeting cannot be drinking deeply of the wells of God's salvation. The church that has no prayer meeting is only a social club with a religious flavor. True prayer could change the world and revolutionize the church. True prayer will change *me.* "Lord, teach us how to pray" (Luke 11:1). (Abbreviated from the author's book, *This I Believe*, pp. 153-171.)

Expository Notes on Paul's Significant Request

And for me, that utterance may be given unto me, that I may open my mouth boldly, to make known the mystery of the gospel, for which I am an ambassador in bonds: that therein I may speak boldly, as I ought to speak (vv. 19-20).

THEME: *Paul's Last Request to His Friends*
OUTLINE:

A. His Delightful Request . . . *"pray for me"*
B. His Definite Responsibility . . . *"as I ought"*
C. His Decided Repetition . . . *"that I may speak boldly"*

It must be remembered that this letter was written when Paul was a prisoner chained to a Roman soldier. His trial before the authorities was imminent, his death assured. All people who have visited the prison where Paul was incarcerated will be aware of the deplorable conditions in which he was obliged to live. This last desire expressed by that indomitable hero of the faith can only amaze the modern reader.

HIS DELIGHTFUL REQUEST . . . "pray for me"

When the apostle wrote to Timothy, he requested, "Do thy diligence to come shortly unto me: for Demas hath forsaken me, having loved this present world, and is departed unto Thessalonica; Crescens to Galatia, Titus unto Dalmatia. Only Luke is with me. Take Mark, and bring him with thee; for he is profitable unto me for the ministry. . . . The cloke that I left at Troas with Carpus, when thou comest, bring with thee, and the books, but especially the parchments" (2 Tim. 4:9-13). Evidently Luke was Paul's only companion during those dreadful days prior to his death. The reference to the bringing of the cloke suggests hardship. Paul knew what it was to be cold at night, and the cloke would be a blanket! It is, therefore, justifiable to assume that Paul could have prayed for various things. He might have asked his friends to pray for better treatment from the authorities; more favorable conditions within his cell; and most of all, release from captivity. It must be significant to all readers of this Epistle that Paul was selfless; he thought only of his task. Many years earlier, when Ananias had been reluctant to encounter the murderous persecutor from Jerusalem, God said to him, "Go thy way: for he is a chosen vessel unto me, to bear my name before the Gentiles and *kings*, and the children of Israel" (Acts 9:15). The forthcoming encounter with the rulers of Rome and possibly Nero himself was to be the climax of the apostle's ministry. He knew that the opportunity was unparalleled, that the dangers were great, and that the difficulties were almost insurmountable. He had no desire to escape, for he was overwhelmed with the privilege of being able to tell his judges about the grace of God.

HIS DEFINITE RESPONSIBILITY . . . "as I ought"

Probably Paul realized that this would be his last chance to proclaim the gospel; any thought of failure was inexcusable. If he could preach Christ in the imperial city, then the proclamation of his message throughout the empire would only be a matter of time. The highways built by the Romans led to the uttermost parts of the world. Therefore, Paul was only concerned with the opportunity God was about to give to him. Thoughts of personal comfort never occurred to him; he considered only the extension of the kingdom of Christ. He urged his readers to pray earnestly that his opportunity would not be lost and that even if he became a martyr, his death would be a grain of wheat falling into the ground to make a great harvest possible. An ambassador is the official representative of his country, entrusted with its secrets and commissioned to speak on behalf of its government. Even in times of stress and strain, ambassadors are allowed diplomatic privileges. That such laws of protocol had been ignored meant that Rome was at war with God; Nero and his leaders would be held accountable for anything that happened to God's appointee.

HIS DECIDED REPETITION . . . "that I may speak boldly"

"That I may speak boldly as I ought to speak" (v. 20b). It was significant that Paul should repeat his request for prayer. Although he had been blessed by God, was famous among believers of his generation, and was efficient in all matters pertaining to the kingdom of God, he, nevertheless, sat in his prison cell, seemingly weak and helpless. He realized that in his own strength he could do nothing. He needed strength to speak *boldly*. The apostle knew exactly what needed to be explained, but was he ever nervous? Did he ever become despondent, believing that his efforts had been in vain? Perhaps it is impossible to answer all the questions which might be asked, but one thing is irrefutable, Paul valued the prayers of his friends, and that was the reason why he repeated his urgent request. He might have desired many things, but to the apostle, at that moment, nothing was more desirable than strength to complete his ministry faithfully and triumphantly.

CONCERN IN THE FELLOWSHIP

THEME: *Paul's Final Words to His Friends*
OUTLINE:

A. A Brother Beloved (v. 21)
B. A Bountiful Beneficence (v. 22)
C. A Beautiful Benediction (vv. 23-24)

Expository Notes on Tychicus, the Beloved Brother

But that ye also may know my affairs, and how I do, Tychicus, a beloved brother and faithful minister in the Lord, shall make known to you all things: whom I have sent unto you for the same purpose, that ye might know our affairs, and that he might comfort your hearts. Peace be to the brethren, and love with faith, from God the Father and the Lord Jesus Christ. Grace be with all them that love our Lord Jesus Christ in sincerity. Amen (vv. 21-24).

A BROTHER BELOVED

It should be remembered that when Paul sent this letter to his friends in Asia, he had visited the church at Ephesus for the last time and, at a later date, had met with its elders on a nearby beach. He knew that they would never meet again on this earth. Now he was aware that this letter would be his final written communication to them. It was amazing that throughout his Epistle, Paul said nothing of himself. Doubtless, he knew of their anxiety on his behalf, but he was so desirous to explain his message that personal matters were excluded from his thoughts. Then, as he neared the conclusion of his letter, he mentioned his friend Tychicus and explained how his beloved brother would answer their questions and describe everything that had happened to him. The appointed courier would visit the churches, read Paul's letters, and tell them what they desired to know.

Three things were said of Tychicus. He was (1) a beloved brother, (2) a faithful minister, and (3) a fellowservant in the Lord (see Col. 4:7). This man had been a constant companion of the apostle and had written what Paul dictated. When he began his journey, Tychicus was accompanied by the converted slave Onesimus. Paul possibly believed that the presence of his trusted companion would help the conciliation which needed to be made between the former slave and his master. He had already rendered invaluable service by being part of the delegation which carried relief offerings to Jerusalem (Acts 20:4-6). The three things said of this little-known Christian challenge our thought. *First*, he was a beloved brother, a description that could only mean that he had captivated Paul's heart and had won an abiding place in the apostle's affections. He was reliable and commendable. *Second*, he was a faithful minister. He could be trusted with finances, counseling, and every facet of Christian service. Difficulties did not deter him from carrying out orders, opposition never silenced his voice, he was a minister who always pleased his leader. *Third*, he was "a fellowservant in the Lord." In spite of his commendable qualities, he remained a humble servant of the Savior. No task was too insignificant and no challenge was too great to accept. Paul loved, honored, and trusted him. It has been thought that he belonged to Asia and that, therefore, this journey on Paul's behalf was in some senses a working vacation in which the faithful courier was given a chance to visit his family and friends.

Expository Notes on Paul's Thoughtfulness

But that ye also may know my affairs, and how I do, Tychicus . . . shall make known to you all things. Whom I have sent unto you for the same purpose, that ye might know our affairs, and that he might comfort your hearts (vv. 21-22).

A BOUNTIFUL BENEFIENCE

During his imprisonment in Rome, Paul received many visitors. Over a period of two years, he had his own rented apartment "and received all who came in unto him" (Acts 28:30). There is reason to believe that if for any reason the Christians of Asia visited Rome, they welcomed the opportunity to visit their former pastor and friend. Paul was aware that the believers in Asia were apprehensive concerning his future; many of his converts were worried because, for the gospel's sake, he was undergoing persecution. Paul was appreciative of their concern and was assured that Tychicus would dispel their fears. Although his future was threatened, the apostle thought of his brothers and sisters in Christ and wanted them to know that he was well and that, rather than being frightened, he was eagerly anticipating the opportunity to preach before the emperor. If they would pray for him, he would be more efficient proclaiming the gospel of God's grace. Paul was selfless and determined to the end; his attitude contrasted strangely with that of Demas, of whom he wrote, "For Demas hath forsaken me, having loved this present world, and is departed unto Thessalonica" (2 Tim. 4:10). There is a law in life which suggests that in caring for others, man strengthens himself!

Expository Notes on Paul's Last Benediction

Peace be to the brethren and love with faith, from God the Father and the Lord Jesus Christ. Grace be with all them that love our Lord Jesus Christ in sincerity. Amen (vv. 23-24).

A BEAUTIFUL BENEDICTION

As Paul finished his Epistle, he used the following wonderful words: peace, love, faith, grace, sincerity. They were shining jewels in the crown that he was about to receive from his Lord! When Elijah was taken up by a whirlwind, his mantle fell upon the servant who watched the homegoing of his master. Similarly, as Paul was about to enter into the presence of his Lord, his spiritual mantle also descended upon his friends. The words used in this final benediction resembled a cascade of shining stars falling from heaven. Paul was aware of the peace of God which for many years had flooded his soul. He had been greatly loved by God and His people, and his faith in the Lord Jesus Christ had grown continually since the encounter on the Damascus road. The matchless grace of God had sustained him through his travels, and now he wished to bestow his riches upon his friends. The apostle had no earthly possessions; he had no family except those who belonged to the family of God. Yet, he was a multimillionaire with unlimited wealth. Such as he possessed, he gave, willingly and gladly, and this remarkable benediction was his last will and testament. If his friends would grasp what he was giving to them, they too, would serve triumphantly and say, "Henceforth, there is laid up for me a crown of righteousness, which the Lord, the righteous judge, shall give me at that day" (2 Tim. 4:8).

A SUMMARY OF THE SIXTH CHAPTER

This study of Paul's letter to the saints in Asia is quickly reaching its conclusion. Each chapter has been briefly summarized; one remaining task involves taking a final look at the apostle's closing message. The Epistle spans time. Paul began in the eternal ages when the church "was chosen in Christ" before time began. The apostle then described the other end of the spectrum when the same church, resplendent in robes of righteousness, will be presented to the heavenly Bridegroom as "a glorious church, not having spot or wrinkle, or any such thing . . . holy and without blemish" (5:27). Paul explained that between the planning, perfecting, and presentation of the Church, spiritual conflicts would be fought in high places and that each Christian would be expected to participate in the final defeat of Satan, the arch-enemy of God. The apostle's final chapter may be divided into three sections.

HIS WISDOM

Paul saw the family as the training ground for battles to be fought later in life. The true value of the Christian worker is seen in the home, not only in the church. Surrounded by fellow Christians, a person's pride may urge him to win the respect of fellow-believers. When he stands before the watching eyes of other people, he is careful to say and do what might be expected of him. Yet, when that kind of scrutiny is absent, the same person may be the opposite of what he appeared to be in church. The apostle emphasized that unless a person gains the respect and admiration of his family, he has little chance of influencing men and women in wider circles of life. Paul covered every aspect of social behavior when he addressed Christian families. The husband should love his spouse as Christ loves the Church. The wife should adore and respect her husband as the Church does the Lord. Children should obey their parents as Christians obey their heavenly Father. Wealthy men who owned slaves should themselves be the bondslaves of Christ; and servants should faithfully serve their masters as though they were actually serving the Lord Jesus. The apostle realized that a radiant family would always be the best advertisement for the Savior and therefore urged his readers to make their homes a sanctuary. Satan could resist and often thwart eloquent preaching, but was helpless against a family motivated by the power of the indwelling Christ. Continuing triumph at home leads to a larger and effective ministry elsewhere.

HIS WARNING

To become a good soldier of Jesus Christ, Christians needed "to put on the whole armor of God." To *remain* a good soldier of the Lord, Christians needed to *wear that armor continually*. Paul gave minute instruction about *putting it on*; he said nothing about *taking it off*! Contentment, complacency, and carelessness are invitations for the enemy to take advantage of our dilatoriness. Even the strongest warrior is vulnerable when he sleeps! The apostle knew that the success of Christian enterprise depended upon the united effort of all believers to resist evil in any form. The world would never be won for the Savior if saints remained motionless. The apostle realized he was about to lay down his life for the Master; if the work he had commenced was to continue, others would need to take his place. To continue Paul's efforts would never be an easy task. Missionaries would need undying courage, a strong faith, and a passion that would burn as a flame within their souls. Christ needed warriors, not weaklings. The efforts of such men and women would hasten the time when the earth would be "filled with the glory of the Lord as the waters cover the sea."

HIS WISH

Paul's final desire suggested maturity. He wrote, "Grace be with *all them* that love our Lord Jesus Christ *in sincerity*." There had been times in the apostle's career when his utterances were not as gentle. For example, writing to the Galatian believers, he denounced other preachers whose message was not exactly in harmony with his own. He said, "As we said before, so say I now again, If any man preach any other gospel unto you than that ye have received, let him be accursed" (Gal. 1:9). Probably Paul was completely justified in opposing what he considered to be heresy, but the apostle had mellowed with age; his attitude had changed. He no longer divided the Church into those who agreed with his doctrines and those who did not. He breathed his fervent benediction upon *all who sincerely loved the Lord.* Arguments, debates, dissension no longer worried the old saint. He was about to go home, and such disturbances were not permitted to spoil his vision. If any person sincerely adored the Master, then he belonged to Paul; they were brothers. Paul's last wish was that the all-embracing grace of God would fall as a protective mantle upon the entire family of God. He set an example which all Christians should emulate.

HOMILIES

Homily No. 16

PAUL . . . Who Met a Runaway Slave

What a pity there is no telephone exchange in heaven! Of course, there is a private line to the palace of the King, and all praying people use it. But what a shame the service is not extended. If only we could lift a receiver, dial a number, and ask the angelic operator to put us through to Paul, the apostle. If only this were possible, the industries of the world would be silent as everyone listened. The people in palaces and hovels would desire to hear the message, and during the conversation all other voices would be hushed. Such a telephone call is certainly wishful thinking and perhaps a little absurd, but it does no harm. It merely expresses the fact that if it were possible, Paul would be able to supply the answers to many of our questions. For example, we could ask him about his convert Onesimus.

GRACE REDEEMING

The Acts of the Apostles closes with the words, "And Paul dwelt two whole years in his own hired house, and received all that came unto him, preaching the kingdom of God, and teaching those things which concern the Lord Jesus Christ, with all confidence, no man forbidding him" (Acts 28:30-31). Probably this was the first Christian pastorate in Rome and was established in a simple home. Were all the meetings held in the house, or was Paul permitted to walk to the market place? Did he ever minister in the synagogue, and where did he find Onesimus—or did Onesimus find him? Had the fugitive become destitute in a strange city, and did desperation drive him to Paul? Had he become contrite, and did he miserably seek advice from the only man he knew in the city? Was Onesimus surprised when he recognized the preacher? Oh, Paul, why can't we get you on the telephone? Surely, you were thrilled to lead that man to Christ!

GRACE REPAYING

Paul wrote, "I beseech thee for my son, Onesimus, whom I have begotten in my bonds. Which in times past was to thee unprofitable, but now profitable, both to thee and to me . . . whom I would have retained with me, that in thy stead he might have ministered unto me in the bonds of the gospel" (Philem. vv. 10-13). It is clear, therefore, that grace had completely transformed Onesimus. He had no wish to escape from Paul, and in contrast to Demas, this new convert loved to serve the man who had won him for Christ. Grace had been shed abroad in his heart. His presence cheered Paul, and his eagerness both to learn and to help demonstrated the reality of his conversion. The transparent sincerity of this babe in Christ and the wholehearted service which he rendered might well serve as an example for all saints.

GRACE RESTORING

Paul was a little sad, and Onesimus had downcast eyes. The apostle was speaking, "Son, I must send you home, but I don't want to do it. I wish you could stay here forever. But Philemon is your master, and the fact that God has forgiven your sin does not release you from the obligation to make restitution for the wrongs of the past. Moral requirements demand that you return to the man to whom you are indebted. My son, you must go home." And Onesimus agreed. Amazing changes had taken place since he had absconded from his master. Punishment might be awaiting him, but he found comfort in the fact that he was about to do his duty. He had written a letter at Paul's dictation, and that Letter—the Epistle to Philemon—was a document destined to become famous.

GRACE REPLYING

Philemon's eyes were misty; the letter from his old friend had stirred his memories. Again and again he read, "I beseech thee for my son Onesimus, whom I have begotten in my bonds. . . . He departed for a season, that thou shouldest receive him forever; not now as a servant, but above a servant, a brother beloved, specially to me, but now much more unto thee, *both in the flesh*, and in the Lord" (vv. 10, 15, 16). The words "both in the flesh" suggest that Onesimus might have been a brother of Philemon—a prodigal brother who had stolen money. One does not need a great imagination to see a cozy parlor where a fire burned on the hearth. The elder brother listens to the account of a conversion in Rome. Former wrongs were forgotten, bitterness of spirit was completely unknown, and love reigned amid boundless rejoicing. Yes, this is a story of grace—wonderful grace overflowing in four hearts. (Reprinted from the author's book, *Bible Treasures*, pp. 151-152.)

Homily No. 17

THE UNJUST STEWARD . . . Whose Stinginess Ruined His Future

Then came Peter to him, and said, Lord, how oft shall my brother sin against me, and I forgive him? till seven times? Jesus saith unto him, I say not unto thee, until seven times: but, until seventy times seven (Matt. 18:21-22).

AN INTERESTING SUGGESTION

It must be emphasized that the entire theme of these verses is the need for forgiveness. Peter recognized this fact and asked his question. Perhaps his inquiry may be appreciated more if we paraphrase it. "Lord, if my brother blacken my eye, how much am I expected to take before I strike him? Do I endure seven black eyes? Must I wait until he is about to strike me the eighth time, and then will I be free to retaliate?" Let it be admitted this was extremely gallant for a man of Peter's fiery disposition. Others might have been unwilling to receive a second black eye!

Jesus listened attentively to Peter's question and then gave His immortal answer, "I say not unto thee, until seven times: but, until seventy times seven." He probably realized that His follower would not have sufficient patience to continue counting until the number reached four hundred and ninety. It would be far easier for a man of Simon's disposition to keep on forgiving. This thought-provoking reply becomes even more interesting when we consider the illustration which followed. When Jesus said, "Therefore," it became obvious the story He was about to tell was the direct result of Peter's question.

Therefore, is the kingdom of heaven likened unto a certain king, who would take account of his servants. And when he had begun to reckon, one was brought unto him, who owed him ten thousand talents. But forasmuch as he had not [anything] to pay, his lord commanded him to be sold, and his wife, and children, and all that he had, and payment to be made. The servant therefore fell down and worshiped him, saying, Lord, have patience with me, and I will pay thee all. Then the Lord of that servant was moved with compassion, and loosed him, and forgave him the debt (Matt. 18:23-27).

AN INTRIGUING STORY

In all probability we would never have received this immortal illustration but for the fact that Peter had questioned the Lord about the necessity of forgiving a brother's indiscretion. The Savior's story was most unusual. He spoke of a man who owed his master ten thousand talents. Throughout the ages theologians have tried to compute the size of the debt. One teacher suggested that it equalled $262,800,000. Another states that a talent was the equivalent of 240 British pounds, and that the entire debt would have been 2.4 million British pounds. When he made his computation, a pound and also the American dollar were worth much more than they are today. Yet under any circumstances the debt was immense, and the offending man must have enjoyed a position of great eminence within a kingdom. The inference was that he had been a Minister of Finance who embezzled a great amount of money. An examination of the royal books revealed the fraud, and the day of reckoning arrived for the offender. In those days the total revenue of even a wealthy province like Galilee was sometimes only 300 talents. Here was a debt which was greater than a king's ransom. The embezzlement made by this high official of state was enormous, and yet when he and his family were faced with slavery, his desperate request for clemency was granted, and the guilty man was pardoned.

But the same servant went out, and found one of his fellowservants, which owed him an hundred pence [denarii]: and he laid hands on him, and took him by the throat, saying, Pay me that thou owest. And

his fellowservant fell down at his feet, and besought him, saying, have patience with me, and I will pay thee all, and he would not: but went and cast him into prison, till he should pay the debt. So when his fellowservants saw what was done, they were very sorry, and came and told unto their lord all that was done (Matt. 18:28-31).

The hundred pence owed by the servant was less than five dollars, and it seems incredible that he who had been forgiven so much should be reluctant to cancel such a small debt. Even the language used by the Lord indicates the vicious character of this unforgiving man, for *he took his victim by the throat* as if to strangle him. We must remember that Peter had spoken of the possibility of forgiving seven times and had been told by Jesus that seventy times seven would be a more appropriate figure. If we superimpose these facts upon the illustration given by Jesus, we discover the enormity of the offense of the unforgiving dignitary. Having been forgiven a sum of money in excess of millions of dollars, he refused to forgive debt which was very insignificant. Had he been more gracious, he would have recognized his need to forgive, not seventy times seven, but at the very least, *three hundred thousand times seven.* It might have been even more, for it is difficult to know fully how great had been his own debt.

These staggering figures were really not of overwhelming importance. It was the thought behind the story which became paramount. Jesus was reminding His disciples that God had already forgiven them many millions of dollars worth of sins! His unfailing mercy had cancelled their debt. If they had been forgiven so much, they should be more than willing to forgive any brother or sister whose debt was minimal. Peter needed a computer to unravel all the suggested financial problems, but the prevailing fact was obvious. It would be easier to continue forgiving everybody. A lifetime of perpetual pardoning would be too short for Peter to forgive others what God had already forgiven him.

Then his lord, after that he had called him, said unto him, O thou wicked servant, I forgave thee all that debt, because thou desiredst me; shouldest not thou also have had compassion on thy fellowservant, even as I had pity on thee? And his lord was wroth, and delivered him to the tormentors, till he should pay all that was due unto him. So likewise shall my heavenly Father do also unto you, if ye from your hearts forgive not every one his brother their trespasses (Matt. 18:32–35).

AN IGNORED STATEMENT

The last verse of the eighteenth chapter of Matthew is frightening! When Jesus had described the fate awaiting the unforgiving steward, He proceeded to say, "So likewise shall my heavenly Father do also unto you, if ye from your hearts forgive not every one his brother their trespasses." It is problematical how far we can go in trying to harmonize this statement with other New Testament verses, but however much we reason or debate, the text remains when talking has ceased. Sometimes Christians take too much for granted! They rejoice in the redemptive work of Christ and proclaim the wonder of His forgiving grace, and yet their treatment of fellow Christians leaves much to be desired. First John 1:7 says, "But if we walk in the light, as he is in the light, we have fellowship one with another, and the blood of Jesus Christ, his Son, cleanseth us from all sin." Unfortunately, many Christians rejoice in the final section of that remarkable verse, but completely ignore the initial statement. It is true the precious blood of Christ actually *goes on cleansing* from sin, but the paramount condition is that men *walk in the light.* John said, "If—IF—we walk in the light," we have fellowship and cleansing. When a person refuses to walk in the light of God's revealed word, and carries grudges against others within the family of God, and stubbornly remains unforgiving, fellowship becomes an impossibility and sin remains unforgiven. This is a truth which the church needs to remember and teach. It is possible for a Christian to be an expert theologian as well as a very enthusiastic speaker and still be bankrupt in his soul. (Reprinted from the author's commentary, *Matthew's Majestic Gospel*, pp. 334-337.)

Appendix

THE WORK OF THE HOLY SPIRIT

Even a casual reader of the Epistle to the Ephesians will become aware that its contents describe various stages in the growth of a Christian. The apostle Paul said his readers had been "without Christ, being aliens from the commonwealth of Israel, and strangers from the covenants of promise, having no hope, and without God in the world" (Eph. 2:12). They had been "the children of wrath, even as others" (Eph. 2:3). Toward the end of his letter, the same people were described as part of the resplendent Church, "holy and without spot or wrinkle, or any such thing" (Eph. 5:27). The journey from the one extreme to the other was clearly outlined as a highway along which various milestones of experience were clearly indicated.

The apostle believed that the Holy Spirit was the unseen, but important, Director of Christ's work upon earth. Deprived of His assistance, a person's best efforts would terminate in ignominious failure. Within this Epistle the work of the Holy Spirit was mentioned twelve times; the verses divide into three categories: *exposition*, *exhortation*, and *expectation.* They promote an understanding of that which God desires to accomplish within the life of every Christian.

PHASE ONE

Ye were sealed with that holy Spirit of promise (1:13).

When Paul described the commencement of Christian experience, he wrote, "In whom ye also trusted, after that ye heard the word of truth, the gospel of your salvation: in whom also, after that ye believed, ye were sealed with that Holy Spirit of promise" (Eph. 1:13). The apostle carefully mentioned four facts relative to a person's salvation. "Ye *heard, believed, trusted*, and *were sealed with that Holy Spirit of promise*." These were the foundational principles upon which Paul based his Christian doctrine. After their positive response to the gospel, the pagan Ephesians had been cleansed by the blood of Jesus and accepted into the family of God. Thereupon, they had been sealed or stamped with God's sign of ownership, which guaranteed their eternal salvation. (See the expository notes connected with Eph. 1:13, p. 45–46.) The child of God cannot be lost; what God commences, He completes. Salvation does not depend upon the ability of a man or woman to remain faithful, but upon the strength of Christ, who said, "My sheep hear my voice, and I know them, and they follow me: and I give unto them eternal life; and they shall never perish, *neither shall any man pluck them out of my hand*" (John 10:27-28).

PHASE TWO

For through him we both have access by one Spirit unto the Father (2:18).

When a man is converted to Christ, the Savior gives him eternal life. When that man grows in grace, he learns about making a full surrender to his Lord. Prior to the death and resurrection of Christ, it was not possible for any man, except the high priest of Israel, to enter into the presence of God. When the Redeemer reconciled people to God, He opened a new way into the presence of the Almighty. The Holy Spirit was sent to be the Guide along that sacred highway. All racial barriers were removed, and, by the transforming power of the gospel, all believers became one family. Paul wrote, "Now, therefore, ye are no more strangers and foreigners, but fellowcitizens with the saints, and of the household of God" (Eph. 2:19). It was wonderful to accept from God's hand the gift of eternal life; it was better to sit at His feet, look into His face, and exclaim, "Abba Father." "Having therefore, brethren, boldness to enter into the holiest by the blood of Jesus, by a new and living way, which he hath consecrated for us, through the veil, that is to say, his flesh; and having an high priest over the house of God; let us draw near with a true heart in full assurance of faith" (Heb. 10:19-22).

PHASE THREE

In whom ye also are builded together for an habitation of God through the Spirit (2:22).

It is impossible to draw near to God and not gain a new appreciation of other people engaged in the same pilgrimage. The Church became the home of those who shared faith in Christ. All Christians became living stones within the sacred structure. The Caucasian could be next to the Black and the Indian adjacent to the Chinese, but with all "fitly joined together," they not only supported each other, but grew continuously into "an holy temple in the Lord" (2:21). There were occasions during Paul's prayertime when the stones beneath his knees seemed to become holy. Yet, even he realized such hallowed experiences could not continue indefinitely. It was wonderful to forget the world with its demands and spend time in the presence of God, but Paul made a greater discovery. It was better to know that when a return to the mundane things became necessary, *God would never leave him.* The Holy Spirit lived within his soul, transforming him into a sacred temple. Through this amazing act, the Lord Jesus was able to fulfill His promise, "Go ye therefore, and teach all nations. . . . and lo, *I am with you alway, even unto the end of the world*" (Matt. 28:19-20). Evidently, the Lord meant what He said. His continuing presence made worship a delight.

PHASE FOUR

> **. . . the mystery of Christ, which in other ages was not made known unto the sons of men, as it is now revealed unto his holy apostles and prophets by the Spirit (vv. 3-5).**

Growth is a continuing process. A balanced diet and proper exercise are necessary requisites for health. The same principles are vital for developing babes in Christ. They need food, understanding, and guidance. That was one of the reasons that God sent the Holy Spirit to supervise everything pertaining to the maturing of His children. The Savior promised, "When he, the Spirit of truth, is come, he will guide you into all the truth: for he shall not speak of himself; but whatsoever he shall hear, that shall he speak: and he will shew you things to come. He shall glorify me: for he shall receive of mine, and shall shew it unto you" (John 16:13-14). This promise was fulfilled when the Holy Spirit revealed the truth of "the hidden mystery" to the leaders of the church. It is refreshing to remember that He is now residing within the hearts of believers and is the Teacher of God's people. One of the most important assets of a healthy believer is *a listening ear*! The Holy Spirit has much to teach, but God's people unfortunately suffer from hearing problems! Was that the reason that the Lord said, "Who hath ears to hear, let him hear?" (Matt. 13:43).

PHASE FIVE

That he would grant you, according to the riches of his glory, to be strengthened with might by his Spirit in the inner man (3:16).

It is an irrefutable fact that unless a baby develops, partakes of food, and becomes strong, its presence in the world is a disappointment. Growth is the natural consequence of birth; strength must succeed weakness. The same principles apply to the child of God. As a baby is helpless and totally dependent upon its parent, so the Christian depends upon his Lord. If God's strength is to be made perfect in our weakness, it is essential that we comply with His instructions.

An unresponsive baby is evidence that problems exist in the tiny body. Similarly, any Christian who fails to respond to the Holy Spirit indicates that within his consciousness there exists a hindrance. Paul drew a line of demarcation between the spiritual and physical natures of humanity when he wrote, "But though our outward man perish, yet the inward man is renewed day by day" (2 Cor. 4:16). The story has been told of the father who would take his child into the darkness of the basement of their home. Evidently, the child disliked the experience for the mother inquired why her husband would do this. He replied, "I love to feel her clinging to my hand!" The father's imparted strength helped to overcome the inherent fear within his daughter's heart. All experiences are valuable if they make us cling to God's hand.

PHASE SIX

Endeavoring to keep the unity of the Spirit in the bond of peace (4:3).

A perfect building signifies that all its stones are in proper alignment; no part of the structure is isolated; each stone contributes to the strength of the structure. Similarly, every part of the human body belongs to the other members. When one member suffers, they all suffer, and when a body is healthy, there is no pain. These facts apply to the Church, which is both the temple of God and the body of Christ. When unity prevails within the spiritual structure, the glory of God becomes visible. Maintaining the unity of the Spirit means that each believer will be careful not to offend others in the assembly; it necessitates an exhibition of loving thoughtfulness, which proves that the believer is controlled by the indwelling Spirit. It indicates the entire assembly is proceeding toward the ultimate goal of the Church—likeness to the Lord Jesus Christ.

PHASE SEVEN

And grieve not the holy Spirit of God, whereby ye are sealed unto the day of redemption (4:30).

It is impossible to make an inanimate object grieve. A person may bang a door or hit a table, but that has nothing to do with "grieving." Paul had this thought in mind when he referred to the possibility of making the Lord grieve. The Holy Spirit was not an influence nor a power within human beings. He was a living Person entrusted with the task of helping individuals conform to the requirements of God. It was the divine will that Christians should "be conformed to the image of his Son, that he might be the firstborn among many brethren" (Rom. 8:29). The believer's body had become a temple of God, and therefore the human sanctuary belonged to the Lord. Just as it was possible for one member of a family to cause another to grieve, so men and women could make the Holy Spirit grieve. There were three ways by which this might happen—by what men were, did, or said. Paul urged his readers to banish from their hearts all manifestations of the old life. If the Christian permitted anything sinful to be dominant within his soul, the Holy Spirit could be hindered.

PHASE EIGHT

And be not drunk with wine, wherein is excess; but be filled with the Spirit (5:18).

Throughout the Middle East, water was often contaminated, and it was customary to drink wine. The words, "wherein is excess" suggest the possibility of drinking too much fermented juice. To exhibit a lack of self-control was a sign of weakness; a believer who allowed this to happen could ruin his testimony and disgrace his church. It was never possible to have too much of the Holy Spirit. It cannot be overemphasized that *NOT to be filled with the Holy Spirit* was as great an offense as being drunk with wine. Nominal church people would be shocked and dismayed to see one of their associates lying drunk in the street, but completely indifferent to see other members without interest in knowing more about consecrated living. It is true that the Holy Spirit resides in our bodies, but, alas, it is possible to confine Him to one small part of the human house. All Christians must choose whether or not to let Him occupy the entire temple. We can live with Him in *His house*; or allow Him a small room in *our house*. If Christians ignore the command "Be filled with the Spirit," they cannot live the victorious life.

PHASE NINE

And take the helmet of salvation, and the sword of the Spirit, which is the word of God (6:17).

A believer filled with the Holy Spirit is controlled by God. Paul carefully explained that the conflict between righteousness and evil continued and that the Lord required dedicated soldiers to drive Satan from human hearts. When military officers vow to be true to their country and obey their officers, their oath is binding unto death. Similarly, when the followers of Christ dedicate themselves to the service of Christ, they promise to be faithful under all circumstances. No man can fight without weapons, and no Christian can prevail against evil unless he is sufficiently equipped to resist the devil's attacks. The most formidable weapon given to the soldiers of the Lord is the Word of God; against its power even the hosts of hell cannot prevail. To possess a sword is one thing; to excel in using it is another. A sword hanging on the wall of a home would never constitute a challenge to anyone. To proclaim that the Bible is the Word of God is a meaningless expression unless the Scriptures are a vital part of our lives. Christ was expert in the use of the Word of God, and if His followers would triumph as He did, they will need to follow His example. The words of God are the "cutting edge" of the Lord's sword of the Spirit.

PHASE TEN

Praying always with all prayer and supplication in the Spirit (6:18).

When a man prays, he invariably asks for something he wants; when he prays "in the Spirit," he seeks something which the Holy Spirit desires. Selfish prayers are an outpouring of hot air and personal ambition. It is not wrong to ask for help to meet emergencies in life, but the Lord supplied a perfect example of praying in the spirit when He said, "Father, if thou be willing, remove this cup from me: nevertheless *not my will, but thine, be done*" (Luke 22:42). Often our petitions are dictated by limited vision. It is possible to seek something which might be ultimately harmful. Occasionally, God gives a negative answer. Babies ask for matches and knives, but wise parents refrain from granting the request. God is a wise, heavenly Father who sometimes refuses to grant the desires of His children. To pray "in the spirit" means to allow Him to control our thinking, to suggest our petitions, and above all, to allow Christ to have the preeminence in our thinking. The Savior made time to pray and never neglected an opportunity to commune with His Father. His major decisions were prefaced by a time of intercession, and, consequently, Jesus never made a mistake. It is better to be sure than to speculate; it is wiser to pray than to pout!

PHASE ELEVEN

For the fruit of the Spirit is in all goodness and righteousness and truth (5:9).

Fruit is something produced by the life of a tree or plant; the Bible had much to say about the fruit of the Holy Spirit. Jesus said, "Herein is my Father glorified, that ye bear much fruit; so shall ye be my disciples" (John 15:8). Paul wrote to the Galatians, "But the fruit of the Spirit is love, joy, peace, longsuffering, gentleness, goodness, faith, meekness, temperance, against such there is no law" (Gal. 5:22-23).

The science of grafting has performed miracles in the realm of agriculture, but, basically, a tree only produces its own type of fruit. Apple trees do not produce blackberries; neither do citrus trees produce cherries. The same truth can be expressed of the spirit-filled life. People who are filled with the Spirit of God never produce "adultery, fornication, uncleanness, lasciviousness, idolatry, witchcraft, hatred, variance, emulations, wrath, strife, seditions, heresies; envyings, murders, drunkenness, revellings, and such like" (Gal. 5:19-21). The Bible says, "Wherefore by their fruits ye shall know them" (Matt. 7:20). Holiness never needs an advertising agent! It does its own publicity, and this is easily understood by the people of the world. Some believers wear buttons announcing they are Christians. This is an excellent way by which to confess Christ, but unless the confession is amplified by a dedicated life, the button becomes a meaningless adornment.

PHASE TWELVE

There is one body, and one Spirit, even as ye are called in one hope of your calling (4:4).

Since the Holy Spirit was destined to play such an important part in the growth of the Christian, it was to be expected that Satan would try to undermine His efforts. The apostle John wrote, "Beloved, believe not every spirit, but try the spirits whether they are of God; because many false prophets are gone out into the world. Hereby know ye the Spirit of God: every spirit that confesseth that Jesus Christ is come in the flesh is of God: and every spirit that confesseth not that Jesus Christ is come in the flesh, is not of God: and this is that spirit of antichrist, whereof ye have heard that it should come; and even now already is it in the world" (1 John 4:1-3).

It is never wise to underestimate the power of Satan. He has the capability of deceiving the elect. I have known cases when evil men confessed that Jesus came to earth, but their utterances were deceitful. The term "the wiles of the devil" covers a vast area of thought, and it might be wise for believers to contrast two verses of Scripture. Paul said, "No man can say that Jesus is the Lord, but by the Holy Ghost" (1 Cor. 12:3). Yet, the Savior declared "Many will say to me in that day, Lord, Lord, have we not prophesied in thy name? and in thy name cast out devils? and in thy name done many wonderful works? And then will I profess unto them, I never knew you: depart from me ye that work iniquity" (Matt. 7:22-23). To contrast these apparently conflicting verses reveals that a man's word is not evidence of his holiness. Supernatural manifestations are not always produced by the Holy Spirit.

The only convincing evidence that a Christian has been filled with the Holy Spirit is *Christlikeness*. Paul wrote of the Savior, "For it pleased the Father that in him [Christ] should all fulness dwell" (Col. 1:19). "For in him [Christ] dwelleth all the fulness of the Godhead bodily" (Col. 2:9). We know the Lord Jesus Christ was full of the Holy Spirit; we shall be equally convinced that others have obtained this superlative treasure when they exhibit the same characteristics which indisputably belonged to Him.

Lord Jesus Christ, grow Thou in me,
And all things else recede;
My heart be daily nearer Thee,
From sin be daily freed.

BIBLIOGRAPHY

Amplified New Testament. Grand Rapids: Zondervan Publishing House, 1958.

Barclay, William. *The Daily Study Bible.* Letters to the Galatians and Ephesians. Philadelphia: The Westminster Press, 1976.

The Bethany Parallel Commentary on the New Testament. Minneapolis: Bethany House Publishers, 1983.

Clarke, Adam. *Commentary on the Bible.* 3 vols. Nashville: Abingdon Press, 1977.

Englishman's Greek New Testament. Grand Rapids: Zondervan Publishing House, n.d.

Gaebelein, Frank. E. (ed.) *The Expositor's Bible Commentary.* Grand Rapids: Zondervan Publishing House, 1978.

Jamison, Robert, Faussett, A.R. & Brown, David. *A Commentary Critical, Experimental, and Practical on the Old and New Testaments.* Grand Rapids: Wm. B. Eerdmans Publishing Company, 1984.

The Jerusalem Bible. Garden City: Doubleday & Company, 1966.

Josephus, Flavius. *The Complete Works of Flavius Josephus.* Grand Rapids: Kregel Publications, 1960.

The Living Bible. Wheaton: Tyndale House, 1971.

New English Bible. New York: Oxford University Press and Cambridge University Press, 1961.

New International Version Bible. Grand Rapids: Zondervan Publishing House, 1978.

Phillips, J.B. *New Testament in Modern English.* New York: Macmillan, 1958.

Powell, Ivor. *Bible Cameos.* Grand Rapids: Kregel Publications, 1985.

_________. *Bible Highways.* Grand Rapids: Kregel Publications, 1985.

_________. *Bible Pinnacles.* Grand Rapids: Kregel Publications, 1985.

_________. *Bible Treasures.* Grand Rapids: Kregel Publications, 1985.

_________. *John's Wonderful Gospel.* Grand Rapids: Kregel Publications, 1985.

_________. *Luke's Thrilling Gospel.* Grand Rapids: Kregel Publications, 1985.

_________. *Matthew's Majestic Gospel.* Grand Rapids: Kregel Publications, 1985.

_________. *This I Believe.* London: Marshall, Morgan & Scott, 1957.

Reader's Digest *Great Encyclopedic Dictionary,* n.d.

Revised Standard Version Bible. Nashville: Thomas Nelson Bible Publishers, 1952.

Tenney, Merrill C. (ed.) *The Zondervan Pictorial Encyclopedia of the Bible.* Grand Rapids: Zondervan Publishing House, 1975.

Thayer, Joseph H. *The Greek-English Lexicon of the New Testament.* Grand Rapids: Zondervan Publishing House, 1983.

Today's English Version. New York: American Bible Society, 1966.

Spence, H.D. & Exell, Joseph S. (eds.) *Pulpit Commentary, Ephesians.* Grand Rapids: Wm. B. Eerdmans Publishing Company, 1981.

Vine, W.E. *Expository Dictionary of Old and New Testament Words.* Old Tappan, NJ: Fleming H. Revell, 1981.

BOOKS BY IVOR POWELL

BIBLE CAMEOS

These eighty graphic "thumb-nail" sketches are brief biographies of Bible people. Pungent and thought-provoking studies.

BIBLE GEMS

You will be captivated by the warm and practical style of these mini-messages with an ample supply of sermon starters, illustrations, and deep truths from God's Word.

BIBLE HIGHWAYS

In this series of Bible studies, Scripture texts are linked together, suggesting highways through the Bible from Genesis to Revelation.

BIBLE NAMES OF CHRIST

This work presents 80 concise studies on the names and titles of Christ. The simplicity and freshness of these mini-messages will provide devotional studies for believers, as well as outlines and illustrations for teachers and preachers.

BIBLE PINNACLES

A spiritual adventure into the lives and miracles of Bible characters and the meaningful parables of our Lord.

BIBLE TREASURES

In refreshingly different style and presentation, these 80 Bible miracles and parables are vividly portrayed.

BIBLE WINDOWS

Anecdotes and stories are, in fact, windows, through which the Gospel light shines, to illumine lessons for teachers and preachers.

MATTHEW'S MAJESTIC GOSPEL

You will find almost everything you need in developing sermons: the theme, outline, expository notes, and preaching homilies. A treasure-book of hands-on help in communicating God's truth to today's Christians.

MARK'S SUPERB GOSPEL

This systematic study offers expositional, devotional, and homiletical thoughts. The enrichment gained from the alliterated outlines will create enthusiasm for communicating Mark's Gospel.

LUKE'S THRILLING GOSPEL

In this practical and perceptive commentary there is a goldmine of expository notes and homilies.

JOHN'S WONDERFUL GOSPEL

Another verse-by-verse "distinctively different commentary" with sermonic notes and outlines.

THE AMAZING ACTS

The Acts of the Apostles become relevant for today in this helpful exposition.

THE EXCITING EPISTLE TO THE EPHESIANS

This work analyzes and communicates, in preachable/teachable units, the great truths of Paul's Epistle. This commentary will benefit those seeking practical insights into the text and will provide easy-to-apply suggestions for preaching and teaching.

WHAT IN THE WORLD WILL HAPPEN NEXT?

An unusual work on prophecy dealing especially with the return of Christ to earth and the nation of Israel's future.